The Sancy
Blood Diamond

Power, Greed, and the Cursed
History of One of the World's
Most Coveted Gems

SUSAN RONALD

WILEY

John Wiley & Sons, Inc.

In memory of my Father, "Appah,"
who taught diamonds to sparkle

Copyright © 2005 by Susan Ronald. All rights reserved

Published by John Wiley & Sons, Inc., Hoboken, New Jersey
Published simultaneously in Canada

The author gratefully acknowledges the following institutions for permission to use their images (numerals refer to page numbers): Diamond Trading Company, London (312). Erich Lessing/Art Resource, NY (210). Museum Boijmans Van Beuningen, Rotterdam (178, 179). National Portrait Gallery, London (80, 90, 144, 145, 166, 173, 264, 275); copyright Tom Hustler (305). Pinacoteca Nazionale di Siena/Lensini (91). Réunion des Musées Nationaux/Art Resource, NY (283); photo Gérard Blot (233); photo Arnaudet (263).

For general information about our other products and services, please contact our Customer Care Department within the United States at (800) 762-2974, outside the United States at (317) 572-3993 or fax (317) 572-4002.

Wiley also publishes its books in a variety of electronic formats. Some content that appears in print may not be available in electronic books. For more information about Wiley products, visit our web site at www.wiley.com.

Library of Congress Cataloging-in-Publication Data:

Ronald, Susan.
    The Sancy blood diamond : power, greed, and the cursed history
of one of the world's most coveted gems / Susan Ronald.
      p. cm.
    Includes bibliographical references and index.
    ISBN 0-471-43651-8 (cloth : alk. paper)
    1. Sancy diamond—History. I. Title.
NK7663.R66   2004
736'.23—dc22   2004001726

Printed in the United States of America

10 9 8 7 6 5 4 3 2 1

Contents

Preface

❧

The Sancy diamond, while little known outside specialist circles, has one of the most fascinating histories imaginable. The fascination does not come from its size—a mere 55.232 carats by modern standards—but rather from who owned it, who lusted after it, and how it helped change the course of European history. From the end of the fourteenth century until 1661, it was the largest white diamond in Christendom, always providing its owner with the most secure and concentrated form of wealth.

It was not always called "the Sancy," and although I give its other names when appropriate, I call it the Sancy throughout this book. The name "Sancy" is thought to come from its original owner, Nicolas Harlay de Sancy (spelled "Sauncy" at the time), though even this simple fact is the subject of some mystery. Some experts say that the diamond was called *sans-si*—short for *sans similitude* (without equal). Still others claim that the diamond was called *cent six*—meaning one hundred and six and pronounced "sancy"—after its original weight in carats. The only certainty regarding its name is that the origins have been shrouded in the fog of time.

As a near-perfect stone and the largest of its kind, the Sancy was indeed a special prize. Originally belonging to Valentine Visconti, daughter of the duke of Milan and duchess of Orleans, the Sancy passed to her mortal enemy John the Fearless, who mounted it in a jeweled coronet called *La Belle Fleur de Lys,* or The Beautiful Fleur-de-Lys. The huge pointed faceted diamond described in various documents as "larger than a nugget of charcoal" was mounted surrounded by four large pearls. In the middle of the central petal above the diamond was a long balas ruby (a ruby spinel of pale rose, red, or orange color) called *La Balais de Flandres*, reputedly the largest in France. The outer petals of the coronet were decorated with eight other large balas rubies, eight sapphires, five emeralds, and thirty-eight large pearls. The ensemble weighed 2 marcs, 7 ounces, and 2 grains—or a stunning 23.2 ounces or 646 grams.

Yet despite the fact that the Sancy appears in at least six official inventories from 1389 beginning with the dowry of Valentine Visconti, historians have failed to look at the diamond's provenance from all sides. I attempt here to record the Sancy's first real history as scrupulously as possible. In my research, I have always taken at least two, and often four, different sources to support the conclusions that I have drawn concerning the Sancy's past. I have based my research wherever possible on eyewitness descriptions of the diamond in official documents that also include the weight of the Sancy, or alternatively, the jewel into which it was set.

When the Sancy disappeared from history—first for a period of nearly 120 years after the last great duke of Burgundy lost it in battle, then a second time for 20 years during the Napoleonic era—I asked myself who the most likely "purloiner" of the stone might be in light of who ended up with the diamond next, and then made the most logical supposition. I have also approached the history of the Sancy from the present backward, using its provenance as documented by the Louvre, where it is currently housed.

For the first period of the Sancy's longest disappearance, there is documentation available that proves my premise, whereas for the second period, where I believe Joseph Bonaparte took the diamond, I have good historical anecdotal evidence but no single document that states, "Here it is." The Louvre makes no attempt to explain these two disappearances, nor has it undertaken research about these periods itself.

My research technique sheds light for the first time on the more enigmatic periods in the Sancy's checkered life. I hope I have cleared up much of its history, one that has been plagued with illicit sales and bargains, out-and-out lies, unsubstantiated rumor, and incomplete research.

I have converted important financial transactions into today's values with expert assistance from the Bank of England Information

Centre, paired with my own research regarding merchants trading internationally at the time of the sales. As we all know, exchange rates constantly fluctuate; consequently, these have been based on the Retail Price Index (RPI). The dollar-to-sterling rate has been fixed at its previous twelve months' average (at the time of writing) of $1.60 to £1, and the resulting conversions have been rounded.

The carat, the means by which gemstones are weighed, has an interesting history of its own. As the successor to such exotic weights for gemstones as ratis, mangelin, tandulas, sarsapas, masas, and surkhs, the carat underwent an evolution from the old carat to the metric carat in the early twentieth century. Weights in the old carat could range from 188.5 milligrams in Italy to 206.1 milligrams in Austria, and it was only in 1907 that the French decided to rationalize gem weights by introducing the metric carat, which is exactly one fifth of a gram (0.2 gram). In 1914 the metric carat was adopted on a worldwide basis, and for this reason, many authors have confused the weights of gemstones.

The Sancy was typically sold when its princely owner needed to raise cash quickly, and these sales—whether illicit or legitimate—can be understood only in their proper historical context. This context is not about the history of impersonal governments, dates, and statutes, but rather the electricity generated in the relationships between the players and power brokers themselves. It is what the king of Portugal *did* to Jacob Fugger—and Jacob's reaction—that is interesting, not the fact that Jacob had won an exclusive pepper contract from the Portuguese crown in 1504. In history as in life, context is everything.

Today nearly every nation has a history of bloodshed, conquest, and human slaughter that we now deplore. This history must be remembered for what it is, undiluted by time, euphemisms, or political correctness. Many of the Sancy's owners or usurpers—though colorful figures—were ruthless and powerful people, using and abusing the rule of law for their own greedy ends. I hope you will agree that I have portrayed the owners in a fair and true light by using original sources, their own words, and eyewitness accounts.

Since the Sancy repeatedly crossed borders, it was extremely important for me to research its voyages across those borders myself, for it is only by studying original sources from as many countries as possible that a complete picture has been created, and romance and fiction have been separated from fact. The Sancy's history is essentially one of power and greed. To tell its story in its entirety for the first time, I have followed the diamond's trail and have conducted research in Belgium, Holland, France, Italy, Germany, Spain, Portugal, and England.

Above all, I have had tremendous fun researching and writing this story, which at times seemed to lean toward a work of detective fiction rather than a true history of one of the world's ten most famous diamonds, and can only hope that you will enjoy reading it.

Acknowledgments

❧

Writing a book is often described as a lonely art. While the act of writing is performed in solitude, getting to that stage can take place only with a raft of supporters. This book would never have been written without my agent, Alex Hoyt, and my editor, Hana Lane, both of whom believed in me and immediately understood that the Sancy's story was so incredible. To you both, my sincerest thanks for giving me this fabulous opportunity to weave the Sancy's tale.

The research for the book was as much detective work as pure research—discerning fact from romance, and trying to understand forensically the most likely path that the Sancy may have taken on its untold travels over hundreds of years. There were myriad disciplines needed to compile this history, and I was fortunate enough to have access to diamond experts and specialized archivists in this task. Without the late Willy Goldberg, former president of the Diamond Club in New York, I may never have had such free access to the legendary Gabi Tolkowsky, whose analysis of the Sancy was truly magical and captivating, making me realize that diamond cutting is one of the oldest arts, and diamonds themselves a holistic art form. He also provided me with an Italian text on the history of Venetian diamond merchants and cutters as well as his Uncle Marcel Tolkowsky's thesis on diamond cutting, which paved the way for all mathematical calculations required for the fifty-seven- or fifty-eight-facet cut that he invented. Gabi, in turn, opened every door possible to me at de Beers; other diamond historians in Antwerp; and at Garrard & Co in London. Without Gabi, many of the mysteries about the Sancy may have remained unresolved and I owe both Gabi and his wife, Lydia, a great deal for their support, kindness, and hospitality.

Through Gabi I met Sabine Denissen of the Diamond Museum in Antwerp, and a former diamond cutter and diamond historian, Hans Wins, both of whom were enthusiastic supporters. Hans introduced me to Ludo van Damme of the Municipal Library in Bruges, whose determination led me to the documents on Charles the Bold at the Archives Départementales du Nord in Lille. To Hervé Passot at the Archives, my sincerest thanks. Also helpful in Belgium were the Staatsarchief Antwerp and the Royal Library in Brussels, which houses the Burgundy Library.

In the Netherlands I must thank Kees Zandvliet of the Rijksmuseum for helping me find Dr. Guido Jansen and Bram Meij of the Boijmans Museum in Rotterdam; their interpretation of the famous Cletscher Sketchbook was illuminating. Dr. Woelderink of the Royal Library at the Paleis Noordeinde Den Haag was also extremely supportive, as were the staff at the Hague Iconography Archive and Mr. van Doorn at the Hague Staatsarchief.

Next, my detective work took me to Switzerland, where Gabriele Keck of the Berner Historisches Museum opened my eyes to the Burgundebeute. This sent me on the trail of documents at the Bern Staatsarchiv, Basle Staatsarchiv, and the Basel Historisches Museum, where Dr. Berke Meier was most helpful regarding the Burgundy Booty that had been held in that city. Mr. Silvio Margadant from the Staatsarchiv in Graubuenden in Chur worked tirelessly with me to help clear up a later mystery in the Sancy's travels.

In France, Martine Chauney-Bouillot, librarian for the fonds Bourgogne in Dijon's Municipal Library, was a breath of fresh air and positively delighted that the Sancy's history was now being thoroughly researched. She kindly helped me at the Musée de Beaux Arts in Dijon as well as the Archives Régionales de Bourgogne. Other institutions and people in France deserving my gratitude are the Archives Départementales du Nord; the Bibliothèque Nationale (particularly Hossein Tengour); the Archives Nationales; the Napoleon Foundation, and especially Peter Hicks, for poring through the library with me; and, of course, the Département d'objets d'art at the Louvre.

In Germany, Mrs. Weiss at the Fugger Privatbank in Augsburg was helpful in putting me in touch with the right people at the Dillingen Archives and the Staatsarchiv in Munich to further the research.

In Italy, the city archives in Mantua and in Rome were useful in providing me with information on the Sancy that was *not* there, as previously supposed by other writers. The Florentine Archives contained a fascinating report on and insight into the Demidoffs and Italian political feeling to foreigners at the time of the Risorgimento, or Italian Unification.

Dr. Miguel of the Torre do Tombo National Archives in Lisbon was absolutely invaluable, not only in locating the inventory that included the Sancy, but also in strong-arming one of his colleagues into translating old Portuguese into English for me, thereby short-circuiting my research in Lisbon from weeks into days. He also patiently helped translate other Portuguese documents that I found difficult to read or understand, and referred me to the director of the Ajuda Palace in Lisbon, Dr. Isabel Jiordano, who, in turn, involved Dr. Ruy Galopim in my search for the truth of the Sancy's sojourn in Portugal.

Matilde Glaston of the Cervantes Institute in London provided me with names, archives, and libraries for all of Spain. Cristina Emperador, subdirector of Los Archivos General de Simanca in Valladolid went to tremendous trouble on my behalf and enlisted the support of Juan José Alonso, subdirector of the archives at the Palacío Réal in Madrid. To Amelia Aranda, curator of the Patrimonio Nacional at the Palacío Réal, my very special thanks. Without Amelia's help and special knowledge of the Spanish crown jewel collection, I might still be leafing through original sources in twenty years' time.

Time, resources, and geopolitics prevented me from going to India to find out firsthand about the Golconda mines, or about the importance of Second Baronet Sir Jamsetjee Jejeebhoy, or indeed to Russia's Demidoff Institute in Ekaterinberg, but the information available at both the Bodleian Library in Oxford and the Oriental and India Reading Room at the British Library was extremely enlightening. Also a special thanks to Jane Rosen, formerly of the SRCSS, who contacted the Demidoff Institute and the museum in Ekaterinberg on my behalf.

In England I was fortunate to have constant access to one of the best national library collections in the world at the British Library; to all its staff, in particular Pat Kuomi, my heartfelt appreciation for your professionalism, assistance, and good humor. To my long-standing friend John Barnes of Historic Royal Palaces, my thanks for putting me in touch with the delightful and knowledgeable Anna Keay, now of English Heritage, and curator of the crown jewels at the Tower of London. Leslie Coldham, Tim Strofton, and Chris Alderman of de Beers also deserve my gratitude for allowing me access to the company's special source material from its library, putting up with my unending stream of questions with such patience, and providing me with photographs. Corinna Pike, curator of Garrard & Co's archives, also has my thanks for explaining the company's historic involvement in the sale of the Sancy in 1865. I also would like to thank Mike Bott of Reading University's Library and Archives for allowing me access to the Astor Papers. To the Bank of England Information Centre, and in particular Chris Thomas, I owe a huge debt for providing me with a stream of exchange rates and inflation rates that enabled me to convert important currency transactions as best possible into today's values. Other institutions in England that merit my gratitude are the Public Records Office, the Victoria and Albert Museum, and the National Portrait Gallery.

My personal supporters include Sue Pfunder for her fabulous and witty Spanish translations at my dining room table over interminable cups of tea; Ika Hibbert for her meticulous German translations of old Swiss German and for her referring the *Burgundgebeute* to Oxford dons too numerous to count; Dominique van Setten for her old Dutch and Flemish translations; and Tim Head for his assistance on "old money" and who, with his brother Giles Head, looked after my home and dogs on my travels. Without the professional support of Peter Morris, Agostino von Hassel, Dr. John Uden, Dr. Sally Edmonds, and Professor Andrew Carr, this book would not have been possible. Rosie Rowland has my deepest thanks for her undying support and for helping me keep body and soul glued together. To my great friends Pam and John Head, my eternal thanks for proofreading my manuscript. To my mom and dad, who gave me a crash course in diamonds, diamond dealing, and endless anecdotes on the "diamond world," and to my sons, Matt, Zandy, and Andrew, for all your special help and support, I can only give my love.

Finally and most importantly, to my husband, Douglas Ronald, without whose forbearance, loyalty, belief in me as a writer and historian, wit, sense of humor, Italian translations, co-research, intellect, driving skills, and willingness to constantly provide the best cups of tea and spaghetti dinners in the world, none of this would have been remotely possible. You have made me feel truly blessed.

1

Golconda

❧

THE SANCY DIAMOND'S STORY, and indeed the history of power and greed behind all large diamonds, begins at the famous Golconda mines in India. These stories are steeped in the mystical folklore and superstition that are the bedrock of the spiritual, economic, political, and social history of gems. The first rumors of Golconda and its huge diamonds trickled westward to Europe through tales of the awestruck Venetian traveler Marco Polo following his visit to several Indian kingdoms in 1292. He wrote in his *Most Noble and Famous Travels* at the time:

> I will pass hence unto the countries of India where I Marco Polo dwelt a long time; and although the things which I will declare, seem not to be believed of them that shall hear it, but have it in a certainty and of a truth, for that I saw it all with my own eyes . . . In the mountains of this country there be found find Adamants [diamonds]. And after they have had much rain, the men go to seek them in the streams that run from the mountains, and so they do find the Adamants, which are brought from the mountains in the summer when the days are long. Also there be strong serpents and great, very venomous, seeming that they were set there to keep the Adamants that they might not be taken away, and in no part of the world there is found fine Adamants but there. . . . No country but this grows diamonds. Those which are brought to our part of the world are only the refuse of the finer and larger stones. For the flower of the diamonds and other large gems, as well as the largest pearls, are

1

all carried to the Great Khan and other kings and princes of those regions [the subcontinent of India]. In truth they possess all the treasures of the world.

By the sixteenth century, as the Portuguese overtook the Venetians in trade with India by virtue of the new sea trade route opened by Vasco da Gama, two Portuguese merchants, Fernao Nuniz and Domingos Paes, reiterated Marco Polo's claim when they reported home that all diamonds weighing more than ten to thirteen carats were destined for the Great Mogul's treasury. They also noted that the local ruler charged a levy on all trade in diamonds—from the mining licenses to individual sales among merchants. A century later, the great French diamond merchant adventurer Jean-Baptiste Tavernier stated, "Trade is freely and faithfully undertaken there. Two percent of every purchase is paid to the King, who also levies fees from the merchants for their mining permits."

Two centuries later, Marco Polo's original observations were again confirmed by another Italian, Niccolo de Conti, who related how all the hill districts were infested with snakes and diamonds. De Conti wrote: "At certain periods of the year men bring oxen and drive them to the top of the hill, and having cut them up in pieces, cast the warm and bleeding fragments upon the summit of the other mountain. The diamonds stick to these fragments. Then come the vultures and eagles which seizing the meat for their food, fly away with it to places where they may be safe from serpents. To these places afterwards come men and collect the diamonds."

But these are not the earliest accounts written about diamonds. At the time when Alexander the Great (356–323 B.C.) made his conquest of Asia, the Greeks wrote about a legend of the Valley of the Diamonds that held a fortune of diamonds in plain sight—a fabulous treasure that was guarded by serpents. This story was told and retold over the centuries and formed the basis for the legendary tales of Sinbad the Sailor in the *Arabian Nights*, written by an anonymous author, now described as a pseudo-Aristotle, who explained:

Other than my pupil Alexander, no one has ever reached the valley where the diamonds are found. It lies in the East, along the great border of Khurasan, and it is so deep that a human eye cannot see to the bottom. When Alexander reached the valley, a multitude of serpents prevented him going farther, for their glance proved mortal to men. So he resorted to the use of mirrors: the serpents were caught by the reflection of their own eyes and so perished. Alexander then adopted another ruse. Sheep were slaughtered, then flayed, and their flesh cast into the depths. Birds of prey from the neighboring mountains swooped down and carried off in their claws the flesh, to which countless diamonds adhered. Alexander's warriors hunted the birds, which dropped their booty, and the men merely had to gather it where it fell.

Over the centuries this fabled tale was frequently recounted by Arab and Persian merchants who adopted several versions of it to help them protect the exceedingly valuable sources of their spice trade; this was a primary motivation behind colonial expansion to India through the Middle Ages.

Diamond sources were jealously guarded, and legends like the Valley of the Diamonds were prolific. Diamond merchants never told anyone where they bought their diamonds, or how else they might have come by them. These merchants risked their lives to ply their trade, as they were easy prey for bandits and pirates while transporting their priceless cargoes. Prior to the commercial establishment of the Portuguese sea routes in 1502, diamond merchants either shipped their Indian gems through the Red Sea or the Persian Gulf into the major Mediterranean or Black Sea ports. The overland route followed an ancient road from southeastern India to the north through Afghanistan. From the city of Taxila (now called Takshasila) the trade route met the Silk Road between China and Persia (modern-day Iran).

Few diamonds trickled out of India to Europe until Roman times, and even then, the majority were small decorative stones. Yet to the Romans, according to Roman writer and philosopher Pliny the Elder (A.D. 23–79), the diamond was "only a speck of a stone, but more precious than gold, known only to kings, and to very few of them." It seems that the Romans believed in the diamond's mystical properties as ardently as the Indians, and certainly the diamond's purported powers would have been part of the spin used to sell the stones at exceptional prices into Europe. Pliny, who may never have seen a diamond himself, was the first European to record the stone's usefulness as something other than a gemstone: "When an Adamas is successfully broken, [it is] much sought after by engravers and [is] inserted into iron tools for making hollows in the hardest material without difficulty." The Chinese, however, had by the time of Pliny been using industrial diamonds for centuries; they were commonly used as bits for finishing and polishing jade and for drilling holes into pearls for stringing.

With the fall of the Roman Empire, the usefulness of diamonds waned rapidly, and by the fourteenth century the diamond's popularity and deemed mystical powers rated well behind those of the ruby, red spinels (balas rubies), pearls, and sapphires.

Yet in the East, the diamond remained the king of gemstones, highly valued from prehistory for its economic and social importance as well as for its mystical powers. The *Artha Shastra* (The Science of Profit), written in ancient Sanskrit by Kautilya in the fourth century B.C., was concerned with details of the economic, political, and legal system of India. In the chapter "The Examination of Precious Articles to Be Received in the Treasury," Kautilya described the most valuable diamonds as "big, crystalline, and brilliant." The less valuable diamonds are devoid of angles and are uneven, such as diamond splinters and those of various colors "like cat's eye or the urine or bile of a cow." He also laid out the importance of strict control over the trade of all gemstones.

But the spirituality of the diamond is best captured in the world's earliest printed text written in Sanskrit, the *Diamond Sutra,* the most profound *sutra* in Buddhist teachings. From the Sanskrit, *sutra* literally means the "string upon which jewels are threaded," and the *Diamond Sutra* is the perfection of wisdom, which "cuts like the diamond thunderbolt and is thus able to cut through earthly illusion." Great wisdom, in Buddhist thought, is characterized by its indestructible nature and enduring truth. The diamond, and in particular all large diamonds, were considered to be sacred by the Buddhists.

The word *diamond,* from the Greek *adamas,* means invincible. Gem-quality diamonds were the most highly prized of all precious stones, from the moment they were first discovered, for their rareness, pure color, brilliance, transparency, and apparent indestructibility.

Diamonds were believed to be gems fit for the gods, and only the most privileged and exalted earthly representatives could possess them. This message was transmitted through the lapidaries—or gem texts written by royal merchants and philosophers since recorded time—in Sanskrit, Persian, Chinese, Greek, Latin, and Arabic, in which the diamond was given the most prestigious position among gemstones.

The power that the diamond symbolizes transcends national boundaries and beliefs, like a golden thread running through the fabric of ancient civilizations. Interestingly, the Sanskrit word for diamond is *vajra,* and *vajra* also describes the Hindu goddess Indra's thunderbolt. The Greek god Zeus brandished a thunderbolt that was inspired by the diamond crystal. In one ancient text, the *Agastimata,* written in the sixth century, the text scrutinizes and grades diamonds according to their shape, cut, weight, clarity, sparkle, color, and beauty. Different colors were ascribed to various deities as well as to the social caste that had a right to own them:

> [The] Diamond has four colors, corresponding to its castes. The diamond with a velvety sheen, like that of a conch shell, a rock crystal or the moon, is a Brahmin. That which is reddish or colored brown like a monkey, beautiful and pure is called *Kshatriya* [of nobles and warriors]. *Vaisya* [farmers and merchants] has a brilliant, pale yellow color. *Sudra* [servants] shines like a well-polished sword: because of its sparkle, experts have assigned it to the fourth caste. Such are the signs which characterize the castes of a diamond.

Hindu sacred lapidary texts also refer to the diamond, providing not only spiritual but also a commercial argument for diamonds being the most valuable of all gems. These texts establish quality criteria for rough diamonds and ascribe beneficial powers to diamonds; today such texts would be considered a sales pitch. These sacred texts carry rich descriptions of the diamond's power to protect against poison, snakes, sickness, and even sinful behavior. According to one of these, the *Ratnapariksha,* "a king who desires happiness must accumulate and wear jewels that have been thoroughly authenticated. A good jewel is a source of wealth for kings, and a bad one is a source of evil." Flawed diamonds, according to the *Brhatsamhita,* a lapidary text by Varahamihira, attract the risks of loss of family, fortune, and life.

The *Brhatsamhita* states that the purest, flawless gems, blessed with perfect octahedron shapes and bearing certain surface markings, called *lakshana*, were considered to be beneficial. Buddhabhatta, a sixth-century lapidary author, believes this to be true as well when he writes, "He who has a pure body, and who carries on his person a diamond that is sharp-pointed, without blemish and entirely flawless, shall daily increase his worth in happiness, prosperity, children, wealth, crops, cows and livestock, to the end of his life."

The Sancy diamond fits this description perfectly. If one is to believe in the mystical power of the diamond described in this ancient text, the Sancy would become a source of evil for those owners who did not thoroughly authenticate its provenance. For those who came by the diamond honestly, it would have been a *lakshana*, daily increasing the owner's prosperity and power. This is the basis of the Sancy's curse, and explains why some of its owners met cruel and bloody endings while others remained wealthy and healthy. While I personally do not believe in curses, this explanation does hold true throughout the Sancy's history.

The Sancy is a pure white and transparent diamond. Its weight, estimated by gem valuers in the fifteenth century to be 106 carats, and color would have destined it to ownership by the Indian king. It was found in the oldest area of diamond extraction near Golconda, but the date of its cutting is unknown. Somehow it reached Europe in the late fourteenth century, making it the largest white diamond in Christendom for well over two hundred years.

According to the legendary diamond cutter Gabi Tolkowsky, the cut is definitely Indian, a forerunner of the briolette cut. He can tell this simply from the fact that like many old Indian cut stones, the Sancy's size was more important than its brilliance: there are fewer facets in the old Indian style, rather than more facets, as in newer European cuts. Further, one side is more flat, and the other side convex. In the fifteenth century, the cutter would have cut his hands off if it had been done in any other way. Tolkowsky says the Sancy was "cut long ago, and most likely in India, and most probably by a Venetian cutter and merchant who would have known its value in Europe."

Tolkowsky explains that it was extremely fortuitous that the Sancy was spared from being smashed with a hammer, as this was the custom to avoid giving large stones to the Mogul ruler in the fourteenth century. The cutter had a high level of expertise and made it limpid and transparent as water when he cut the Sancy. To retain the weight and size of the stone, Tolkowsky believes that the Venetian cutter polished one side flat and one side as a briolette. The entire process would have been conducted in the greatest secrecy and the stone smuggled out of India, since the large stones became legend rapidly.

The Sancy would have been transported to Venice by the merchant and sold to the wealthiest, most powerful ruler to whom he could gain access. At the end of the fourteenth century, Florence was at war with Milan and Lucca. Venice sided at times with Florence, at times with Milan and Lucca, depending on whose expansionist threat it chose to curb. Precisely when or how the diamond reached the phenomenally rich and powerful John Galeazzo di Visconti, duke of Milan, is shrouded in the fog of history. But when John succeeded in expanding his sphere of influence to France through the marriage of his stunningly beautiful and perspicacious daughter Valentine Visconti to the rake and rogue Louis, duke of Orléans, brother of Charles VI, king of France, he gave her a dowry beyond belief.

Valentine had been accustomed to the Milanese court, which was reputed to be the grandest and most luxurious in Italy. When she arrived in France, she initiated a new era that was different from the poorer French court, coming with jewels beyond compare and art objects of unimaginable value. She also brought with her a dowry in cash of 450,000 Milanese florins ($218.3 million or £136.4 million today) and sovereignty of the town and province of Asti.

Hidden among Valentine's vast array of jewels was one jewel (item 6195) that is described in her Blois inventory dated 1398 as: "A girdle surrounded with a halo of gold on which are mounted at either side four large balas rubies and in the middle of these is one very large balas ruby above which hangs a clasp with four extremely large pearls and in the middle of these is an exceptionally large diamond, and from this clasp hangs a porcupine and from eight points from the said girdle 88 large white pearls are hanging, and this girdle belt is also embossed in gold and white and red enamel."

This "exceptionally large diamond" is the first reference in Europe to the Sancy diamond.

2

Valentine and the Dukes

1389–1409

✥

THE SANCY'S FIRST EUROPEAN OWNER, the wily and unreliable John Galeazzo di Visconti, was an enlightened despot. His oligarchy of Milan was based, like those of Florence and Venice, on trade. Valentine's Milan was approaching the pinnacle of its renaissance, when the artisans' guilds were more powerful than at any point in history. In the summer the bankers would sit at their green cloth-covered tables in the sun-drenched piazzas to show that they were open for trade. Booths with colorful awnings protected fishmongers, bakers, and fruit and vegetable merchants from the blazing heat as farmyard animals and people from all walks of life mingled in the alleyways. The often unpleasant smells wafted on the summer air, with the only means of escape along a narrow lane where feather, silk, tapestry, and jewel merchants lined the passage—the Rodeo Drive of its day.

Whether the Venetian merchant carrying the Sancy traveled these pathways we will never know, but he certainly sold the diamond to Valentine's treacherous father. The Visconti family crest of a snake opening its mouth to devour a child tells their story well, I believe. From the thirteenth century—aside from brief periods of exile—the Visconti had been dukes of Milan and absolute rulers. Following the succession of John Galeazzo di Visconti in 1378, the family expanded their power: from 1378 to 1395, the duke acquired Siena and Bologna by force, and Pisa through outright purchase.

John Galeazzo had above all a fine political mind, if also a penchant for intrigue, and he plotted incessantly to overwhelm Florence, fortunately without success. His reign was marked by bloody clashes and, paradoxically, by the high ideals and beauty of Renaissance Italy. His wife, Isabelle, the daughter of the French king, John the Good, and sister of Charles V, was effectively purchased for 600,000 Milanese florins ($291.1 million or £181.9 million today) to ransom the French king from the clutches of the English. The French themselves did not have the ready money to free their own king, so when John's father offered to help in exchange for marriage between the wealthy Milanese duchy and the impoverished French crown, the French court leaped at the opportunity. The fact that the Milanese people were taxed heavily to pay for it did not matter to John Galeazzo's father.

Valentine was their second child, born in 1370 at the castle of Pavia. Two years later, however, her mother died in childbirth. Although Valentine would never rule Milan, she was a great marriage prize for any prince. Valentine was reputed to be a great beauty; intelligent; and, by all accounts, a talented musician, as deduced from the golden harps she would later carry with her from the Milanese court to France. She spoke Italian, French, and German, and took a keen interest in the affairs of the court. Milan was already an important commercial center that attracted many foreigners, particularly German-speaking soldiers in the pay of her omnipotent father. Like that of Venice, Milan's court was wealthy, and Valentine was one its major beneficiaries, with a jewel collection beyond belief.

The palaces in the duchy were unlike any others in the medieval world. Whereas most castles were built to be fortresses meant to withstand invaders, the castles in which Valentine grew up were filled with light, splendor, art, and ideas. Life was punctuated by sumptuous entertainment, with jugglers, poets, musicians, artists, and magnificent feasts. The castle at Pavia was surrounded by a huge park and several villages where hunting, shooting, and riding were norms. It was a fairy-tale world, an oasis filled with swans, pheasants, ostriches, peacocks, and wild boar. There were fine furniture, tapestries, baths made of white marble—and, of course, jewels.

Yet storms were brewing. John Galeazzo was tremendously jealous of his uncle Bernabo, and had already taken the duchy away from him by force. In order to consolidate his sphere of influence, however, he needed powerful allies, and the best way to assure himself of their fidelity was through marriage. So Valentine was put on the wedding market.

Although a German prince had initially been sought, John Galeazzo settled on the brother of Charles VI, Louis, duke of Touraine (later duke of Orléans). Louis was thirteen, Valentine fifteen. On August 26, 1386, terms were agreed, with Louis signing the marriage contract on January 27, 1387, and John Galeazzo ratifying it on April 8. The couple were married the same day by proxy in the palace of John's mother, Blanche of Savoy, in Lombardy.

Aside from the payment of 450,000 florins, two-thirds of which was due on April 9, 1387, Valentine's personal treasures needed to be inventoried, packed, and prepared for her voyage to her new home. Among her personal riches, in addition to her silk and velvet cloth and dresses adorned with precious stones, were gold and silver plate, and a treasure trove of jewels of ivory, jasper, mother-of-pearl, amber, coral, crystal, diamonds, rubies, pearls, sapphires, enamel brooches, and cameos. In all, she had more than 150 diamond jewels, 28 emerald and 310 sapphire pieces, 425 rubies in various settings, and 7,000 pearls. It was a massive inventory to compile. Yet, it was only in the summer of 1389 that she arrived in Paris and at last came face to face with her husband, with whom she reportedly fell in love at first sight.

But why was there such a long delay in their meeting? The unofficial answer is simple: it had taken John Galeazzo some considerable time to acquire his daughter's cash dowry through taxation. The official excuse to the French was that the northwestern provinces of Italy and the regions in France through which Valentine would have to pass were filled with marauding bandits and mercenaries in search of plunder. Since Valentine would be carrying the two-thirds of her vast cash dowry and all her personal treasures and jewels, guaranteeing her security was of paramount importance. She would have been a tempting target, and her life could not be assured—even with her father's sizable army to protect her.

Her journey in the summer of 1389 was like a royal progress, taking place with tremendous pomp and circumstance. Homage needed to be paid as she passed through diverse provinces ruled by other petty autocrats; ambassadors had to be welcomed and sumptuous feasts organized. Anyone who was anyone wanted to glimpse the young beauty and her riches, and they frequently went into debt with Jewish moneylenders to buy cloaks or dresses or even to rent jewels to have the pleasure of her company, if only for a fleeting moment.

The first feasts of the journey took place in Milan itself. The Venetians sent their ambassadors, who were given, according to a decree of June 7, 1389, 50 ducats ($7,000 or £4,400 today) each to have silk clothing made, as well as 150 ducats ($21,000 or £13,100 today) for gifts and tips. These sums were deemed by the doges as being "quite sufficient," meaning paltry, by the normal Venetian standards.

The France that Valentine married into was not the country we know today. It had been ravaged by generations of barbaric war among its petty fiefdoms, and most especially against the English, who had laid claim to the French throne itself. France was a harsh land, her people uncivilized and accustomed to vulgar ways. Barely larger than the Île de France region that surrounds Paris and the Loire, France was dominated by its powerful vassal states, whose dukes were all part of the Valois line of princes. These rival dukes would eventually plunge France into a civil war with the unwitting aid of Valentine and the Sancy.

The most treacherous uncle, Philip the Bold, had been granted Burgundy and Franche-Comté on the death of his father, Charles V. Philip's three older brothers, the dukes of Berry, Armagnac, and Anjou, were Charles VI's regents, and they plundered France for their own ends.

While Philip was seemingly content with his lesser status, since his first priority was to unite his two duchies and expand his territories into Flanders, his power and greed were imperceptible at first. As the contemporary writer Bonet wrote, "When I was a young man, you were called Philip Lackland: now God has generously bestowed on you a great name, and placed alongside you the mighty ones of the earth." By the time Philip had married Marguerite of Flanders, heiress to the wealthy provinces that included the bustling northern trading capital of Bruges and the nearby city of Antwerp, he had become a mighty force with which to be reckoned. The fact that he had allowed his brothers to busy themselves with the affairs of state of France did not mean that he would allow them to erase him from the political or economic picture.

The dukes of Berry and Anjou undoubtedly had been squandering France's wealth and resources for their own personal gain. When King Charles VI inherited the crown in 1380 at age twelve, his tyrant uncles the dukes of Berry and Anjou ruled not only their own lands but also France, as Charles's regents. Referred to by history as "the old men," they loved courtly extravagance and spent vast sums of money on court entertainment, jewels, and plate. Given the extreme poverty outside of court—France had already been at war for decades with England in what became known as the Hundred Years' War—their greed could lead only to further bloodshed. The population had been heavily taxed in life and pocketbook, and the dukes' callous governance led inevitably to a series of antitax revolts in Paris known as *les maillotins*. "The old men" were loathed by the common man, adored by their court cronies for their lavish spending, and thieved from the French crown.

Then, with startling suddenness, the situation changed. King Charles fired his regent uncles in a public ceremony at Rheims in 1390. Philip the Bold placated his older brothers by saying, "Brothers, we must bear the situation. The king is young . . . the time will come when those who will advise him will be sorry."

This alarming coup had been engineered by Charles's brother and Valentine's husband, Louis, recently elevated to the title of duke of Orléans. The teenage Louis took over the court ceremonies and organized the festivities and the pomp of all external affairs, while his minions were left to the boring business of bookkeeping, tax collection, and administration. His uncle the duke of Anjou had died, and the duke of Armagnac seethed in his domains. The duke of Berry skulked back to his own lands in Languedoc. This left Philip alone to confront Louis in the Council of State.

Matters were made worse when Charles VI began to suffer from intermittent bouts of madness, the first episode of which was noted in 1392. By then Louis had had several years to taste power and greed, and thanks to his marriage to Valentine, had felt the thrill of territorial expansion when Asti had come under his rule as part of her dowry. During his first period of madness Charles VI had feverishly and sentimentally bestowed vast lands and wealth on Louis, who now had his own designs on the duchy of Milan, the Ardennes, and Luxembourg. Louis's uncle Philip of Burgundy felt that his nephew was going too far, since the Ardennes and Luxembourg bordered on his own provinces.

Yet an uneasy truce settled in between uncle and nephew, with each tending to his own affairs and consolidating his own domains until Philip's death in 1404. In Philip's last testament, he willed half of all his worldly goods to his beloved wife, Marguerite, and the other half to his son, John. Although Philip was cash poor, in debt by hundreds of thousands of *livres,* he still passed on to his wife and son a fabulous illuminated library, tapestries, paintings, and jewels beyond imagination. The most precious of his jewels, *La Belle Balais de Flandres* (the Beautiful Balas Ruby of Flanders), had been in the duke of Flanders's family since "old times," according to the will. Despite the fact that this gem had come to Philip through his wife, he left it to John, the new duke of Burgundy and Flanders, stipulating that it would remain with the dukes of Flanders in perpetuity. All his other jewels, valuables, and plate were to be divided equally between his wife and son, with each also assuming responsibility for half of his debts.

The new duke became known as John the Fearless, duke of Burgundy and Flanders, who ushered in a new era of antagonism with France, and more particularly with Valentine's husband, Louis, duke of Orléans. The hostilities would result in a family rivalry and loss of life that would end in a bloody civil war. And the Sancy would become one of its hostages.

3

Valentine's Revenge

1407–1419

❧

THE SANCY BECAME the central instrument in the family power struggle and the symbol of power lusted after by the new duke of Burgundy, John the Fearless. John was an ugly, ungainly, vulgar man endowed with his father's prominent chin—a feature that would become the trademark of the Habsburg princes. He had a quick mind and innate ability to take pleasure in inspiring terror in others. More often than not, he took no trouble over his appearance and clothing. Yet when he wanted to make an impact, he would clean the grime from under his fingernails; perhaps wash; don his crimson, green, and gold cloak adorned with jewels; and cut an incredibly impressive figure. He was jealous, clever, treacherous, militarily fearless, and astoundingly astute politically.

John loathed the king and Valentine's philandering husband, Louis, viewing both as unworthy of holding high office. The power struggle that had begun between Louis and John's father, Philip, had come to a head when Louis bought the duchy of Luxembourg in 1401, thereby threatening the "heart and soul" of Burgundy.

After Philip's death in 1404, Louis felt the ecstasy of unbridled power and promoted a renewal of hostilities against England. Louis had even initiated the folly of challenging King Henry IV of England to a duel—a folly fortunately laughed off by the English monarch. Valentine's husband knew that by ending the truce, he would curtail

14

the lucrative trade that had built up between Flanders and England, and thereby cut off John's supply of wealth.

The plan was Machiavellian. John's objective was to lower taxes and increase trade with France, as his father had so successfully done with England. Since John had signed a treaty with England in April 1407, he was able to set himself up as the champion of the people, winning the hearts and minds of Frenchmen by arguing vociferously for tax cuts that could be granted if the king paid no heed to Louis's warmongering against England. When Louis replied by proposing new taxes to pay for his war, John refused to levy taxes on the Burgundians, claiming that if that were not proof enough of his sincerity, he would pay *all* the taxes on behalf of *all* his people to stop the madness.

It was an unprecedented populist maneuver for medieval France, and it worked. John's popularity soared, while Louis's crumbled. The two dukes were on a collision course, and it would be a fight to the death. John's ideas were bound to win popular support, whereas Louis's represented the status quo at court. In a pamphlet, John accused Louis of promulgating widespread corruption, wasting precious capital from the public purse, and embezzlement from the crown.

France's security hung in the balance. Charles VI's wife, Queen Isabelle, renewed the "special relationship" with Burgundy, while remaining devoted to Louis of Orléans in the hope that the two warring cousins would see sense and declare a truce. John pretended to go along, but only until he could gain the upper hand. But first he would have to sideline the observant and virtuous Valentine.

Although Valentine was seen by her enemies as a voluptuous temptress, she was not. She was most certainly a sensual beauty, with her heavy-lidded eyes, silken hair, and lithe figure, but above all she was perceptive, intelligent, and loyal. Her devotion to Louis and their family was complete, yet this very fidelity would become her undoing. She had had several children by Louis, and ignored rumors of his affairs, including the persistent rumor of his love affair with the queen of France. Louis was forever in Queen Isabelle's company, but history is divided over whether there was a romantic entanglement between them.

When Valentine administered herbal remedies to attempt to cure the ailing, insane King Charles VI, it was interpreted by her enemies as black magic. Her most important detractor, John the Fearless, claimed she was a witch. When her newborn daughter Marie died suddenly in 1407, probably of sudden infant death syndrome, Valentine was indirectly accused by Duke John of poisoning her own child. These ridiculous accusations did the trick. Even Louis believed them, and eventually exiled Valentine to Neufchâtel.

Once Valentine had been removed, John chose his moment to strike. It happened on November 25, 1407, at the Château de St.-Pol in Paris. A gang of thugs in John's pay, led by the king's own *valet de chambre,* came to Louis's quarters claiming that the king wanted to see him at once. Louis never suspected a thing, and followed the valet into John's trap. Louis was accompanied by five or six of his own servants when he was set upon by John's eighteen to twenty men. Louis identified himself and demanded to be allowed to pass. The lead assassin replied, "Ah, you are the man we want!" Two of Louis's servants were killed before the others fled. The duke's head was smashed open, his body mutilated, and his remains left in the mud while the murderers made their getaway.

The morning after the assassination, John took his place at the funeral service alongside the king and queen, showing the respect due his slain cousin, despite whisperings linking him to Louis's murder. Two days later, John confessed to his uncles the dukes of Anjou and Berry that he had instigated the crime. The following morning he left Paris for Flanders.

When Valentine heard of her beloved husband's assassination from her exile at the Château-Thierry in Neufchâtel, she immediately feared the worst for her children. She ordered her most trusted servants to remove them to Blois, in the heartland of Orléans, to protect them from John. Once she had word that they had arrived safely at her castle there, her mind turned to vengeance.

On the icy winter morning of December 10, 1407, the beautiful widow, dressed in her black velvet mourning weeds, arrived in Paris at the château in Paris where her husband had been murdered. The "old men," the dukes of Berry and Anjou, were present, and the king appeared quite sane to her. Valentine threw herself down at the king's feet and in a torrent of tears demanded justice for her husband's assassination. The king cried as he listened to her impassioned plea, knelt down, and raised her up to him, promising her the vengeance she deserved. A petition was put before the council to punish John, and it seemed as if Valentine would have her revenge.

But John the Fearless was a master spin doctor. He successfully circulated the scurrilous tidbits that Valentine was the temptress witch who made the king mad; that her husband had been a tyrant; and that he, John, was only doing his patriotic duty to France to rid her of the man who wanted to plunge the country into another barbaric war with England and tax her people into oblivion. At a stroke, he had become the voice of the downtrodden, and the king would not go against him. Charles threw out the petition to punish John and embraced him for saving France from wickedness. Valentine was stunned by the outcome, changing her motto to "Nothing more for me, for I am nothing more."

She retired to Blois, apparently a broken woman. But when an uprising in Liège forced John back to Flanders, Valentine cobbled together a stronger Orléanist faction that persuaded Charles to revoke his previous stance in favor of the Burgundy duke, and Valentine returned to the capital. The queen and Valentine became firm allies, and it looked as if John had lost at last.

When John returned from Liège, the people of Paris mobbed the streets in his support, again reversing the tide in his favor. Valentine knew she had been crushed and returned to Blois, sliding rapidly toward death. As she felt the end approaching, she assembled her children around her and made them swear to avenge the death of their father. After they had pledged to carry on her vendetta, Valentine Visconti, duchess of Orléans, died of a broken heart, aged only thirty-eight.

John was victorious, but had not reckoned with Valentine's legacy. Her great jewels and wealth were put at the disposal of her children, and her eldest son, Charles of Orléans, who had recently married into the Armagnac family, became allied to a man of power comparable to that of the Burgundy duke. Charles's father-in-law, Bernard VII, duke of Armagnac, turned the Orléanist cause into one that suited the Armagnacs. A treaty was concluded at Gien on April 15, 1410, among the dukes of Orléans, Armagnac, Bourbon, Berry, Clermont, and Anjou to raise an army and remove John from Paris "for the good, the honor and the advancement of the king, the kingdom and the public weal." Valentine's great diamond (the Sancy) and myriad other jewels were used as security with Parisian merchant lenders to buy this army to oppose John's absolute power. The first known civil war partially financed by the Sancy was imminent.

John's spin machine worked overtime, maintaining to his adoring public that the Orléans/Armagnac faction was interested only in pillaging the countryside, and used examples of their transgressions to support his claim. In reply, in July 1411, Charles of Orléans threw down the gauntlet by issuing letters patent (a royal decree) holding John responsible for his father's murder. The duke's response was immediate: "You and your brothers have lied, and you are lying now, like the traitors you are." John prepared for the war, and for complete control of France.

Now John excelled himself in cleverness. He waited . . . and waited. The Armagnac faction marauded into Paris with its pillaging mercenary horde, and the people fought back without assistance as best they could. At last the king begged John to enter the capital to save his kingdom. And so on October 28—three months after the civil war had begun—John marched his army into Paris and "freed" it. His first decree was to apply the pope's edict against brigands to the looting Armagnac army. Meanwhile, John's own lieutenants pillaged in his name, and jewels and valuables were strewn at John's feet. John's reaction when he beheld Valentine's great jewels, including the Sancy, was not recorded, but this must have made his victory very sweet indeed.

Perhaps it was in the hope that he, or his heirs, would sit upon France's throne that John had the Sancy diamond mounted into a larger jeweled piece called *La Belle Fleur de Lys de Flandres*, or The Beautiful Fleur-de-Lys of Flanders. This jewel united his largest gemstone, the beautiful balas ruby of Flanders, with the largest white diamond in Christendom, now named *La Balle de Flandres*.

The Sancy, as part of *La Belle Fleur de Lys de Flandres*, was pledged by John on July 2, 1412, as security with other jewels to Laurens Caigniel, a merchant from Lucca, for 2,000 livres ($65,500 or £41,000 today) plus interest of 270 livres ($24,000 or £15,000). For the second time in just five years, the Sancy was used to finance the civil war.

The Beautiful Fleur-de-Lys was effectively John the Fearless's coronet. It had three large petals in the middle and two smaller ones on either extremity. In the middle of the central petal above the diamond was Philip the Bold's long balas ruby *La Balais de Flandres,* reputedly the largest in France. The outer petals of the coronet were decorated with eight other large balas rubies, eight sapphires, five emeralds, and thirty-eight large pearls. The ensemble weighed 2 marcs, 7 ounces, and 2 grains—or a stunning 23.2 ounces or 646 grams. With no idea of how much gold was contained in the coronet, it is impossible to assess the weight of the various stones, but the 646 grams converts into an astronomical 3,230 carats!

As in the U.S. Civil War, the civil war between Burgundy and the Armagnac pitted brother against brother, with the lines of battle fought along principle and belief rather than geographic family location. The fog of war claimed its victims on both sides, with the Armagnacs, the Parisian rabble and John alternatively in charge of the capital between 1411 and 1413. In the end the Armagnacs gained the upper hand and possession of Paris.

Once barred from the capital, John initiated the most heinous of crimes for a medieval Frenchman—a secret treaty with the new English king, Henry V. When Henry then laid claim to the French throne through his Capetian ancestors, John was the only major power broker not to take part in the ensuing war. The Armagnacs took charge of France's defense, resulting in the disastrous defeat at Agincourt in 1415, which paved the way for Henry to be crowned king of France. With Charles of Orléans captured at Agincourt (he would spend twenty-five years in England as its prisoner), and the dauphin dying shortly afterward, the Valois dynasty succession passed to his fifteen-year-old brother, Charles.

At dawn on May 18, 1418, John's Burgundian troops entered Paris—for the first time since 1413—initiating a bloodbath. Bernard VII, duke of Armagnac, was assassinated; banks and merchant lenders were pillaged of all their riches; and anyone who stood in John's way was massacred. Less than a year later, on September 10, 1419, John agreed to meet the dauphin Charles on the Yonne bridge at Montereau to discuss how a renewed oath of friendship and alliance between them would work. There are dozens of accounts of what happened that day, yet only one fact remains: John the Fearless was assassinated with a blow from an ax.

4

The Last Great Burgundian Dukes

1420–1476

✦

IN THE INVENTORY TAKEN at John's death in 1423, the huge diamond from The Beautiful Fleur-de-Lys of Flanders appears, but no longer as part of the jewel. It is described as "a large faceted diamond squared with a point, and surrounded in a circle of gold, and the diamond is as large as a nugget of charcoal." John's son Philip the Good had remounted the Sancy diamond in an agrafe, or large clasp, which could be worn as a hatpin or cloak clasp, or attached to a necklace.

Georges Chastellain, the best of the Burgundian chroniclers, refers to the diamond as "the purest and largest in Christendom." Use of the word *pure* meant that the diamond was white rather than completely without flaw. Colored diamonds were not prized at all yet and would never have been described as pure at that time. Philip's son and heir, Charles, wore the large white diamond mounted as a hat ornament, sometimes with a large oriental pearl hanging from it. This mounting has recurred several times throughout the Sancy's long history.

The new duke of Burgundy was quite different from his father. On hearing the news of his father's murder, Philip uttered a blood-curdling cry. A shadow fleeted across his face, and his eyes rolled back in their sockets. Philip was in shock, and his court mourned and wept as much for his reaction as for the loss of the mighty Duke John.

21

Philip was a sensitive prince, full of spirit, extremely handsome and well built, and of noble bearing. He also held a deep love of precious stones. As his court chronicler Chastellain wrote, "He knew how to make the most of jewels, fine horses, splendid armor . . . the crowds gasped at the dazzling display . . . he outshone all his predecessors. His guests were astounded by his array of jewels, tapestries, plates and dishes, and his gold-filled coffers." He was also known as "lickerous," or leacherous, with thirty known mistresses and fifteen biological children.

Philip battled brilliantly against France, allying himself to the king of England. Within a year of John's murder, Charles VI had been compelled to sign a treaty that handed over to Philip vast territories between Burgundy and Paris, as well as the towns of the Somme, Ponthieu, and Boulogne, which could only be redeemed for 4 million ducats ($970 million or £606.2 million today). Importantly, Philip and his heirs were exempted from paying the homage due for his French fiefs during the king's lifetime.

Philip, like his father, spent years making it possible for the English king, Henry V, to conquer French territories. He fought for Henry V, and it was Philip's lieutenant in charge of the Burgundian troops, John of Luxembourg, who accepted Joan of Arc's sword in May 1430. It was Philip who agreed that Joan should be handed over to the English for 10,000 golden crowns ($7.3 million or £4.5 million today) and was, therefore, responsible for her betrayal.

Philip was the best loved of the Burgundian dukes and consolidated John's empire, moving the main court to Bruges because it was the center of commerce. There Philip transformed Burgundy's court into a major "luxury industry" for its members and suppliers. The court set the pace for a generous and diverse patronage system, and merchants made their crust of bread off of its conspicuous splendor.

On Philip's death, Charles, now Charles the Bold, inherited fabulous wealth comprising duchies, counties, châteaus, precious tapestries, illuminated manuscripts, paintings, objets d'art, and exceptional jewels. His library was considered by his contemporaries to be the richest of any, comprising more than nine hundred manuscripts and illuminated books. His fifteenth-century Burgundy had become the wealthiest "nation" in Christendom thanks to the ruthlessness and intellect of its first three dukes, and if it had not been for Charles the Bold's absolute conviction of his invincibility and blind ambition when he became duke, he would have successfully transformed the European map as we know it today.

This last great duke, like many tyrants, had a sense of historic destiny that was well documented by a number of court chroniclers in his pay. Philip de Commines described him as:

> [A] prince not as tall as his father, but strong, well-built and sturdy; strong of arm and spine; narrow shouldered; with a low center of gravity; good legs with powerful thighs, long fingers and small footed, not too heavy, nor too thin, with a lithe body that is suited to all work and forces. He has . . . clear blue, laughing, truthful eyes which are angelically clear, and one can see his father alive in them again. He has a dark beard, with a healthy olive glowing skin. . . . When he walks, he looks down at the ground. . . . He is intelligent, soft-spoken, but once he decides to talk, is quite eloquent. His voice is velvety and clear. The duke loves music, literature and art, and is wise and discreet, and speaks often of a grander destiny. . . . He is . . . sour sometimes when he does not obtain that which he wants, and sharp with his words on these occasions . . . and carries a grudge. . . . To cross him is to court peril. He loves art and the game of checkers and other games of chance, as well as money.

Charles—like all medieval men—was also highly superstitious, partly by virtue of the general lack of scientific understanding of natural events, partly instilled in him, as in others, by the all-embracing church. As a superstitious man, for him diamonds—the indestructible, invincible jewels of the gods—took on an almost religious importance in his mission to conquer Europe. An avid student of ancient history, Charles devoured tales of conquest and pored over stories about his hero Alexander the Great. Charles believed the fables about Alexander and his troops finding the Valley of Diamonds, and like so many before and after him, attributed mystical powers to diamonds.

This legend would have enhanced his reverie about diamonds as an irresistible force. By adopting them as symbols of his own power, he would project onto others the diamond's aura of invincibility. Diamonds also furthered his grand design by being precious talismans of good fortune. He took great care of all his jewels, as their commercial value was only a fraction of their real worth. His detailed house account from 1467 states: "My Seigneur has a jewel repository with a head servant as its *valet de chambre*, who answers only to my Lord. This valet has one assistant guard for the jewels who serves under him. A *sommelier de corps* [bodyguard] always stands guard by him with a second *sommelier de corps* standing guard as well. A third sommelier guards the many jewels of my Seigneur as described in the accounts. Another valet is always present in front of the jewels."

Charles employed these six men not only to protect the jewels but also to keep watch on one another. His chamberlain and chronicler Olivier de la Marche, who had the key to Charles's bedchamber, described the duke's detailed security arrangements. The wages for the duke's inner circle of forty individuals cost a staggering 800 *livres* daily ($65,000 or £40,000 today).

Among the illuminated manuscripts there is a portrayal of a single large diamond mounted on a hat, in a work by Guillaume Fillastre titled *The History of the Order of the Golden Fleece*; the portrayal appears in both volumes one and two, which were completed in about 1473. An earlier illuminated work, *The History of Charles Martel* (Charlemagne), written by David Aubert between 1463 and 1465, also shows Charles the Bold wearing his famous diamond. Charles had kept the diamond, as his father had had it mounted in a gold setting as a single separate stone to be worn as an agrafe.

According to the Swiss chronicler Diebold Schilling, the diamond was *sans similitude* or *sans-si* (without equal). A Basel archival record from 1477 states that it weighed *cent six* (pronounced "sancy") carats (one hundred six carats). The diamond was described as being "roughly the size of a walnut."

Charles's fabulous jewel collection, the largest of any royal collection in Europe at that time, had been amassed from the time of his great-grandfather Philip the Bold, who, like many of the benevolent tyrants of his time, had an eye for beauty and a love of stones. Yet this love never transcended monetary value. When the stones had to be put up as security to fight the latest war, or make the latest conquest, Charles, like the three previous dukes, used his gems to gain and retain power.

By the time Charles became duke in 1467, Bruges was a large town with a splendid port and forty-five thousand inhabitants. Merchants flocked there from all over the world to sell their goods in northern Europe. Permanent commercial offices were established with Venice, Genoa, Lucca, Castile, Navarre, Portugal, England, and the German Hansa. The Brugean world market was supported by a well-developed money market, with Italian bankers producing the newest financial instruments and ample capital. The rich court culture started by Charles's father, Philip the Good, thrived, with hundreds of skilled craftsmen and experts producing high-quality finished goods. Commines explained the wealth of the people of Bruges: "the subjects of the House of Burgundy were very prosperous because of the lasting peace and because of the goodness of their prince, who did not tax his subjects heavily." For merchants to cross Charles would have been financial suicide.

The earliest record of diamonds being sold in Bruges dates back to about 1370 and is linked with Venetian imports. The Venetian ambassador to the Burgundian court wrote back to the Doges Palace in the late fourteenth century:

> I saw oranges and lemons from Castile as fresh as if they had just been picked, food and wine from Greece as abundant as their homeland. I also saw pieces of cloth and spices from Alexandria and all corners of the Levant as if one would really be staying there. Moreover, there were as many furs from the black sea regions, as if they were produced in Flanders. I could find everything I could imagine from Italy—brocades, silks, weapons and precious stones. In a word, in Bruges, one can find all goods produced anywhere else in the world.

This portrait of Bruges contrasts sharply with those of other European capitals of the time. Europe was only beginning to recover from the ravages of the Black Death, which had killed more than a third of the Continental population a hundred years earlier. Most people in the fifteenth century worked the land under the dominion of a powerful aristocracy and an all-powerful Catholic Church.

Furthermore, by 1467, the basic principles of social and financial hierarchy and institutions and the organization of roads and towns would be readily recognizable to a twenty-first-century person. Trade had developed between regions, but the nation-state was in its infancy, with only England, Wales, Scotland, Portugal, and Switzerland maintaining much the same borders that they do today. Italy was divided into its city and papal states, with Germany (the Hanseatic States) and Spain divided into regions.

The economies of England and Flanders were interdependent, with a brisk trade in luxury items such as jewels, wool, and fine cloth well established. Exchange based on money in different European currencies had already developed. Simply put, the economic world as we know it today is based on foundations laid before Charles the Bold's time.

Charles's world was, without doubt, treacherous, yet every court in Europe tried to model itself on that of Burgundy. Edward IV's English court was patterned on that of Philip of Burgundy, which was described as "being a royal court worthy of leading a kingdom, full of riches and men from every nation." The duke's total income was estimated to be 900,000 ducats ($218.2 million or £136.4 million today). This vast sum was equivalent to the total revenue of the Republic of Venice. The Republic of Florence had only a quarter of that sum, and the pope half.

When Charles inherited his domains on the death of his father in 1467, he immediately set about putting his finances in order, just as another French warrior, Napoleon Bonaparte, would do 333 years later, and his first priority was to assess the value of his jewels and plate. The role of jewelry, and most especially precious stones, went far beyond giving pleasure and ensuring status. Jewelry was above all a negotiable asset honored by banking houses and moneylenders, and was frequently the only acceptable collateral. John had pawned the Sancy to raise an army, and Charles intended to do the same if necessary.

As with his predecessors, Charles's archenemy was the king of France—this time Louis XI, nicknamed "The Universal Spider." Louis's mistrust of Charles was equally deep-rooted, and his main ambition was to conquer the upstart duke of Burgundy and absorb the duchies back into the kingdom of France. He both resented and feared the power of Burgundy, and he mistrusted Charles. Louis was a man of uninspiring appearance, with a long, hooked nose; a mouth that showed an expression of perpetual disdain; a double chin; and heavy-lidded, wary eyes. He was determined to conquer his renegade vassal and would entangle the whole of Europe in his web of intrigues within ten years of Charles's inheriting.

Charles, for his part, was obsessed with conquest, and therefore needed his riches to help him achieve that goal. Commines, in defense of Charles, wrote: "As money is the ruler by which one can arm oneself and guarantee against such vagaries of life . . . our prince's need for money and to guard it dearly is not only for himself but also for the fruit that it can bring in more opportune times."

Charles's gems were essential to his future. As a dynamic ruler, always thinking, plotting the way forward toward his goal of reestablishing the Middle Kingdom of Lotharingia as intended by Charlemagne when he divided the Holy Roman Empire among his three sons, Charles was single-minded in this purpose. When he became duke of Burgundy, he was thirty-four and had already been married twice. His first wife, Catherine of France, daughter of Charles VII and sister of Louis XI, died without giving Charles an heir. His second wife, Isabella of Bourbon, bore him a daughter, Marie, before Isabella's untimely death.

From the outset there seemed to be a haste, a rashness, in Charles's actions, as if he knew that he was somehow running out of time to achieve his aims. This haste would prove his downfall. Charles never acquired even the superficial heartiness of his father that had made him so loved by his subjects. Charles was passionate but reserved, and held himself apart from his court, cultivating neither friends nor confidants. Olivier de la Marche once wrote that the duke had "an indefinably barbaric cast of countenance which was in perfect keeping with his passion for storms and surging seas."

Yet above all, Charles was recklessly ambitious and headstrong, and was renowned for not taking any of his advisers' counsel. He could often be seen storming through the castles where he lived, his black cloaks flowing like sails, shouting orders, pacing like a caged bear when he could not get his way immediately. Commines claimed that "even half of Europe would not have satisfied him." These traits, combined with the suspicious nature that he had inherited from his mother, Isabella of Portugal, who was called "the most suspicious lady who ever lived" by Charles's father, made life in the Burgundian court tumultuous.

By 1470, with Bruges flourishing, the phenomenally wealthy Burgundy was nearly completely estranged from its overlord, France. This led Charles to believe that Burgundy could afford to go its own way. Yet he also felt that his success was dependent on the failure of France. To annoy and disorient his enemy, Charles claimed to be English, since he was a descendant of John of Gaunt. At other times he claimed to be Portuguese, through his mother. Of France, he often stated that he "wished her to have six kings." A smaller, weaker France would be easier to conquer if it were turned against itself in civil war, he reasoned. His dream was to establish the Kingdom of Burgundy on the ruins of royal France, and in 1474 he delivered a speech at Dijon setting out how this would be achieved.

Though perhaps unclear to others, Charles's plan had been put into action from the outset of his reign. Using marriage to further his aims, he put his ten-year-old daughter Marie on the blocks in 1467, so that he could have reliable political alliances. In fact, the matter of Marie's marriage forms one of the most curious anecdotes in fifteenth-century European history. By following the long and tortuous procession of her French, Austrian, English, and Italian fiancés, it is easy to follow Charles's rash thinking, daring adventures, and fleeting coalitions.

Unable to decide which potential suitor would make the best ally through his daughter's marriage, Charles remarried for the third time, in 1470, to Margaret of York, sister of the Yorkist King Edward IV of England, in a ceremony that was guilty of the most conspicuous ostentation. The wedding lasted ten days, with thirty-course feasts twice daily. The jeweled gowns, handsomely dressed men, and diamond-studded horses were described in great detail by the Burgundian chroniclers Molinet and de la Marche.

Charles wore his hat with the "largest and purest diamond in Christendom" in a gold setting with a large oriental pearl hanging from it, attached to the middle above his brow. Georges Chastellain not only referred to the diamond as the purest and largest in Christendom, but also clearly described it as a pear-shaped stone. In the nineteenth century, lapidary writers claimed that this diamond was the citron-colored Florentine without taking into consideration the fact that a yellow diamond would never have been described as "pure."

It is believed that Charles also wore the Sancy to his coronation in 1468, though it was probably worn under the coronation robes rather than as a hat ornament. According to various inventories, Charles had three diamonds in excess of forty carats, and would have worn all of these for the most important occasion of his wedding—symbolizing his indestructible ties to his strong ally England.

England and France had ended their Hundred Years' War only thirty years earlier, and for nearly a generation England had been in the throes of its Wars of the Roses, essentially a civil war spurred on by the personal feudal rivalry between the Houses of York and Lancaster for the English throne. By uniting with the Yorkist English king, Charles was making a challenge to Louis, who was allied to the Lancastrian English king, Henry VI.

But the storm over France had only just begun to gather force. Louis XI also had incurred the wrath of John II of Aragon by supporting the House of Anjou against John. In October 1469, John's son Ferdinand married the powerful Isabel of Castile, who would during their own reign see the height of the Spanish Inquisition and finance Columbus's first voyage to the New World. It now looked as if France would find itself in a pincer attack among Burgundy to the east, England to the north, and the first two united provinces of a new Spain to the south.

The tense situation for France was defused temporarily when Louis struck a masterful blow to Charles by promoting the treachery of the earl of Warwick, called "The Kingmaker" in England, in support of the Lancastrian Henry VI. Edward IV was forced to flee the country, and was given safe haven in Charles's commercial capital, Bruges. Louis had, at a stroke, not only stopped Charles's plan of conquering France but also had prolonged the English Wars of the Roses.

Charles retaliated by using his vast wealth. He gave Edward IV 50,000 crowns ($1.8 million or £1.1 million today) and an army that enabled him to successfully reconquer England, putting Louis directly into the English king's vengeful sights. Within four years, the pendulum had swung against, then in favor of Duke Charles.

Charles, while less devious than Louis, portrayed himself as Edward IV's and John II of Aragon's powerful champion purely to serve his own needs. A letter dated March 28, 1473, from Charles to John shows clearly how Charles was able to turn the situation to his advantage:

> Having been asked on several occasions by my very dear brother and cousin the Duke of Brittany, on behalf of the King of France, our common enemy . . . to conclude truces with him until the 1st April 1473 . . . I agreed to do so, but on the express condition that Your Majesty's name be included, with your consent, as one of my confederates and allies. . . . I learned also that the said King of France was proposing to send against you the army which had been made available through the surrender of Lectoure.
>
> On hearing this, I immediately ordered a thousand lancers recruited in Italy. . . . It is my intention that these troops should cooperate with the Burgundian contingents against our common enemy, if he breaks truces by attacking Your Majesty.
>
> I shall be at the head of my forces to see that he is given no rest. . . . I have sent letters and messengers urging them [the king of England and the duke of Brittany] to bring a common pressure to bear. . . .
>
> I wish our common enemy to know that Your Majesty's cause and mine are so closely linked and our policies so united that no one can attack either of us without the other intervening at once.

With this letter, Charles had launched the first NATO-style alliance in Europe. He undoubtedly had a military mind, and had built up his army carefully, but he lacked the patience and subtleness for diplomacy, and the decisiveness to lead a large army into battle, eventually reducing his extraordinarily powerful military machine to dust.

Whatever Charles's revenues, they could never finance a pan-European war. Year after year Burgundy's deficit increased, in the same alarming way that national deficits do today in similar circumstances. But unlike many kingdoms, Burgundy had recourse to outside sources of capital—advances from merchants or moneylenders who accepted securities and other forms of guarantees, such as jewels, in exchange for gold. We should view these collateralized operations as the same sort of manipulation of gold reserves employed by nations until the mid-twentieth century. The merchants of Bruges and Antwerp were, simply put, Charles's gold reserves.

Merchant lenders—or merchant bankers, as they preferred to be known—who were headquartered in Bruges included a number of Italians from Florence, Lucca, and Venice. They also began to set up shop in Antwerp as the Schelt River began silting up, thereby making sea trade from Bruges more difficult. Portuguese families like the Rodrigues d'Evora, originally of Jewish extraction, were obliged to emigrate during the Inquisition and found homes in Antwerp. The great German merchant banking house of Fugger also was established in Antwerp. The Low Countries—modern-day Belgium and Holland—were seen as fast-growing economic miracles. These merchants and their cities were all to play a critical role in financing Duke Charles's wars, and most of them were to benefit from the spoils afterward.

When the duke of Lorraine died in 1473, Charles's war aims suddenly became succinct: to seize the Duchy of Lorraine. This would make him the ruler of ancient Lotharingia and Burgundia, stretching southward, he hoped, to Provence. Clandestine maneuvers were set in motion to obtain the inheritance of René, the duke of Anjou, who was the father of Queen Margaret of England, wife of the feebleminded Lancastrian Henry VI, who was now languishing in the Tower of London.

Charles dreamed of Marseilles being Burgundy's port on the Mediterranean, as it had been in the fifth century. And the dream of kingship, once offered as a sop to his father, Philip, looked as if it might at last be realized. Like so many later tyrants, those who knew him said that Charles was lost in his dreamlike follies of glory and the paradoxical pursuit of his destiny.

An aggression treaty aimed at France had been signed between Charles and the Yorkist king Edward IV. The only missing piece in the duke's geopolitical puzzle was an alliance with the Holy Roman emperor, Frederick III. And like Napoleon and Hitler, he mistakenly turned to the east before consolidating the empire to the west.

Charles arranged to meet Frederick on September 20, 1473, at Trèves on the pretense of discussing the marriage of Marie to the emperor's son Maximilian. As he contemplated his own dazzling and ostentatious retinue, Charles took great comfort from the fact that the Holy Roman emperor arrived with a humble suite. The duke's horses were covered in diamond-studded headgear, armor, and saddles with velvet blankets, while the emperor's were merely saddled with leather livery. Charles dismounted and greeted the Holy Roman emperor on bended knee, secretly opening talks to raise his ducal state to a kingdom.

But the duke hardly expected that Louis XI had already poisoned Frederick against him. After two months of Charles's exorbitant demands and Louis's whisperings that the bellicose duke intended to take over the Holy Roman Empire, Frederick III panicked and took flight in the dead of the night on November 25. His boatmen rowed him across the murky and freezing waters of the Rhine, setting in motion the next move for both Charles and Louis.

Incredibly, Charles did not perceive the emperor's undignified exit as a bad omen. He was preoccupied with his own designs to become king. After all, everything was ready: the thrones, the coronation garments, all the pomp and circumstance befitting such an important occasion. Undeterred, he approached his goal with renewed vigor, according to de la Marche, in "forging himself a kingdom." Charles's motto—"I have set my hand to it"—emblazoned on his crest, shields, and livery, spoke of his determination.

So when Charles made his first official progress into his capital, Dijon, on January 23, 1474, some two months after Frederick fled for his life, his speech delivered on the stone steps of the Hôtel de Ville reminded his faithful subjects that "the former kingdom of Burgundy had for a long time been usurped by the French and made a duchy of France, which should give all his subjects cause for sorrow."

It was nothing less than a declaration of war. In Commines's words, "His thoughts were grand, but no man would know how to accomplish them."

5

Playing into the
Hands of Thieves

1474–1477

WHILE CHARLES PREFERRED TO WEAR JEWELS on his silk- and velvet-clad person, and thus display his power, more often than not, his riches were used as financial instruments to buy arms, men, and food quickly to build a kingdom. As he was superstitious, he had a mortal fear of being portrayed in paintings wearing his precious jewels and finery, either for fear of enticing thieves or, more likely, in fear of his enemies being able to understand the source of his power.

His wars to become king of the Middle Kingdom of Lotharingia (as originally intended by Charlemagne) began with the signing of the Treaty of London in 1474 with his brother-in-law Edward IV. It provided for Edward's invasion of France no later than the summer of 1475, with a force of ten thousand men. Charles would supply another ten thousand to assist Edward in France's conquest. The duke also recognized Edward as king of France, an empty title that all English kings kept using until Charles II in 1660.

While Edward prepared his army at Calais, England's last possession in France, Louis XI had no doubts that Charles and Edward intended to destroy him. Louis, who could never muster an adequate army to defend France against England and Burgundy, retaliated by making Charles's uneasy neighbors worry to distraction about the unstable and hot-tempered duke's next move. Louis's insinuations and innuendos worked. The duke of Lorraine was the first to be roused against Burgundy's duke, whose ambition, as Louis XI intimated, was to become the elector of Cologne. Next, Switzerland became allied to Austria—its mortal enemy. Then Louis loaned Austria enough money to repay the debt to Charles on Austrian territories in Alsace. Yet, rather than return these lands to Austria, Charles quickly mobilized to defend what he felt was his by right, and attacked the town of Neuss in Lorraine. Meanwhile, France and Austria incited the Alsatians to revolt against Charles's cruel and tyrannical bailiff, Peter de Hagenbach. When de Hagenbach was brutally executed by an outraged mob, it provoked one of Charles's most incendiary rages.

With his machinations, Louis had duped Charles into withdrawing his gaze from France. The rash duke stormed headlong to Alsace and into Louis's trap, taking most of his vast wealth to war with him for four reasons: to protect himself from defeat by keeping close by his "invincible" diamonds; to display his power and opulence to the impoverished rebels; to guard his treasures from theft; and, most importantly, to use his riches, if required at short notice, to finance his war.

Charles was informed by messenger that the English king was preparing his invasion for the summer of 1475, as planned in the Treaty of London. Instead of joining Edward at Calais, as had been agreed, Charles battled on in Alsace, obsessed with the fear of defeat or retreat. Commines expressed the duke's state of mind succinctly when he said, "God had allowed his mind and judgement to become disordered, for all his life he had striven to open a way to France for the English, and at this moment when the English were ready, he remained stubbornly determined to embark on an impossible undertaking."

When Edward and the "finest army to ever cross the Channel" (according to the Calendar of State Papers of England) landed, Charles at last suspended the siege of Neuss to join his brother-in-law, leaving the finest of his men-at-arms in Alsace. During a three-day marathon discussion that followed, the duke browbeat his royal brother-in-law into believing that a change of battle plan would be to their mutual advantage, and Charles rushed back to pursue his battles in the East. And so while Edward advanced his troops southward as agreed, Charles became bogged down in Lorraine. By now, Edward IV viewed his brother-in-law's behavior with downright suspicion. After all, he had now been in France for two months without Charles's help. The brief and victorious campaign promised by Charles was becoming a nightmare for Edward: the French were resisting steadfastly, while casualties and disease in the ranks were rife. Charles, for his part, remained wholly engrossed in his pitched battles against the duke of Lorraine, ignoring his main ally.

Edward decided that he had no choice but to act in the best interests of England, and sent word to Louis that he would like to open talks for a treaty between their two countries. Louis was in his element, and began the clandestine negotiations. Edward put his terms on the table immediately: if, within two weeks, Louis paid him seventy-five thousand crowns—the sum spent to date on the war—and granted Edward a pension of fifty thousand crowns annually for life, the English king would be happy to make peace. Louis agreed, as long as his son could marry one of the English princesses, who would be granted a dowry of sixty thousand crowns. They shook hands on the deal, there and then, and the Hundred Years' War between France and England was finally at an end.

When Charles heard what had happened he was enraged, and made for Edward's camp, berating his brother-in-law for being a turncoat. Edward replied in kind, reproaching Charles for failing to honor the Treaty of London. Charles flew off in a fury, asserting that he did not need the English to attain his purpose, nor would he conclude a peace with France until at least three months after the English army had retreated home. Edward left Charles to his tantrums and returned to England.

Stepping into England's place against France with his other allies, like the king of Naples and John of Aragon, Charles battled on. Yet he remained obsessed with the Lorraine and Swiss insurrections, and determined to fight on there until victory was his.

Without the financial assistance of his allies, Charles's jewels had to serve their primary purpose: to buy mercenary armies. But because it was the ultimate symbol of power, the Sancy remained in Charles's possession. Charles subjugated Lorraine with a vengeful and bloody hand, making full-scale war between the Swiss and Burgundy inevitable. The duke made no attempts at diplomacy, and in fact relished the prospect of a pitched battle.

In January 1476 Charles made his first campaign into the Swiss cantons with fifteen thousand men, whose loyalty was purchased with his gold and jewels. The duke made his first cruel and ruthless attack at Grandson, where his triumphant forces executed four hundred of the town's defenders by hanging and threw hundreds of other victims into the lake to drown. Fueled by this cruel victory, he then marched on Neufchâtel.

The Swiss cantons, which for centuries had agreed to come to one another's aid, had created a confederate army and marched together to meet the Burgundian tyrant at Neufchâtel. They hurled Charles's forces back in confusion to Grandson on March 2. The next morning, by all accounts, a heavy mist hung over the lake, which ran the full length of the right side of the floodplain that would become the battle-field. Charles's forces were caught unawares by the Swiss, who came up by way of a ravine and rushed into attack sounding their horns, which reverberated against the walls of the mountains. The din was deafening and disoriented the Burgundians. Charles fatefully ordered his men to give ground, claiming later that his orders had been mis-understood, and caused a general panic. The Burgundians were pushed back—some into the river, others into the lake and surrounding swamps. The Swiss attack in a mountain pass meant that there was no freedom of maneuver and made the Burgundians easy prey. According to the chronicler Paradin (1510–1567), "all seemed to flee in a marvel-lous disorder, as if they were being chased from the spot by some invis-ible force. The Burgundians fled faster than the Swiss could follow."

The jubilant Swiss overran Charles's camp and spent the next three days in an orgy of rape and looting of the greatest treasures of the time. According to Charles's chronicler Molinet, who was taken prisoner by the Swiss at Grandson, "and the Duke René of Lorraine, extremely joyous and proud of his people, stayed for the night in the camp of the Duke Charles of Burgundy, which he found to be well served with provisions, rings, jewels and plate and utensils. And for retribution of this service, which he made to the Swiss, these Swiss gave him a park and the spoils of war from the Burgundians, such as he had found on the field of battle."

The Swiss chronicler Jean de Troyes reported, "It is here that he lost all his wealth—gold, silver, plate, jewels, tapestries, all of his artil-lery, tents, pavilions and generally all that he had taken to Grandson."

Olivier de la Marche, who was a faithful servant to Charles until the bitter end, wrote shortly after he rejoined his downtrodden master from the battlefield: "The duke is terribly sad and quite melancholy having lost this day, where his rich rings and jewels were pillaged from his broken army. The Swiss won, on this day of the battle, jewels, the wooden Palace of the duke with its very rich plate, all of his pavilions, tapestries and riches of the Duke Charles."

But it was perhaps Commines, who rarely wrote of Charles's jewels or wealth in detail and who had already deserted his Burgundian master for the patronage of Louis XI, who summed up the situation best when he wrote, "now we can see how the world changed after this battle."

It is Paradin, however, who provides us with the fate of the Sancy that day when he tells the story of what had been passed down to him. He interpreted for posterity the very importance of Charles's loss of power when he wrote:

> Since, on this particular voyage, he [Charles] had to take everything he owned with him, in order to demonstrate his excessive grandeur to the foreigners. . . . The loss the Duke incurred this day was estimated in cash terms at thirty times one hundred thousand *écus* [$2.2 billion or £1.4 billion] which made the Swiss rich, since they had never before had any knowledge of this kind of wealth and the value of the booty: they divided into pieces the most beautiful and sumptuous pavilions that the world had ever seen in separating the booty, which they could then sell again very expensively to their personal profit. . . . Amongst them was one Swiss soldier who picked up the private jewel-box in which the large diamond belonging to the Duke with a big pearl hanging from it lay. He took the diamond out of its box, looked at it, then put it back inside the box, then threw it under the wheels of a moving cart, and after went to fetch it. He sold it to a priest for a florin, and the priest gave it to his Masters, who paid him three francs for it. There is a huge market for this, the most beautiful of diamonds in Christendom. It is one of three jewels of incredible size. The first is named The Three Brothers, the next, a jewel named *La Hotte,* and the third a balas ruby named *La Balle de Flandres* [the Sancy] which are all the most beautiful stones that one could hope to find.

Paradin's account has led to centuries of confusion about the Sancy's loss at Grandson. He correctly refers to the three largest jewels belonging to Charles by name, but misleads—undoubtedly unintentionally—in their description. The Three Brothers was a large ruby and diamond jewel, most prized for its rubies. *La Hotte* was a very large ruby, not a diamond. By referring to the "balas ruby named *La Balle de Flandres*" he had mistaken the *Belle balais de Flandres* [the Flanders balas ruby] with the diamond *La Balle de Flandres*. The most beautiful diamonds in Christendom were undoubtedly lost on that day at Grandson— along with the most beautiful rubies—but Paradin, alas, has not given posterity a cast iron description on which to hang its hat. It is certain that Charles had a new setting created for *La Belle Fleur de Lys de Flandres*, the coronet originally crafted for John the Fearless, from which he could extract *La Balle de Flandres* (the Sancy) to wear on its own. Yet this is no reason to completely discard Paradin's account.

While Charles skulked off in a near-catatonic state, the Cantons agreed among themselves to compile a complete list of booty, known as the *Burgunderbeute*, or Burgundy Booty, which describes down to the most minute detail who took what from whom and how much of what they took had been handed over. The Swiss soldiers were under penalty of death if they did not hand in their loot. Hundreds of pages describe the wealth that Charles had taken with him to Grandson and lost so senselessly that day.

Among the booty to reach Lucerne, where it was to be divided equally among the Swiss, were silver pots, plates, bowls, mugs, and other silver tableware; gold tableware; and candlesticks that were weighed and estimated at four hundredweight (which makes eight hundred marks or half pounds in silver or gold). But for every item that was counted in Lucerne, it was estimated that ninety-nine other items of inestimable value were secreted away by the victorious Swiss soldiers. Even by the most conservative Swiss reckoning only a hundredth part of the booty was ever documented. The Lucerne booty had some silver and golden cloaks and other silk and golden cloth and clothes and many edible delicacies that the impoverished Swiss had never seen before and found difficult to describe in a written record. There were also many large tapestries, one of which was made entirely of gold thread with six beautiful large pearls and six large rubies sewn into it along with a religious relic.

The *Burgunderbeute* list is quite staggering, describing with Swiss efficiency who acquired which pieces, which Swiss contingent they belonged to, the number of men in that contingent, and then the pieces themselves as best they could. Not surprisingly, while there are well over a hundred jewels mentioned in the *Burgunderbeute*, there are few large diamonds. There is, however, reference made to one of the duke of Burgundy's diamonds and staff, which are described as "inestimable." This diamond is described as "half a walnut," mounted in gold with two large pearls hanging from it as a pendant that could be separated from the diamond by a clasp. It was arranged in a setting with seven large diamonds, seven large rubies, and fifteen large pearls and was described as "something wonderful and invaluable."

Could this have been the Sancy, previously described as a "walnut"? There is no record of Charles having cut the large diamond, nor would he have had reason to do so. While there are diamonds and other priceless jewels on this list, none of Charles's great jewels appear, and certainly the three great jewels described by Paradin are not in this comprehensive and compelling litany of the duke's phenomenal wealth. The jewel for the Order of the Golden Fleece is missing. The White Rose jewel given to him by his brother-in-law is nowhere. The *Federlin,* or little feather jewel, which is known to have been in his possession, does not appear. *La Hotte* and *La Balle de Flandres,* or the coronet *La Belle Fleur de Lys de Flandres,* do not rate a mention. If the Swiss precision dictated that *all* the booty needed to be reported under penalty of death, then surely all the loot would be on the list.

It seems likely, therefore, taking Paradin, Schilling, and other Swiss chroniclers as a point of departure, and where the Sancy next surfaced, that the "priest" referred to was a priest from the Bishopric of Basel. While Basel contributed its own contingent of men to the battles as a junior partner in the Swiss venture, it was widely understood that it would not receive a "full" share of the booty. The priest, having proven that the diamond was real when it did not shatter when it was thrown under the wheels of the cart (as the "indestructibility" of diamonds was never doubted in those days), would have gone to the bishop or his chamberlain to tell him the good news of his find. The priest was amply rewarded in his eyes, since he had no concept of its value. The bishop, however, seeing the extraordinary booty that had been laid before him of the Three Brothers, *La Hotte,* and *La Balle de Flandres* [the Sancy], knew precisely what he had to do. The terms of the division of the spoils meant that everything would need to be transported to Lucerne, and from there divided *equally* among all the participants in the battle, as well as any other battles to come. The bishop of Basel had an easy choice to make; he sat tight, did nothing, and waited.

Within nine months of losing his precious treasures at Grandson, Charles fought his last battle, at Nancy, where he was utterly defeated, and hacked to death by the townspeople as he lay mortally wounded on the field of battle.

Word of mouth and superstition spread throughout Europe like wildfire. The mighty Duke Charles had lost his indestructible diamonds, his wealth, and a kingdom the likes of which had never been known. Surely he must have been cursed to come to such an end.

Meanwhile, the Sancy and the other gems found in the crushed jewel box of Charles the Bold would remain locked away in secret for another fourteen years.

6

The Diamond Vanishes

1476–1507

⌘

DEEP WITHIN THE BASEL ARCHIVES lies a secret bill of sale dated 1504 to Jacob Fugger, the head of a great merchant banking house headquartered in Augsburg, Germany, for the purchase of four jewels from the Bishopric of Basel. The method of payment, when the sale had to be completed, and the conditions under which Jacob could have access to the jewels are all set out in this secret document.

The Fugger *Ehrenspiegel* (Inventory) of 1508 describes this trans-action and gives us the first clue as to the whereabouts of the Sancy:

> By and large the Swiss have defeated him [Charles], scattered his army, seized all his possessions, weapons, valuables worth well over ten times a hundred thousand gulden or florin. The silver riches went unnoticed for their value as the Swiss believed them to be pewter. The splendid silk pavilions and other princely household items were part of the Swiss booty. Whatever form the distribution of the loot took, it somehow contained the large and pointed dia-mond, the one that was renowned in the whole of Christendom [the Sancy]. The Three Brothers jewel, called thusly for its three large rubies that are the same size, thickness and weight was also in the booty. It is embellished with three of the largest Oriental pearls according to the old custom. The first diamond [the Sancy] was not immediately sold off, but was secretly sold some years later. The next jewel was offered to Jacob Fugger who was famous everywhere

41

for his vast wealth. While this jewel with its pure stones, so large and magnificent had also belonged to the Duke of Burgundy, the same Jacob Fugger bought, as is described in the following, the gem, plus a ruby and feathered gem for 47,000 Gulden [$34.2 million or £21.4 million] from the Swiss citizen Kauffweiss and kept it for a number of years.

The Fugger *Ehrenspiegel,* like all other chronicles of the times, depicts the Swiss as unworldly in terms of the booty they possessed from the battles at Grandson, Morat, and Nancy. Indeed, the fact that they physically sliced up the priceless tapestries that came into their hands into various shares is testimony to this fact. Although the bishop of Basel would have known that the Sancy was precious, he would have been unaware of the true market value for such a gem, or the other jewels he held. Wisely, the bishop waited . . . and waited. The Burgundy Booty was tallied, recorded, and divvied up at Lucerne, while more and more Swiss "soldiers" donned gold and silk jerkins, ate off gold plates, rode fine horses, and sported other forms of wealth far beyond their means.

As the accumulated wealth in the countryside began to disappear over the years, the bishop assumed that the jewels he possessed would eventually be forgotten, just as the cantons "forgot" to persecute those who had so overtly stolen from the Burgundy Booty. The canny bishop knew that when it came time to sell his precious cache, he should sell through a fellow Swiss. This would give him the most leverage by threatening the buyer with hellfire and damnation, not to mention sharing in the penalty of death as engrossed in the Edict of Lucerne of March 21, 1477, which set out the punishment for all those who stole from the Burgundy Booty.

And so it was in 1491, some fifteen years after Charles's defeat, as the Basel records show, that the Sancy, described as "a very large white diamond the size of a walnut," was sold to the Hertenstein family of Lucerne, who were merchants, for just over 5,000 florins ($606,000 or £379,000). The Hertensteins were not one of the great merchant banking families who dominated European trade at that time and would never have had access to that kind of capital. They could best be described as second-tier middlemen acting as agents for smaller profits than the international merchants on behalf of the grand families like the Fuggers.

Hertenstein, while no expert in fine jewels or diamonds, would have certainly known how to turn a tidy profit on this opportunity. He would not have contemplated, for a moment, being a turncoat and collecting a paltry reward by notifying the cantons of the bishop's lapse. He would have known precisely who would buy it from him *outside* Switzerland for the greatest profit—and may have even been the intermediary for the eventual purchaser. With language being one barrier and trade relationships another, Hertenstein would have had a natural preference for a fellow German-speaking merchant. And the greatest of these was Jacob Fugger.

Jacob was the shining star of the family business, which he brought to preeminence early in the sixteenth century. The Fuggers were not one of the ancient well-connected merchant families of Augsburg like the Welsers, Herwarts, or Lagenmantels. According to his 1409 will, the clothier Hans Fugger left a considerable fortune of 3,000 florins, but still well short of what was needed to create a great merchant banking empire. Hans's younger son, Jacob (the Elder), a modest and hardworking man, married the daughter of the treasurer of Augsburg, who, according to Fugger's biographer Victor von Klarwill, "had grand relations and business dealings with all sorts of merchants." Jacob's father-in-law ended up in the Tyrol, where Jacob and his wife followed, making the first family fortune mining silver.

On his death in 1469, his three oldest sons—Ulrich, Georg, and Peter—continued in the family business. The two youngest sons, Marcus and Jacob, were destined for entry into the church. But when Peter died suddenly in 1473, the distraught Jacob abandoned the prospect of becoming a priest to join the family business. By age fourteen, Jacob had attended the Fondaco dei Tedeschi (the German Foundation) in Venice, learning about business as many young Germans did, with the added advantage of watching the family business in operation at its Venice office and warehouse. By the time Jacob had come of age, he had shown a genius for business far beyond that of his older brothers. He was like a master chess player, always seeing at least three moves ahead of his opponents and always winning. It was said that no large transaction occurred in Europe without Jacob

Fugger's knowledge, and that if he could carve a role for the House of Fugger in any transaction for financial or political gain, he would do so.

When Georg died in 1506, followed shortly by Ulrich, Jacob found himself in sole charge of the family empire. Quiet, highly intelligent, and thoughtful, Jacob was able to capitalize on the relationship that Ulrich had first cemented with the Habsburg Holy Roman emperor Frederick III in 1473, when Jacob provided the fine silk cloth for Frederick's meeting with Charles the Bold at Trèves. There is no doubt that Jacob followed the defeat of Charles with an eye to the main chance, especially as Charles's son-in-law Maximilian I was the reigning monarch with whom he had to deal for the Tyrolean silver and copper mines.

By 1496 Jacob had departed from his usual prudential financing arrangements, and agreed to advance 121,600 florins ($14.7 million or £9.2 million today) to back Maximilian's folly to be crowned Holy Roman emperor in Rome. The only reason for the wise financier to become embroiled in such a costly episode would have been to gain political advantage. In the end, Jacob needed to advance only 40,000 florins in total, which would have been a sound investment for the extension of his financial empire into Italy.

So when a diamond described as "the size of a walnut" was sold to Hertenstein, there is little doubt that Jacob Fugger knew of the transaction and was one of the few merchants in Europe with the political and financial means to purchase it. As so often was the case, no bill of sale survives, if one ever existed. The transaction could easily have been part in cash, part in favors, or as settlement for many unpaid accounts, and we may never know which it was.

By 1502 Jacob had been approached by "men of confidence" and was negotiating directly with the Bishopric of Basel for the purchase of four other jewels that had been stashed away along with the Sancy. This in itself is further evidence that the bishop believed Jacob to be the end purchaser of the Sancy, and one of very few men with a sufficient fortune to acquire his remaining jewels in secret. Jacob had established a flourishing trade with the pope from 1500, and was already known as "banker to the pope." He was also banker to the Habsburgs and Maximilian.

Having trained initially for the church, Jacob spoke the prelates' language, and had been recommended to all other princely curates as a "man with whom one could do business." The bishop could not have wished for a better recommendation for Jacob's fortune or discretion. On September 16, 1504, the secret bill of sale between Basel and Jacob Fugger was signed, giving Jacob the rights to the other four jewels "from the treasury of Charles the Bold," namely:

1. the Order of the Garter, a collar of the order created by Edward III which on January 10, 1459, Edward IV, king of England, conferred on his future brother-in-law Charles of Burgundy;
2. the White Rose, which represented the coat of arms of the royal family of York, kings of England, made of precious stones; also probably a present of Edward IV, King of England;
3. the *Federlin* (or Little Feather), a small hatpin arranged with precious stones and more than seventy pearls, also of provenance from Edward IV, King of England;
4. the Three Brothers, with rubies acquired by John the Fearless; the jewel, created by Philip the Good, was inherited by Charles the Bold, duke of Burgundy.

The purchase price for these jewels was 40,200 Rhinish florins ($10.7 million or £6.7 million today), of which 19,000 florins would be paid in gold and the rest in silver coin minted in Milan, Zurich, Lucerne, Fribourg, Saint Gallen, or in the Valais district of Switzerland. Until the entire amount had been paid, the jewels would remain with the seller, and the Fuggers would be permitted to view the gems but not allowed to alter them in any way. An interest payment would apply to the outstanding amounts due, and the sale would need to be completed within five years.

These negotiations, as well as the agreement, were kept entirely secret. Most of Jacob Fugger's money was used to pay the debts of the city of Basel to Strasburg in particular, for services that Strasburg had rendered to the Swiss border town. A proportion of the payments were made in gold, and interest of 3 percent was charged on the silver coin payments made over time. On October 15, 1506, three "men of confidence" from the House of Fugger arrived with the final installment in silver and took possession of the jewels.

But what was Jacob's motive in collecting so many valuable gems from the last great duke of Burgundy's inheritance? Certainly Jacob had been noteworthy for his distaste for personal luxury goods and his long-established prudence. He would even later ignore the title of "Count" when it was conferred on him. One reason may have been to create a readily transportable "reserve of capital" through the gems in the tumultuous times in which he lived. However, there is little doubt that Jacob saw the value in these fabulous gems as instruments of political and financial power, to be wielded to enhance his own financial empire and the House of Fugger.

By January 1502, a likely "acquirer" for the great diamond of Flanders had emerged. Don Manuel I, king of Portugal, who for the past seven years had consolidated a tremendous royal treasure chest for the emerging thalassocracy of Portugal, became Jacob's next financial target.

The Kings and
the Counting Houses

1507–1522

THE CHRISTIAN WORLD HAD BEEN changing rapidly since Charles the Bold's death in 1477. Charles's son-in-law Maximilian I had consolidated the Burgundian empire and added it to his own, which stretched from the Kingdom of Naples to Austria in the east, with the principalities of Milan, Florence, Genoa, and Venice remaining independent. The French had repelled the English from their shores but remained weak and divided by provincial warlords. Henry VII, the first Tudor king, had usurped the English throne, ending all hope of a revival of the Wars of the Roses by the houses of Lancaster and York. Ferdinand of Aragon and Isabel of Castile had joined their crowns for a united Spain, and put their religious zeal into practice by intensifying the infamous Spanish Inquisition in 1492. The Portuguese, under the auspices of the pope and the all-embracing Catholic Church, had since the time of John II (1481–1495), predecessor of the current monarch, Don Manuel (1495–1521), either enslaved or expelled the Moors from its lands. And the Sancy diamond played its own important role at the heart of power in the shifting sands that changed Western civilization.

As a contractual condition of Don Manuel I marrying Ferdinand and Isabel's eldest daughter (also named Isabel), he, too, had to institute the first official Inquisition and it was decreed in 1497 against the Jews. Some were fortunate enough to flee to Flanders, while others

were forcibly converted to Christianity and became known as Mar-
ranos (Portuguese for pigs) by their brethren.

This mass forced conversion and expulsion of what was Portugal's
mercantile class combined with other factors to hasten commercial
changes that were afoot elsewhere in Europe. Bruges had slowly lost
its preeminence to Antwerp as the progressive silting up of its river,
the Shelt, had made access to it by sea difficult. The Venetians, who
for centuries had maintained a stranglehold on the importation of
most luxury goods from the Orient and India, were eclipsed by the
most important shift in power—the birth of the Age of Exploration
and the dominance of Portugal.

Charles the Bold's maternal uncle Prince Henry the Navigator gave
birth to the Portuguese thirst for exploration. The simple desire for
scientific discovery often attributed to Henry was, in fact, inextricably
linked to his compulsion to fight the Muslims on their own soil in an
unofficial holy Crusade. Commercial imperatives that came with the
growth of the Portuguese state and national pride under King John II
were translated in an insatiable search for an alternative route to the
rich spice trade of India, and the formation of a slave market in
Africa. Much of this commercial expansion was rationalized by the
need to convert the "unenlightened" people of Africa and Asia to
Christianity.

King Ferdinand and Queen Isabel of Aragon and Castile financed
the Genoese Christopher Columbus's voyage to the West Indies in
1492. Don Manuel I of Portugal financed the voyages of Vasco da Gama
to India in 1497 and 1500, opening up for the first time a sea trade
route that threatened the Venetian stranglehold.

Yet the financing of this phenomenal Age of Exploration did not
come, as commonly believed, from the royal purses of the kingdoms
of Spain and Portugal, but from the likes of merchant bankers called
Fugger, Affaitadi, Rodrigues d'Evora, Schetz, Hochstetter, de' Medici,
Strozzi, and Balbani, among many others. And the hotbed for these
financial transactions was not Madrid, Lisbon, Venice, or Naples. It
was Antwerp—the new commercial center of Flanders.

While the Age of Exploration was still in its infancy in the last
decade of the fifteenth century and the first decade of the sixteenth,

the map of Europe, and the powerful dynasties ruling it, had been redrawn and transformed through marriage and war. Despite Louis XI's best efforts to usurp Marie of Burgundy's inheritance on the death of Duke Charles, Marie married the Holy Roman emperor's son Maximilian, as Charles had planned, and together they ruled Flanders, Holland, Zeeland, and other parts of the former Burgundian Empire. On Marie's premature death, her Burgundian lands and titles were subsumed into Maximilian's Holy Roman Empire, giving him rights through his royal inheritance to Austria and parts of Germany and Naples.

Maximilian's and Marie's son Philip the Fair had taken the title king of Holland, and from 1504, on the death of Queen Isabel of Castile, he inherited the crown of Castile through his marriage to Joan the Mad (another daughter of Ferdinand and Isabel) and became Philip I of Spain. Through marriage and without bloodshed, Maximilian had achieved an inheritance long dreamed of by Philip's grandfather Charles, duke of Burgundy.

While Maximilian was consolidating his new land empire through war with Hungary in the east, Don Manuel I of Portugal was creating a dominance of the seas that would make his country wealthier than any other in Europe for thirty years. By 1517 Don Manuel presided over a commercial empire in Brazil, the western coast of Africa known as the Guinea Coast, Mozambique, the Congo, Angola, Malacca, the Moluccas (Spice Islands), Goa, and Hormuz, and had discovered the islands of Madagascar, Tristan da Cunha, Cape Verde, and St. Helena (where Napoleon died). Trading posts were established through a brutal messianic Crusade against the Muslims, who were Asia's primary trading partners. Gold, precious stones, silver, silks, and spices would be heaped on board Portuguese vessels and brought back to the mother country. Portuguese supremacy was wholly attributable to its legendary commanders, like Albuquerque, Cabral, da Gama, and Magellan, as well as to the unsung heroes of Portuguese shipbuilding and armory manufacturers who outfitted sleek vessels with guns and cannons beyond the enemy's capability.

Yet the Sancy's next owner, Don Manuel I, remains a shadowy figure, eclipsed by the household names of the navigators and merchant adventurers of his times. The humanist chronicler Damaío de Goís described Don Manuel in 1567 as

> [A] man of good stature, of a body more delicate and refined than large, with a pleasant rounded head and chestnut colored hair. His brow protrudes, casting a shadow over his lively hazel eyes. He has a white smile and beautiful lips, corpulent arms, as rich and as long as those of the most chivalrous gentleman. His legs are richly adorned and well formed, well proportioned to his body, and no man could be more handsome than he.

The illuminated books and chronicles of Rui da Pina portray the king as a person rather than by his physical attributes:

> This king of men works hard and long and continues to write his dispatches into the small hours of the morning. He eats little and drinks only water. In the beginning it mattered little to him if he was rich or poor, and it was only much later that he woke up before dawn and that his bad disposition grew. This is when he fell into the vice of luxury and ostentation and became oblivious to the risks of India. The only thing that he obviously enjoyed was music and dancing. He often protested that he wished to go on voyages to Asia, but when his advisers convinced him of the need to stay in Portugal, his ships brought him back five elephants and a rhinoceros from Africa, and Persian horses from Asia.

Manuel had a colossal five-thousand-person royal household. He took a keen personal interest in commercial life, setting up the Casa da India in Antwerp for da Gama's second voyage. The Casa da India was effectively the state-owned monopoly for the sale and distribution of all goods and products imported from Portugal's expanding empire. Don Manuel could frequently be heard referring to "his places over there," with a flourish of his hand and looking out to sea. These "places" were primarily churches, palaces, trading posts, and fortresses in his overseas domains. It mattered little to Don Manuel if these places were completed edifices or not, since from the moment they were under construction they represented an extensive source of revenue—a personal subsidy—to his royal purse.

According to the contemporary historian Virgilio Correira, "the Manuelian era built more than romance." Yet, like so many rulers who are out of touch with the mood of the country and its needs, it was in Don Manuel's reign that the seeds of the rapid destruction of Portugal's brief empire were sown.

In his *Origins of the Portuguese Inquisition*, Alexander Herculano portrays Don Manuel's Portugal as a corrupt land:

> The administrative and judicial abuses that were practiced in all cases were more than less, and no more so than in the secular world, although the ecclesiastical world was almost as bad. Our kingdom became idle and lived opulently without knowing the art of how to do so. Our predominant failure of judgment in all classes, with fatal consequences robbed us of self-respect, created disharmony and domestic misery. Our taste for luxury went wild and knew no bounds. Our livers cried out from the excesses, the way one's arms groan under the strain of working the land hard. With each voyage, this king would look for his subsequent victim amongst us poor people to see whom he can get next to go along with his latest whim.

Don Manuel was undoubtedly king of conspicuous consumption. Nicknamed "The Adventurer" by posterity and "The Fortunate" during his lifetime, he was determined not to be outdone by any other monarch. Selfish, powerful, and single-minded, Don Manuel created a court that was unparalleled in European history for its wealth and frivolous expenditure, and the young king saw only the pleasures that the wealth would bring him personally rather than how it might better his people.

Don Manuel's most fondly held dream was to reunite the kingdoms of the Iberian Peninsula under *his* rule—a dream he came close to achieving. Having witnessed how Maximilian had consolidated his power base by marrying Marie, duchess of Burgundy, Manuel negotiated a marriage contract with Ferdinand and Isabel for the hand of their eldest daughter, putting his children in line for the Spanish throne.

In the provision for the institution of the Inquisition in Portugal, where many of Spain's Jews had taken refuge, Jews were given ten months to either convert to Catholicism or be killed. They were hunted down if they attempted to go into hiding, and any non-Jews found harboring them were also subjected to the death penalty.

Many bought their way to freedom and "sold" their entire estate—businesses and possessions, as they were not allowed to own land—for a new life in Flanders. Jewish children under age fourteen were torn from the family home and "resettled" in other towns and villages, to be brought up as good Catholics by strangers. More than twenty thousand Jews converted within two years and thousands more emigrated or were killed.

The "free" Moors who remained in Portugal were also victims and found the same fate as the Jews. Few practicing Muslims remained in the country unless they converted and, even then, were often targets of racial hatred and bigotry, common throughout the Christian world of the day.

Those who had escaped with their fortunes intact to Antwerp were made to feel grateful because they could from this safe distance maintain good relations with the Portuguese crown. Others, less fortunate, lost everything. This unspeakable pogrom provided Manuel with a rapid influx of capital, jewels, gold, and plate that would help to finance the first voyage of Vasco da Gama in 1499, thereby limiting Manuel's own financial risk. Like most monarchs before him as well as those to come after, Don Manuel was learning to master the art of spending other people's money.

Riches and jewels were to remain essential to Manuel's power and purpose, and he believed that the only way to get these was through the Indian trade. The king and his newfound wealth, with the indispensable financial assistance of the great Portuguese merchant banking families in Antwerp like Ximenes, Lopes, Rodrigues d'Evora, and Nuñes—many of whom were also expelled Marrano Jews—bankrolled Vasco da Gama's first voyage to India in 1497. When da Gama's sails billowed over the horizon some two years later, in September 1499, he ushered in the new era of marine commerce.

Interestingly, da Gama said nothing at first about the cool welcome the Asians gave to his half-starved, scurvied Portuguese crew reeking of sweat, filth, and the sea after ten months aboard ship. These Europeans would have appeared like extraterrestrials to the Asians, and seemed to have inspired them with fear equal to that an alien from another world would do for us today. Nor did da Gama mention that the trinkets and cloth with which the Portuguese had been trading in Africa were merely curiosities to the Asians and of no value whatsoever to them.

As an ever intelligent and perspicacious but as yet not a wealthy monarch, Don Manuel knew that to attain his own dreams of Iberian domination and riches beyond his own fertile imagination he would have to market his Indian riches that da Gama brought back in Antwerp. The king summoned the trusted private secretary to the king's household, the nobleman Thomé Lopes, a relation of the merchant banking family in Antwerp, to set the ball in motion. Lopes hired Lucas Rem, a German merchant, as the king's agent in Antwerp to conclude a deal with the local merchants.

Don Manuel could not afford, literally, to alienate the power-hungry and bellicose Maximilian, who ruled Antwerp, nor let him know his plans for expansion as a seafaring nation. Involvement in a European power struggle would be costly and only deter Portugal from becoming the great thalassocracy envisaged by da Gama. This made it a simple decision for the Portuguese king to wisely steer a noncommittal course when asked by those opposed to Maximilian for his assistance. France in particular wanted a Portuguese alliance, but the king remained steadfast.

The Sancy's rightful heir, Maximilian, had his own dream, or rather folly: to be crowned Holy Roman emperor in Rome at the head of his powerful imperial army. Naturally, the strongest resistance to this ludicrous idea came from the duchies of Genoa, Milan, and Florence; the Venetians; the French (who under Louis XII felt that they were just as threatened as in the time of Maximilian's father-in-law); and Ferdinand of Aragon, who had already assumed the title of His Most Catholic Majesty. Maximilian refused to understand what effect his imperial army's march down to Rome would have on the various city-states it would have to cross to get there.

Still, the king of the Romans, as Maximilian liked to be called, remained uncompromisingly attached to the idea. He was described by the Venetian ambassador Quirini as a man "who finds solutions to his problems. But all of the solutions that he finds confuse him, he does not know which is the best, and as he has a rich imagination, he executes all of them perfectly and at the same time." King Ferdinand was heard to say of Maximilian that "when he has thought of something, he believes that he has done it." But Prince Machiavelli was the most scathing when he said Maximilian "is a wastrel of his goods above any of our time or previous times. . . . If all the leaves of all the trees in Italy were transformed into ducats, they would not be enough to satisfy his needs."

The personal wealth of these two kings was the best means of displaying their power and prestige, and acquisition of riches led them invariably to Jacob Fugger. Jacob, for his part, was happy to make a royal accommodation. After all, Maximilian was the monarch with the greatest sway over European politics, while Don Manuel represented the promise of a brighter financial future to come. Jacob Fugger harbored his own dream—to have a monopoly on the pepper contract from India.

Pepper was and is the most important of all spices. Today it represents a quarter of all spice imports worldwide, with the United States being the single largest importer. In Jacob Fugger's time it was known as the king of spices. Like salt, it was a precious spice worth its weight in gold. Arab traders and merchants grew rich providing the Romans with pepper, its value so high that Roman grocers were known to often blend juniper berries with their peppercorns to stretch the product and increase their profits. Don Manuel himself called pepper "the light of the Portuguese spice trade." And if pepper was the light, Jacob Fugger wanted to be its shining star.

By 1506, Fugger had acquired the Sancy and the four other great jewels of Charles the Bold. Fugger also had sold one of Charles's diamonds to Maximilian in 1504 for 10,000 florins and another to Pope Julius II for 20,000 florins. Fugger's gem purchases were not, however, for show. Fugger, the original workaholic, had a razor-sharp business mind and knew that such easily transportable wealth would in a first instance provide him with a ready escape, but more importantly, the gems would provide him with the competitive edge he would need to buy into lucrative contracts that sooner or later would be put up for sale by greedy and powerful monarchs. The fact that the monarchs needed these gems as part of their perceived power utterly suited him. It was the perfect symbiotic relationship.

By the beginning of the sixteenth century, Jacob Fugger also had set up an intelligence system to rival that of any well-run government. Like the Venetian and Milanese duchies, Fugger had his own "ambassadors," who were his commercial agents in important fair towns and capital cities throughout the Christian world. Their missives contained important social, political, and commercial information that would allow him to steal a march on the competition. Fugger was running a multinational company on which hundreds of employees and their families relied, and any knowledge he could glean to give him the upper hand was seized. He was often accused behind closed doors by envious competitors of espionage, but in medieval Europe it is safe to say that one man's espionage was another man's initiative and vision.

There is little doubt that Fugger had tremendous intelligence on Don Manuel's plans to build a sea empire for the importation of luxury goods and spices from the various Portuguese forays around the globe. Jacob knew about Don Manuel's extravagance for jewels and fine clothes, and knew the Sancy would represent the ultimate prize to the greedy king.

In 1502 the first contracts to be given for the expansion of the spice trade were proposed to the top merchants of Europe by Don Manuel's agent Lucas Rem. By that time Don Manuel had already decided to expand his horizons beyond the Portuguese merchants of Antwerp, and Thomé Lopes was en route to India with Vasco da Gama, on his second voyage of conquest, as the explorer's diarist.

Fugger knew that the Affaitadi family from Cremona and other Genoese merchants in Antwerp would be considered along with himself for the contracts. Putting together his intelligence reports, not only on Don Manuel but also on the competition, Fugger worked relentlessly to figure out how best to entice Don Manuel with the Sancy to win the lucrative first pepper contract. Pepper, more valuable than any diamond to Fugger, was the future. It was the one spice besides sugar that could best preserve food. Pepper was more than a luxury item; it was the one imported spice that had mass consumption appeal.

It is likely that the Affaitadi family of Cremona, now trading in Antwerp, provided Fugger with his solution. They were close friends of Fugger. Jacob honored friendship and respected wise business acumen

above all else, and remarkably possessed a commodity in as short supply today as then: business ethics. The Affaitadi, for their part, had
been trading with Don Manuel for a number of years and had been
merchants specializing in sugar, moneylending, and gems. In fact, the
Affaitadi had their own diamond cutter, a German named Franz
Mesingh, working full-time for them. The Affaitadi family were also
one of the few Antwerp merchants who distinguished uncut diamonds
from cut ones and from other mounted jewels, gold, silver, rubies, and
amber in their inventories. And like Fugger, the Affaitadi made commercial reports, but in their case, these documents were sent to the
Doges (Senate) in Venice. Other merchants who did not dedicate
the same resources to market research like Fugger and Affaitadi called
them both espionage merchants who sent "spy reports" to foreign
rulers. These reports, like the Fugger newsletters, remain amazing
sources of the social history of the era.

Fugger's competitive edge to win the pepper contract depended on
three things: first, to appeal to Don Manuel's power and greed; second,
to neutralize the competition as much as possible; and third, to pro-
pose a deal that would make Fugger and his partners unstoppable.
The first step was to approach and persuade the Affaitadi, who knew
good gems with their expert diamond cutter Mesingh, to help Fugger
minimize his losses by recutting the great *Balle de Flandres* (the Sancy).
Fugger had to handle these delicate operations in total secrecy, or Maximilian would learn that he had Charles the Bold's most powerful and
largest white diamond in Christendom—an inheritance that Maximilian might well believe to be his. By cutting the diamond, hopefully in half, Fugger would to be able to give away half of the valuable
gem, keeping the other half—whether as one large jewel or several
smaller ones—and not be out-of-pocket at all. Since Hertenstein of
Lucerne had acquired the gem for 5,000 florins, it is probable that for a
quick sale to Fugger he sold it for 8,000 florins ($970,000 or £606,000
today)—or clearance of a debt that he may have been unable to pay
otherwise to the powerful merchant from Augsburg. In simple mathematical terms, Fugger would expect to make 100 percent profit mini-
mum on such an item, and would have valued it for 16,000 florins
($1.9 million or £1.2 million).

By bruting, or sawing, the diamond in half from its original 106-carat weight (21.2 grams), even if one of the halves would need to be sold as smaller stones due to loss from the bruting, the larger half, hopefully more than 50 carats, would still be the largest diamond in Christendom and have the added benefit of being completely untraceable. Once the cutter had polished the newly cut stone, no one would know that it had been Charles's great diamond, which was now shrouded in mystery. Jacob Fugger could offer it to Don Manuel as a "sweetener" to accept his proposal for the pepper contract.

While the Affaitadi and their diamond cutter were working the stone, Fugger began to organize the second step: neutralizing the competition. His agents hovered closely around the Portuguese merchants, and reported back which spice contracts interested them. Fugger's men worked their spin, discouraging these merchants from bidding for the pepper contract by reasoning that they would come up against the mighty Fugger and other German merchants, who were, after all, the bankers to Maximilian. The implied threat would not have gone unnoticed by the immigrant merchants.

Jacob Fugger formed his pepper consortium with the Welsers of Nuremburg, as well as a select group of Italian merchants including the Affaitadi, and secretly negotiated satisfactory terms between themselves. This was undoubtedly a pivotal deal for Fugger, and as he had an extra-special present to impart to the king of Portugal, he wanted to open the negotiations in person.

Fugger met with Don Manuel in January 1502 and struck, or so he thought, a very favorable deal for himself as well as his partners. The newly cut 54-carat (old carats) diamond with facets could not fail to impress the king, whose greedy eyes saw only the promise of many other such jewels to come on the back of the voyages he had planned to India. By February the "privileges" conferred by Don Manuel on the German consortium formed the basis of the future lucrative relationship between the Portuguese state and its exceptional German and Italian merchants.

Yet despite the deal being by and large agreed, Don Manuel hesitated in providing his share of the bargain—the ships and soldiers to protect the commercial vessels. Marauding pirates from other nations

presented constant threats—and English pirates, or merchant adventurers, were notoriously active. A frustrating two years ensued until
finally the king's agent Lucas Rem signed a contract on April 1, 1504,
with the Welsers and Fuggers to fit out three merchant vessels for the
voyage to India. Interestingly, the records show that the Welsers contributed 20,000 cruzados toward this undertaking, while their 50 percent partner Fugger put up only 4,000 cruzados—the difference being
the assumed approximate value of the diamond at 16,000 cruzados.
When precisely the Sancy was handed over to the Portuguese king we
may never know for certain.

The flotilla of three merchant ships with sundry soldiers aboard
accompanied by fighting vessels sailed at last in 1505, returning in
1506, laden with 13,800 tons of spices, to Antwerp. But on its arrival
at the "India Dock," all the spices aboard were seized by the Portuguese crown's Casa da India for resale to the merchants at "His Most
Catholic Majesty's pleasure." Fugger and his partners were outraged at
such a grotesque flaunting of their understanding with Don Manuel.
Yet the cargo remained protected by the king's men, and there was
little they could do to remedy their losses except to play along.

Lucas Rem undoubtedly conspired with the king to try to gain the
most from this first major commercial venture to India, not thinking
for one moment of the far-reaching repercussions that this would have
for Portugal in the long term. According to a dispatch that Rem made
to the crown, their merchant partners "nonetheless made a profit of
175 percent."

Fugger steadfastly refused to ever deal again directly with Don
Manuel despite entreaties by Rem, and later Thomé Lopes and Rui
Fernandes. For Jacob Fugger, his handshake was his bond, and a contract was a contract. It was normal to try to drive a hard bargain, but
it was beyond comprehension to set out to thieve from one's own
partners. Fugger knew that he would get justice in his own way, and
would wait for it.

Yet Fugger's move to gain the upper hand for the pepper contract
through the sale of the Sancy—despite Don Manuel's actions—was
not without its ample rewards. Having consolidated his political and
economic position with the pope, the Catholic Church, Maximilian,
and now Portugal, Jacob Fugger began to back a number of Spanish

mercantile expeditions to the New World. He provided financing for several expeditions to Colombia and Peru to the Spaniards, now ruled by Maximilian's son Philip I of Spain. Fugger made the transition in banking arrangements from Maximilian to Philip with ease, and the House of Fugger continued to finance the imperial courts of Austria for the remainder of the sixteenth century.

As Portugal created trading settlements throughout Africa and on the western coast of India, Don Manuel justified the barbaric treatment of the inhabitants of these lands, with papal approval, as a means of bringing the heathens to Christianity and salvation. When, in 1517, Martin Luther nailed his ninety-five theses to the church door in Wittenburg against the sale of indulgences (whereby sinners would be absolved for a fee), thereby forever changing the face of Europe, Don Manuel was busily revising his Ordenaçõs Manuelinas, or Manuelian Laws, to centralize power by giving the king a neo-Roman absolute authority. Don Manuel by now took little interest in European affairs, and had turned his attention to improving the judiciary and its account-ability to the crown. With the exception of establishing trade links with China, the Portuguese thalassocracy was complete.

Yet slowly, almost imperceptibly, the influence that Portugal had exerted in Europe eroded. Antwerp flourished with, and briefly with-out, Portuguese trade when Don Manuel tried to move all his custom to Lisbon. The Antwerp merchants refused to pay for the overland haulage to the north from Lisbon, and bought through the Venetians and Genoese again, who had reestablished their links with Egypt. Don Manuel remained in his ivory tower at Lisbon, not understand-ing the significance of his loss of commercial influence. He had riches beyond compare, and no monarch was wealthier.

But Rui Fernandes understood the strength of Fugger's commer-cial position in Europe and especially the depth of Fugger's mistrust of Don Manuel. Rui Fernandes knew well enough how the merchants had been alienated over the years by continued unfair dealing. He also knew that despite repeatedly awarding Fugger the ongoing pepper contracts from India, Don Manuel might have irretrievably reversed Portugal's fortunes. He tried to communicate this to the Portuguese monarch from Antwerp on February 11, 1521, when he wrote: "On the negotiations with the Fuggers, this is the age of that powerful man of Germany, and all the princes have already found the time to be his friend. This age has much affected the same gentleman, and he would remain very contented from his side for me to communicate this to you."

Some fourteen years after the initial double-cross, Fugger still maintained a lively dislike for the Portuguese monarch, and as it would seem from this letter, Don Manuel knew it. But he thought he was powerful enough that he could do without him.

On Christmas Day 1521, Don Manuel died in Lisbon. His trusted secretary Thomé Lopes, now the keeper of the jewels, made an inventory of all of the valuables the king had owned. The inventory is more than a hundred pages long, detailing not only fabulous gems—especially emeralds—but also illuminated manuscripts, gold and silver plate, and other valuables. The first item on the list is the Mirror of Portugal, a fabulous table diamond with a ruby and a large Oriental pearl hanging from it. The diamond is encrusted with white, green, and blue enamel that from the obverse side is dark gray. This jewel weighs, together with its setting, 1 ounce, 5 octaves, and 37 grains.

The second item is: "A great cloak clasp with a great and pointed diamond with a large balas ruby hanging from it as a pendant and the weight of this diamond and ruby together with its gold setting in the shape of a flag is 2 ounces and 11 grains."

This jewel weighed more than 56 grams. The Sancy alone, at 55.232 metric carats, weighs 11.06 grams, and is the only possible diamond known today that could have made up this jewel.

The two great jewels of Portugal, the Mirror of Portugal and the "unnamed" diamond that Jacob Fugger had passed on to the extravagant king, both mounted with rubies hanging from them, were now in elaborate settings at the head of the inventory.

8

The Coveted Touchstone
of Power

1522–1578

DON MANUEL WAS UNDOUBTEDLY AWARE that he owned Duke
Charles's great diamond. How he discovered that the largest diamond
in his fabulous collection was from the great warrior Charles the Bold
we may never know. The most likely source of the information was
not Jacob Fugger, who lived for another four years after the Portuguese king's death, but rather the Portuguese merchants residing in
Antwerp. While gossip and idle talk spread more slowly in the sixteenth century than now, it was more pervasive and often taken
as fact, undiluted by sound bites or round-the-clock news. By the
time of his death in 1521 Don Manuel was able to console himself
with the knowledge that Charles's all-powerful diamond had found
its way into his hands. Unfortunately for Manuel, the secrecy surrounding its sale to him meant that he could not advertise the origin
of his great diamond without risking the wrath of its true inheritor,
the Holy Roman emperor. Yet, as with Charles the Bold, this knowledge would have lulled the superstitious and extravagant king into
a false sense of security—believing that as long as the diamond
remained in the crown jewel collection, his and Portugal's fortunes
were safe.

But Portugal was not safe. The spread of Lutheranism and the religious strife it engendered became the foci of tremendous unrest and spurred a new type of Continental war. On the Italian Peninsula, the Renaissance in art and architecture led by da Vinci and Michelangelo and financed by great merchant rulers such as the de' Medici, Strozzi, and Borgia was gaining in importance and influence. The Turkish sultan Suleyman the Magnificent was knocking at the gates of Vienna in his own holy war. Religious wars and marriages continued to change the geopolitical complexion of Europe with new ideas and the emergence of more powerful monarchs. Don Manuel's son João III soldiered on with Portuguese dreams of an overseas empire in much the same way as his father had done, oblivious to any lack of influence in Europe.

Notwithstanding this, Portugal remained a rich prize for any ruler who could legitimize a claim to its throne. At the end of the day it would be Charles V (1500–1558), the last European monarch who would seek to unite the European continent as a single nation under his rule, who laid his claim to Portugal by marrying João III's sister and Don Manuel's daughter Isabel in 1526. Charles, like his paternal great-grandfather, Charles the Bold, believed it was his destiny to fulfill the Burgundian grand design to dominate European affairs. For him to acquire the "largest diamond in Christendom" or any of his great-grandfather's stunning jewels would be seen as "proof" that his purpose was blessed by God.

His quest for power brought him into direct conflict with François I (1494–1547), king of France, and it could safely be said that the period when their rules coincided was punctuated by only brief periods of peace. Their feud began when François lost the election to Charles for Holy Roman emperor on Maximilian's death—an election lost due to the phenomenal campaign contribution of 544,000 guilders ($44 million or £27.5 million today) by the Sancy's previous owner, Jacob Fugger, out of a staggering total of 852,000 guilders ($68.9 million or £43.1 million today) spent. It ended with Charles imprisoning François for years, then exacting onerous terms from him, successfully demanding that he hand over half of France and his infant sons for their own terms of incarceration.

Other new and powerful rulers, too, had heard rumors that Duke Charles's jewels had begun to resurface, and they began their own quest to find and possess these gems. The third mighty European ruler vying for power with Charles and François I of France was England's Henry VIII (1491–1547), also an avid lover of gemstones. Henry, remembered mostly for his disastrous marriages, also believed in the importance of a navy, and followed the Portuguese colonization of India with keen interest. Henry's financial agent in Antwerp, Stephen Vaughan, knew all there was to know about trade, and was an expert in the jewel market. He was often guilty of "news management" relating to the persistent rumors about Charles the Bold's great diamond as well as other large stones, and his release of information to Henry was usually dependent on the king's ability to pay.

Despite all the changes throughout Europe in the 1520s, Antwerp and Flanders retained their stranglehold as centers of trade and thereby commercial knowledge and innuendo. Antwerp also prospered by Henry's explosion onto the scene. His marriages, wars, and skirmishes were to fuel the shipbuilding, iron, wood, and copper industries, and his taste for opulence and wives would create a luxury cloth and jewel industry such as the world had never seen.

Henry VIII was a veritable powerhouse, ambitious for European glory by conquest. Yet he had a great deal in common with the Portuguese monarch. Portugal had been England's closest ally for several hundred years by the time Henry ascended the throne in 1509, and the thalassocracy of Portugal was the envy of most nations, especially England. Henry was married to Don Manuel's sister-in-law Catherine of Aragon and could possibly, given the right circumstances, stand in line for the Spanish throne. Above all else, Henry Tudor resembled Don Manuel in his ostentation and ruthlessness in obtaining what he wanted. Orders went out from Henry to the effect that anything the Portuguese could do, Henry could do better. His biggest challenge came when he ordered the formation of the English navy, which, unlike all other countries besides Portugal, would be a standing navy for the defense of the realm.

As relations with France deteriorated toward 1513, the Venetian ambassador wrote to the Doges, "The new king [Henry VIII] is eighteen years old, a worthy king and most hostile to France. . . . it is thought that he will indubitably invade France." Huge coastal fortifications were built at Portsmouth and Dover. At Henry's beck and call were the largest and best-armed ships of the day, the *Mary Rose* and the *Peter Pomegranate,* which had been built three years earlier for the invasion of France to reclaim the French crown for England.

Henry also was a great admirer of Jacob Fugger and his intelligence-gathering devices. Whereas Portugal did not seem to care what her European neighbors did, Henry, like Fugger, was well aware that knowledge was power. Since there were no permanent English embassies abroad except in Paris, Henry imitated the Fugger example and established a primitive spy network to help him gain the upper hand.

By Don Manuel's death in 1522, Henry knew that diamonds from the Portuguese trading posts along the Indian Malabar coast had made their way through Antwerp for sale in greater number and bought not only diamonds but also other precious stones in abundance. Meanwhile, the Venetians had reestablished their trade links with some Arab merchants who had survived the Portuguese onslaught and were again making inroads into the jewel trade at Antwerp. The proliferation of gemstones meant not only that more were available for sale, but also that more people could wear them.

Diamonds, rubies, sapphires, and pearls were now worn by all the nobles of Europe, with some members of the merchant classes also beginning to wear precious stones, despite arcane laws across the Continent prohibiting nonnobles from the practice. Jewels and jewelry-making were being swept along in the tide of the Italian Renaissance. Earrings were jeweled, and collars of gold and precious stones indicated noble rank and royal prestige. Cancanets and necklaces were worn close to the neck, gold and precious stone bracelets on the wrist. Golden chains, pendants, and jeweled crosses also adorned the neck. The tablet, an essential part of court dress to wear at a lady's girdle as a double-sided opening jewel designed to reveal its contents (more often than not a miniature portrait), also could be worn at the throat or on the breast. Henry VIII ordered cipher jewels with his initial and those of his wives; these were jewels with the point of the diamond directed outward to enable the wearer to write secret messages with it. These became the rage with the wealthy. Religious iconography was as common as in Duke Charles's time, and jewels were separated in inventories as "secular" or "religious" adornments.

Anyone who was anyone, or who wanted to become anyone, knew that the way to Henry's heart—or, indeed, to that of any other European monarch—was to give him jewels. And when good relations were withdrawn, so, too, were the jewels. When Cardinal Wolsey was disgraced in 1530, and sent to the Tower of London by Henry to die, the king did not neglect to appropriate the cardinal's jewels, just as he had done with those of his first queen, Catherine of Aragon.

In 1520, when Henry met François I at the Field of the Cloth of Gold to negotiate peace, his array of jewels caused a tremendous stir. From 1527 to 1530, Henry continued to spend phenomenal sums on jewelry—some £10,801 ($7.9 million or £4.9 million today). At Henry's second meeting with the French king, in 1532, François would not be outdone, and even brought a large diamond for Henry's sensual new queen, Anne Boleyn.

This rapid growth in the sale of jewels in England, as well as the rest of Europe, put huge pressure on Portugal, with other crowns plotting to own or dominate the export of gemstones from India. This royal avarice would soon bring economic and political pressure to bear in the quest for gemstones by European monarchs and their noble classes.

Like the Portuguese, Henry did not come by all his riches by fair means. When his argument with Pope Clement over "the king's great matter," as his divorce to Catherine of Aragon was known, had taken on epic proportions, the bombastic Henry decreed that papal authority ceased to exist in England and that the king was now head of the church there. Thomas Cromwell, who had been keeper of the jewel house since 1532, masterminded and designed the provocative and effective Dissolution of the Monasteries and ensured that the treasures of the church were "acquired" by the crown. An estimated 289,786 ounces of plate and jewels were plundered and an estimated one-sixth went directly to the Royal Jewel House to be reset as jewels, with the remainder going to the mint for coining. As was so often said, Henry VIII stopped at nothing to achieve his aims.

The rumors that the crown of Portugal had obtained some of Duke Charles's notorious and fabulous gems continued to resurface over the years, and each time these came to Henry's ears, he would order

Stephen Vaughan to find out more. Henry simply wanted the largest and most important gems to make all see that he was the greatest monarch alive. He knew that whatever had passed into the Portuguese crown's possession was beyond reach, at least while he needed Portugal as an ally, but if there were other great and historic gems to be had, he wanted them.

Vaughan received word sometime during the early 1540s that the Fuggers had been intimately involved in the sale of some of Duke Charles's jewels. When he imparted this news to Henry, he was ordered to ask Anton Fugger, Jacob's nephew now in charge of the great merchant banking house, about the truth of the rumors. Vaughan and Henry were not disappointed with Anton's reply. It was confirmed that Jacob had indeed procured a number of Duke Charles's great jewels, but that some of these had been traded or sold to other monarchs since the time of purchase.

But Henry's buying power had become limited due to his profligate spending on wars against France. This was masked by the fact that large numbers of jewels that had been confiscated from the church had arrived in the royal coffers as a result of the Dissolution of the Monasteries in 1547, the last year of his reign. Still, Henry remained obsessed by Duke Charles's great jewels. The Fuggers were silent on the precise whereabouts of the great diamond and the *Balle de Flandres* (the Sancy), but Henry may have guessed, as Don Manuel and his son João III had done, that it now resided with the Portuguese crown.

Henry bought many jewels from the Fuggers over the years, and others were offered by a variety of Antwerp merchants, including one Florentine merchant, Jasper Duchy—a man described by Vaughan as "inconstant," which today would mean he was a hanger-on. Duchy was a man who was close to power but who never quite achieved the credibility or station of a main player. When, in 1547, as an intermediary of the Fuggers, Duchy tried to sell Henry diamonds worth 50,000 florins ($4 million or £2.5 million today), Anton Fugger wrote a scathing letter to Duchy about his proposed commission:

> About the 3,000 florins which you ask, besides the 5,000 florins of gratuity which Guido Horl on the writer's part promised to pay him,

I think the 5,000 more than sufficient, and that you should rather complain of your own liberality in leaving all to the King of England. . . . I am sure that the King would have willingly given from 12 to 13 percent interest both for jewels and money, as before, and as he has bargained with others.

Duchy, it would seem, also was in the pay of Charles V, and may well have been a spy for the Holy Roman emperor. Henry most likely knew this, but needed agents who could communicate directly with Charles on financial matters, since the all-important Antwerp was still in Charles's dominions. Even if Henry wanted to move money from Antwerp to his own domains in Boulogne and Calais, he would need a license from the regent of the Netherlands. In fact, Vaughan wrote to Henry in February 1546 that he and Duchy "thought it expedient to remind your highness to write to the Lady Regent for licence, in case your agents make any money here, to convey 200,000 crowns to Calais or Boulogne."

In other words, if you want to move your cash through Antwerp to English possessions, then you will need to guarantee safe conduct to Charles and his ships through the Channel. This marrying of economic to political interest had already become common, and monarchs were directly involved in medium to large transactions. Commercial negotiations were frequently intermingled in political correspondence, as can be seen from another of Vaughan's letters to Henry from February 1, 1546:

Since Jasper Duchy's return from the Emperor's Court, I have received his promise to serve you. I was at once in hand with Duchy to know if he could serve you with 40,000 pounds in ready money upon such obligations as were given to the Fugger. . . . The Fugger who lately loaned you the 100,000 florins will loan you a further 30,000 florins in ready money with 10,000 florins in fustians [cotton velvets] at their present English price, for such interest as you are wont to give. . . . Duchy offers to serve you next summer for six months . . . with 100,000 crowns monthly upon the obligation of London, if you will take therewith a jewel which he values at 100,000 crowns [$8.1 million or £5.1 million today].

While this power struggle was going on among Charles, François I, and Henry, João III of Portugal's role was a mere footnote in a European context, as he demanded fair rates in Antwerp and audiences with the three powerful monarchs for better treatment of Portuguese nationals in their countries. Although João had expanded the empire in the 1530s, he did not have an army that he could call upon for his defense in Europe, and resorted to the old alliance with England or Spain in time of difficulty.

By 1547 Henry had been engaged in numerous acts of piracy against the Portuguese and the Spanish, but this needs to be understood in the context of the mid-sixteenth century, a particularly difficult time. There was famine throughout the Continent brought on by a harsh winter, wars, and poor distribution channels for goods. The rise of Protestantism was turning militant, leading to riots in many cities. Charles V had resolved with the pope to put down the heretic Lutherans and Calvinists with an armed force of thirty thousand Italian mercenaries and ten thousand Spanish crack troops. This meant that there was precious little food to go around, and England was using its newly founded naval might in Europe to feed itself. Stephen Vaughan wrote to Henry from Antwerp in July 1546 based on information he had received from Jasper Duchy that "[t]he Fugger, who dwell in Augsburg, have been greatly threatened by the inhabitants for loaning money to the Emperor." The thought that less should be spent on court opulence by any of the monarchs, and more on staples for survival, seems never to have been contemplated.

It would seem that Duchy was now trading with João III from Antwerp regularly, and at this precise time, began to offer a number of precious stones that were remarkable for their quality and size. Duchy tried to offer some of these directly to Henry, but was stopped from successfully concluding deals by the ever vigilant Vaughan. Still, one of Duchy's clients, Juan Carolo, approached Vaughan with a remarkable gem in an incident that Vaughan described to Henry's minister Paget:

> I dined yesterday with John Carolo, who showed me among other good jewels "a table diamond set in an inch of gold little less than the paper squared on the other side [illustrated as 1 inch by 1¼ inch

in size] which I think is of the greatest sort that lightly is to be found. If the thickness answered the length and breadth it would be a jewel of wonderous price. He [Carolo] holds it at 40,000 crowns [$3.2 million or £2 million today]. It has a great fair and oriental round pearl hanging from it. . . . I do not write to the King's Majesty of the largeness of this diamond.

The reason for Vaughan's reluctance to tell Henry about the diamond was twofold. First, the king needed cash, not jewels, to feed his country. Second, Henry was still desperately searching for Charles's powerful jewels, and this large table diamond, which sounds remarkably like the Mirror of Portugal—which could well have been part of Duke Charles's collection at one time, and later shared a common history with the Sancy—would certainly have attracted the greedy king beyond common sense. Carolo was desperate to get rid of the stone, only since it had been given to him unexpectedly in payment for grain and, according to the Calendar of State Papers, "through payments of money to the factor of Portugal for spicery."

Whether this gem was indeed the Mirror of Portugal we will never know, but it did appear on the market at the same time as another fabulous diamond, which had been valued at 100,000 ducats, and which Vaughan described to Henry's minister Paget as "a great pointed diamond set about with other pointed diamonds like a rose." Could this have been the Sancy? It is possible, since owners were constantly changing the settings of their jewels. If it was, Vaughan was right to have hidden the potential sale of the stone from Henry, who could have ill afforded its purchase. Similarly, it is entirely possible that both of these stones were from the Portuguese crown, who by now were reduced to pay for foodstuffs with pawned jewels due to their poor fiscal management of the country's empire and profligate spending. In any event, neither jewel was sold to Henry or any other monarch, and both disappeared back into the Portuguese treasury.

King João responded to the tense religious and economic situation by assiduously preserving Catholic orthodoxy as a means of countering the spreading Lutheran doctrine, and reimplemented a Portuguese Inquisition. While it had been instituted as early as 1536, it was only in 1548 that it was put under the fanatical direction of João's wicked brother Cardinal Henry (later King Henry). By 1555 the Jesuits had founded the College of Arts of the University of Coimbra, and Jesuit dominance in Portuguese education would remain paramount for centuries. The Jesuit influence also dominated the colonies, with a messianic devotion to conversion of the "heathen" indigenous populations.

The failed harvests, rural depopulation, and other indications of national decay had taken hold by the end of João's reign. João's answers to all of the calamities that befell him were to increase the use of African slaves and to ignore his debts. But the debts grew well beyond his means to pay them, and several of his most prized jewels again found their way unofficially onto the Antwerp market for pawn.

Portugal slid farther downhill as the next potent economic world power, England—despite its debt—continued to rise. Henry, a confused religious "convert" who thought he had remained Catholic but whom other nations perceived as Protestant, was superstitious, like everyone of his time. His precious stones, and particularly his diamonds, were his "insurance policy" against his loss of authority. And this belief in turn fueled the flame in the quest for Charles's omnipotent gems. Despite his best efforts, Vaughan was not entirely successful in shielding Henry from his own avarice.

When the Fuggers "reluctantly" divulged that they still had the Three Brothers—the jewel made by Philip the Good with three perfectly matched balas rubies set without foil around a high-point diamond, and three round pearls between the rubies, with a fourth pearl as a pendant—Henry simply had to have it. By now he owed the Fuggers astronomical sums of money—well over 200,000 florins ($16.2 million or £10.1 million today). The Fuggers adamantly stuck to their guns, insisting that some of this would need to be repaid before they would deal with Henry. Within short order, Henry agreed that monies due the Fuggers would take precedence over payments to other merchants.

In the end, Henry's quest for Charles's great jewels ended with his son and heir Edward VI, aged fourteen, completing the purchase of the Three Brothers in 1553. The innocuous annotation in Edward's State Papers notes: "To the Fuggers £26,700; (payable 15 nov 1552) To the Fuggers £20,000; interest £1,400 total payable 15th February 1553. To the Fuggers—£24,000; interest £2,360—total £27,352.13.4 [sic] payable 15th August 1553."

Charles V retreated to a monastery in Spain in 1556, having fought for and won domination over most of western Europe, including all of modern Germany, the Netherlands, Belgium, Luxembourg, much of northern Italy including the duchy of Milan, the Kingdom of Naples (which represented most of southern Italy), Hungary, parts of France, and, of course, Spain. He had been battling wave after wave of Lutheran and Calvinist converts to Protestantism in his German provinces at a huge cost of human life and ready funds with little success. He had grown old and weary, and prepared to leave his empire to his son and heir, the future Philip II. In 1555 the Peace of Religion was signed at Augsburg, decreeing that the religion of the ruler would be shared by his subjects in the future, despite the fact that many of his subject princes were now Calvinist or Lutheran.

That same year, aged twenty-seven, Prince Philip was honored throughout the Holy Roman Empire, including in the rebellious Protestant states, as Charles's heir, in myriad ceremonies of supreme pomp put on by the emperor himself in a propaganda exercise to persuade his subjects of his son's ultimate power over them. To ensure their loyalty, Philip remained in the Netherlands for the following four years, ruling personally. After all, Antwerp—and by now Amsterdam—represented the most important financial centers in Europe. Further, Antwerp was the main port from which the gold and silver wealth from South America was distributed. Philip could literally not afford to have rebellious subjects in the region.

By 1578, the balance of power and empire had evolved from Portugal to Spain, with England and France sniping at each other's heels. The Sancy had remained in the hands of the House of Aviz for more than seventy years and been central to the reigning monarch's perceived invincibility. Within the next two years it would become one of the most important financial instruments in the pan-European troubles that had been brewing for the previous fifty years—coveted by Elizabeth I of England and worn by Henry III of France.

9

At the Heart
of the Struggle for Power

1560–1580

DON MANUEL'S DREAMS of dynastic wealth and power for his House of Aviz were about to come to an end. His son João III, profligate in his spending, had been reduced to pawning the family jewels to eat and heat the royal palaces. Nevertheless, the empire was expanding, and the need for more money and riches finally led João to explore, colonize, and exploit the crown's huge undervalued asset called Brazil. But the riches from that far-off land proved elusive. The expeditions and Jesuit settlements were costly, pushing the kingdom ever closer to financial ruin. It would be another 150 years before diamonds would be discovered in the Americas, and then another 20 years before large quantities of all gemstones would be brought back to Europe for sale. When João's grandson Sebastian became king at age three on João's death in 1557, Portugal was guilty of some of the worst excesses of colonization. The nobles were highly corrupt, lining their own pockets at the expense of the country, and eventually its freedom. In 1561 the Portuguese aristocracy begged Sebastian's mother, Isabel, to return from the Spanish court to take her place as regent, but she refused, sending word that she could "not leave this court at present."

Sebastian's grandmother Catherine, sister of Charles V, soldiered on as regent for the boy king, but by 1566 grew tired of the warring noble factions at court and retired to a nunnery. João III's brother, the cruel and ruthless Cardinal Henry of Evora, moved into the palace, placing himself in pole position as her successor.

When the colonies in Brazil and India revolted in 1568, Sebastian, now fourteen, finally stole power back from the nobles and ruled in his own name. To make matters worse for the young king, Portugal was not only suffering from internal turmoil and financial difficulties, but also was eclipsed by Spain and under threat of Spanish invasion. If Sebastian did not produce an heir, Philip would have been next in line for the throne since Philip II of Spain and Sebastian I of Portugal were both descendants of Joan the Mad and Philip I. All haste was made to betroth the child king to a suitable bride, and in the end another distant cousin, the daughter of the Roman emperor Ferdinand, uncle of Philip II, was settled on.

At this time there were only two tremendously powerful and charismatic rulers in Europe—Philip II, and Elizabeth I of England. One ruled by divine right entrusted to him by the Catholic Church, the other by sheer wit, grit, and determination as a formidable woman living not only in a man's world, but also as a Protestant queen in a Catholic one. For his part, Sebastian, who was largely influenced by his avaricious uncle Cardinal Henry, had rapidly become a fanatically religious zealot, and was destined to play an even smaller role on the European stage than his grandfather. He left what he saw as European secular squabbles to the likes of Philip and Elizabeth, feeling that he was above the secular world. Sebastian was primarily motivated by military and religious exercises that would, in his mind, lead to his glorious conquest of Morocco, which had for so long eluded his grandfather João III. For him, the Sancy diamond—and indeed any other of the jewels in the crown jewel collection—could have only one purpose: to purchase cannons, men, and ammunition for the conquest of Morocco. Thereafter, the jewels would be dazzling illustrations of his power to the defeated Muslim infidel.

On the other hand, Elizabeth's and Philip's "war" was hardly secular. Philip took his title of "His Most Catholic Majesty" very much to heart. He also had been the Catholic king of England during his brief marriage to Elizabeth's sister, the devoutly Catholic and bitter Mary I. To Philip his rabid intolerance of Protestantism, or other heretical religions, and his stalwart enforcement of the Inquisition had been, and would forever be, entirely justified. He was a man of intractable disposition, not favored by the Italians, thoroughly disliked by the Flemish, and positively loathed by the Dutch and Germans. It was only on the admonitions of his father that he tempered his severity toward anyone who was not Spanish, and even this concession was only accorded out of sheer necessity.

Philip, along with all of Catholic Europe, viewed Henry VIII's half-hearted Protestant legacy as having been taken up in earnest by his two youngest children, Edward VI and Elizabeth I. Edward had plans to make England a Lutheran state, and Elizabeth, who had been first under house arrest then thrown into the Tower of London by Mary, was now the devoted Protestant queen of England. When Mary lay dying in 1558, and Philip had communicated to her from Spain, he had shown little thought for his wife, and every concern for his adopted country's religion. He sent word to Mary to tell the imprisoned Princess Elizabeth that neither he nor the queen had believed her guilty of plotting against the queen. When Philip followed the gesture with the gift of a large diamond ring for Princess Elizabeth, it was not a gift of love but rather a peace offering, with the diamond representing her purity of thought and deed. Philip knew that he would be obliged to leave England in Elizabeth's hands, and hoped that if he could appear to have been instrumental in her accession she would remember his intervention fondly.

But Elizabeth would not be swayed. As the daughter of the beheaded queen, Anne Boleyn, she felt that her entire life—and even her sovereign power—was fragile, and she became devoted to making England Protestant and strong enough to defend itself against the Catholic princes of Europe. But Philip was not to know this, since Elizabeth had sworn to her sister on Mary's deathbed that "the earth might open up and swallow her alive if she were not a true Roman Catholic."

When Elizabeth had become queen in November 1558, she decided to overtly practice the Protestant faith. Among her first acts was to determine how to reform the church. Inventories were drawn up showing her assets, views taken as to who should remain her advisers and who should go, and, most importantly, what she could then afford to do to take hold of her realm absolutely. The queen's revenue was small, her debts large. There was no way she could rule England by force of a standing army, or even by what would become known as her highly regarded but exaggerated "omnipresent network of spies," according to Lord Burghley. In fact, her entire wealth amounted to less than Philip's annual income extracted from his duchy of Milan.

Elizabeth Tudor had survived childhood and life as a Protestant under Mary by her wiles. As monarch, detested by the pope, both envied and admired by Philip, Elizabeth had made powerful enemies for herself and for England, while the English began a forty-five-year love affair with their queen.

Philip believed in God's obvious design, which he was convinced would, over time, lead to Spanish world domination. There was a true asceticism in the way he worked for "Spain, Inc." into the small hours of the morning, with red-rimmed eyes, and with fingers aching from personally written dispatches as the self-imposed chief clerk of the Spanish Empire. He believed in the Inquisition and returning the "heretics" to the Catholic fold. The fact that the renewed fervor of the Inquisition meant that thousands of merchants fled Antwerp (still in the Spanish Netherlands) to city-states like Cologne, Amsterdam, and Hamburg for protection by Protestant princes meant nothing to him.

But this piety came after decades of profligate spending. In fact, Philip had been bankrupted twice—the first time in 1557 and the second in 1575. During the crisis of 1557, Philip suspended all payments in Antwerp on behalf of the Spanish crown. The entire amount due in Antwerp was judged as a result of payments made later as being approximately 1,275,000 ducats ($106.5 million or £66.5 million today).

The situation was precarious for Philip; without the Antwerp merchants it would have been impossible to wage war. The fact that the Antwerp merchants were dwindling due to his religious persecution again went unnoticed. So, as a half measure, Philip provided the merchants with letters of exchange for 850,000 ducats, to be paid over time on a royal installment plan.

Like Philip, Don Sebastian also was in dire financial straits. In the same missive that communicated Philip's financial difficulties to the Doges in Venice, the Venetian ambassador expressed his latest worries surrounding the young Portuguese king, who had not as yet begun to rule in his own name:

> The King of Portugal had taken from his subjects as a deposit about a million of crowns, for which he paid them ten per cent per annum, and he has now declared that he will no longer pay them more than five, affirming that he does so to disburden his conscience, his theologians having reproached him with this sin. This thing has much frightened the merchants, most especially the Genoese, to whom he owes considerable sums, lest he fail in his promise to them likewise . . . they will certainly be paid by means of the pepper contract, for there is a very great quantity of pepper on board the fleet whose arrival is expected from day to day, it is nevertheless strongly suspected that henceforth this King will lose much of the credit given to him hitherto, as no one more easily than he got money in exchange for produce, so that at the last fair of Medina he obtained about 900,000 crowns.

In light of the Spanish bankruptcy three years earlier, the nervousness in the Antwerp market about Sebastian was understandable. To compound the problem, the steady loss of Antwerp's importance in trade to Amsterdam also was taking its toll. The Fuggers still thought that *they* had the lock on the pepper contract, and were to discover from this message to Venice that the queen regent was prepared to forget her prior commitments. Similarly, the Genoese knew that their exposure to a potential bad Portuguese royal debt could bring them down. Everyone was rushing for cover, yet little protection from the impending storm was to be found.

In 1566, when Sebastian's uncle, Cardinal Henry of Evora, had been put in charge of the Portuguese Inquisition, he had been able to quench his desire for an active administrative role in the empire while lining his pockets with its riches. Within two years the cardinal's influence and greed became so loathed by the nobles that the teenage Sebastian assumed power in his own right—to the great relief of his people.

While the change was welcomed, it was widely recognized that Sebastian was still a child, and his government was plodding and plagued by indecision on any matter that did not touch his passions for military conquest and religion. Sebastian's older biological cousin, Don Antonio, prior of Crato, emerged as a temporary favorite at this time and took part in the first wave of Portuguese nobility who sought military adventures in Morocco.

Don Antonio—later named "The Determined"—became the central figure in the final debacle to overwhelm Portugal, its independence, and the Sancy's future. He was above all else an opportunist with little to recommend him and frequently described by those who met him as having a "character and morals of doubtful origin." Antonio frequently argued with both Henry and his cousin Sebastian, and ironically had to take refuge on more than one occasion in Spain to avert their wrath. But between 1571 and 1574 Don Antonio was in his element, swashbuckling his way across Morocco as the governor of Tangier, having refused to take up his religious orders in the church, to the great consternation of the pope. Don Antonio's appointment as the governor of Tangier allowed him to participate in the ill-fated Portuguese Moroccan expedition from its inception, putting him at the heart of the Crusader-style struggle.

Sebastian's war against the "infidel" Moors began in earnest in 1578, when he joined the fifteen thousand Portuguese noblemen already in battle. The king was only twenty-four years of age, and promised to marry the Holy Roman emperor's daughter on his victorious return. An eyewitness account by the Jewish physician to the king of Morocco tells the story of the decisive Battle of Alcazar (now Ksar El-Kebir), remembered in Portugal as the Battle of the Three Kings:

> We heard that the king of Portugal was marching from Argilla towards us, and so we unpitched our camp and pitched it again by Alcazar. After dinner, the king had tidings that the Portuguese were beginning to march; and he called for his raiment and appareling himself in cloth of gold, and wrapped upon his head his *tora* and set upon it his brooch with three precious stones and his feathers. He took his sword also which was very rich, and was sent him from Turkey, and his dagger of the same work garnished with precious stones, turquoises and rubies and finally arrayed himself as if it was Easter Day with great rings on his fingers full of precious stones, and went on horseback against my will.

As the battle progressed, the king of Morocco, the king of Fez, and Sebastian were all slaughtered. Sebastian died of two head wounds, with a third wound in his arm, and was buried at Alcazar in a plain wooden chest. All three kings died in the first hour of fighting, their bodies pillaged of jewels, and the survivors were sold into slavery. Don Antonio was one of the survivors.

The eyewitness account continued:

> All the nobility of Portugal, from the Duke of Braganza's son to the squires are slain or captive; a thing never seen or heard. God miraculously took the kingdom of Portugal and delivered them to our people. The slaughter, for anything that we have seen may be some 15,000 men. As for the captives I can give a judgement because every lieutenant ["Wildmore"] has a Christian as his page, every cavalry man has pages going after him. To that every handicraftsman has two or three Christian captives as do the citizens for their gardens. The value of them was from 100 to 150 ounces [$3,234 to $4,849 or £2,021 to £3,031 today] and some of them ransom between 300 and 500 ounces [$9,699 to $16,165 or £6,062 to £10,103 today].

Cardinal Henry, by now an old man, was crowned king as soon as the news reached Portugal. Not only had the flower of Portuguese nobility been killed with Sebastian, but also those who remained alive—including the heir presumptive to the throne, Don Antonio— were now hostages of the Moors. Henry had little time to react. If he did not ransom his remaining nobles, there would be riots. He arranged to send to the Casa da India in Antwerp a huge quantity of jewels with instructions to sell them for gold, and made any other arrangement he could by the sale of spice contracts and future shipments to get the hundreds of thousands cruzados required for the release of nobles held hostage. As a panic seller in a shaky financial market, Don Henry certainly did not get full value for any of the precious ornaments and jewels that were snapped up. Despite the huge quantity of jewels that were disposed of on the Antwerp market and elsewhere, the most fabulous and largest of the crown jewels remained cloistered in Lisbon, including the Mirror of Portugal and the Sancy.

By the time the first nobles trickled back from Morocco, among them Don Antonio, Cardinal Henry lay dying of tuberculosis in Lisbon. Duchess Catherine of Braganza had the strongest claim to the throne along with Philip II of Spain, as they were both legitimate children descended from Manuel I, while Don Antonio de Crato was the biological son of João III's brother Luis. While Catherine's claim was favored by the Portuguese nobles, she did not press it, since she was well aware of Philip's plans. The struggle for the crown ensued, with King Henry applying to Rome for the purchase of a papal bull to favor King Philip. Queen Elizabeth's temporary ambassador to Portugal, Edward Wotton, aptly wrote to her minister Walsingham:

> Concerning the succession in Portugal, I know not what to say; so much may be said both in favor and in disfavor of every one of the pretendants, by which I mean the King of Spain, the Duke of Braganza and Don Antonio, their parts are least in the pudding. . . . The things which are to hinder Don Antonio are . . . The King favors him not because of his dissolute life. He has many bastards by base women, most of them by "new Christians" [Jews]. It is feared therefore by the nobility that if he should come to be King, being unable by ordinary means to make them all great, he will seek to advance them by extraordinary means, and perhaps take dignities from the rest of the nobility to give them. He is very poor, and therefore not able to win such of the nobility as are to be won by money; nor if it should come to force, would be able to maintain a power in the field.

Don Antonio's success depended, or so he thought, on being proclaimed "legitimate" by Pope Gregory XIII. In the event, King Henry wrote to Antonio that no marriage had taken place between his father, Luis, and his mother, Donna Violante, and that "our late brother in his will always refers to Dom Antonio as his natural son, and there are notorious reasons and strong presumptions against any such marriage; we pronounce and declare that there is no proof of marriage, but rather a very violent presumption that the whole thing is a machination, and we pronounce Dom Antonio illegitimate and conformably impose on him perpetual silence in the matter."

Philip II, King of Spain, preparing
to take the throne of Portugal.
Painting by unknown artist, c. 1580.

Don Antonio remained resolute and hungry for power, and as a
man without fortune, saw the jeweled crown of Portugal as too tempting to let go of without a struggle. He fought back with a powerful
message that struck a chord with the commoners:

> You commanded me to avoid the Court in the nighttime because I
> should find none to pity my case, and kept me a banished man all
> the time of my pretension, to the great discredit of my person when
> all other pretenders openly requested their justice of you; being
> "well seen" and favored by you and accompanied by their friends.
> You also got against me a Bull from the Pope, as shameful as was
> seen, in which you showed yourself forgetful of the honor of the
> Infante [my father] and your brother.

Don Antonio truly believed that he was the only legitimate heir to the throne, and on Henry's death two months later, he proclaimed himself king.

An irate Philip made it clear to the world that the Portuguese throne was his, and prepared an army to, he asserted, "take what was his by right." According to the Venetian ambassador in the court of France: "The King was in hopes, without recourse to arms, to become master of Portugal, and from there to attack France; and now that this attempt has failed, he is seeking to occupy that country [Portugal] by force, both against the will of the nation and against right."

To complicate the succession even further, the scheming mother of the dissipated King Henry III of France, the queen mother, Catherine de' Medici, also pretended to have a claim to Portugal's throne. Through her intrigues she had already obtained the crown of Poland for her son Henry seven years earlier, in 1573. The queen mother, even if she lost the crown of Portugal, would ensure through intrigue that Philip would never be able to keep it.

By January 1580 Don Antonio had hidden away the court's treasures—including the Sancy and the Mirror of Portugal—for his own personal use, and prepared the country for a war he was confident he could win. Portugal still had the strongest merchant fleet in Europe, and her independence was tantamount to that of Portugal's oldest ally, England, as well as France. Surely, he reasoned, both powers would stand proud alongside Portugal. And as surely as he so reasoned, he was surely wrong.

10

The Pawn on the Chessboard of Giants

1580–1584

⋖⋗

WHILE THE CROWN JEWELS OF PORTUGAL were reputed to be unparalleled for the size and quality of the stones, by 1580 it was widely known that Charles the Bold's great diamond, the Sancy, was among its treasures. Both Henry of France and Elizabeth of England lusted after this gem and the other crown jewels, and they conspired against each other to get them. Diamonds remained the ultimate symbol of power and purity in the sixteenth century, and the Sancy, as the largest white diamond in Europe, was the pinnacle of that power.

We must not forget that superstition and folklore continued to surround jewels of all values. Elizabeth wore many jewels that had "magical" powers, including two that were reportedly made of "unicorn horn" as agents to detect poisons and toadstone rings as an antidote to poison, and she gave rings that were "blessed by the royal touch," as her father had done to safeguard her favorites. Jewels and gems were not only things of beauty, but also talismans to protect and promote the wearer.

Jewels also represented strength and greed. Catherine de' Medici had already lost to Elizabeth the famous de' Medici pearls she had once given to her former daughter-in-law, the defeated and imprisoned Mary, queen of Scots, and was determined not to lose any others to her. Henry III also was keen to get his hands on the invincible diamonds of the Portuguese crown to help him consolidate his slipping hold on a wartorn France. Now the battle for Portugal neared; royal horoscopes were taken in England, France, and Spain; and the race was on between the French crown and Elizabeth to procure the Sancy and Don Antonio's other treasures. Whoever gave the most in military support and money would succeed in obtaining the jewels—even if Philip were to be successful in conquering the country.

Don Antonio, as the possessor of the most powerful gemstones and jewels in Christendom, believed in his own infallibility and was oblivious to his greed. He thought himself clever enough to manipulate Philip II; Queen Elizabeth; the queen mother of France, Catherine de' Medici; and her third son, the weak and debauched King Henry III. Don Antonio never recognized that he would prove to be the most formidable weapon in the hands of Philip's enemies, and an expendable pawn on the chessboard of giants.

Within a month of Don Antonio's ascent to the throne, the Venetian ambassador in Spain indicated in a dispatch to the Doges that the Spanish fleet amassing in the Mediterranean was not bound for Ireland to foment trouble for England, as previously had been feared, but was heading for Portugal. Then he added in cipher:

> And this greed of the King of Spain is too prodigious, for he is not content with the many kingdoms which he possesses, but is now endeavoring to seize the kingdoms of other sovereigns and to make himself monarch of all Christendom.
>
> Having a King so powerful and so ambitious as your neighbor [Philip of Spain's Duchy of Milan], and should he seize Portugal, what will become of your commerce? For if it received great injury when the Portuguese took possession of the Indies, think what will happen when the Spaniards who have the power to reduce these countries to subjection will be masters there.

Philip represented a clear and present danger to Portugal as well as to other European nations. He was after the riches that Portugal represented—including its depleted but still fabulous collection of crown jewels. The importance and symbolism of these jewels was significant to the aging Spanish ruler, who, after all, bankrupted the Spanish crown twice—the second time only four years earlier. The

Portuguese trading posts in India were churning out thousands of precious gems along with a vast fortune in spices and shipping these to Europe regularly. This luxury trade symbolized a significant rolling income to the financially overstretched Philip, and a tempting prize.

Queen Elizabeth, too, was alarmed by Spanish domination, and was also tempted by Portugal's riches. Philip had paid for a papal bull that condemned the queen for her religious practices, reducing all of England to the status of a rogue state. Francis Drake's monumental achievement in circumnavigating the globe from 1577 to 1580 became a "state secret" to hide from the Spanish England's design of becoming masters of the high seas.

An economic war, dressed up as a dynastic one, was about to begin.

By 1580, Drake's name struck terror in the hearts of the Spaniards, and particularly Philip's, as *El Draco* (The Dragon), had made his hatred and vendetta against Spain highly personal. Drake's escapades against the Spanish galleons returning from New Spain were no more than piracy, benefiting his crew, financial backers, and Elizabeth herself.

Also in 1580, the opulence of Elizabeth's court as expressed through her clothes kept her power timeless, and supposedly kept her "youthful" appearance changeless. The queen was exceedingly vain, and with the passage of time, this vanity stretched the credulity of her court. Above all else, Elizabeth needed gemstones, which were essential to her timeless image and power, and she gratefully received many of these as the "booty queen" of Europe—generously provided by Drake's escapades. It would be Elizabeth's vanity that would set the course to break Philip's world domination, a road that would end in victory with the battle of the Spanish Armada in 1588. But to begin on that course, she needed to manipulate Don Antonio. By April 1580 the Venetian ambassador reported that large provisions were being sent by sea to Portugal in merchant ships and that the queen of England was arming.

Simultaneously, Elizabeth embarked on an exceedingly clever subterfuge, by reopening talks to marry the duke of Anjou (formerly the duke of Alençon), the youngest brother of Henry III of France. Anjou pandered to her vanity, showering her with diamonds he could ill afford to give. Elizabeth, having been led to expect a hunchback with a huge nose and a face deformed by smallpox, found an intelligent equal who was bold and exotic with an insinuating sexuality. It would have been a match made in heaven and one that deeply worried both Henry of France and Philip of Spain.

When Anjou stormed off from court at Blois against his mother's and brother's wishes to conclude the marriage contract with Elizabeth, raging at Henry, "If Your Majesty went to Poland to obtain that kingdom, why should not I go to England with a similar object?" it was reported back to Venice in an open dispatch that:

> Monsieur [Anjou] went to England not so much on account of the marriage as for the affairs of the Low Countries, because the Queen had held out hopes of advancing him money and of assisting him in order that he might make himself master of some part of Flanders; the Queen desiring to harass the Spaniards as much as she could, both to expel them and also to divert them from any prospect of disturbing her tranquility, as they appear to show signs of intending to do, and likewise that they might abandon their project of taking possession of Portugal by force of arms.

When Anjou arrived in London, the queen presented him as a token of her trust and love with a large golden key with which he could privately open and enter every apartment in the palace. Anjou, not to be outdone, placed a large and perfect diamond on the queen's finger, and Elizabeth gave him a small, jeweled harquebus (jewel box) of tremendous value. All courtiers and ladies-in-waiting were then dismissed, to their great consternation, and the queen and her suitor were left alone for the better part of two days. While there is no doubt that there was a great deal of lovemaking, a political plot was hatched to put Philip's ambitions in check and procure a kingdom for Anjou. By the time he departed England a month later, Anjou had given Elizabeth a jeweled headband worth 8,000 crowns ($388,000 or £242,000 today), and Elizabeth had given him a heart-shaped diamond.

The queen, for her part, was prepared to finance a kingdom for Anjou—Flanders—and wrest the north's most important commercial region from Philip's control, providing Anjou would take an active interest in the affairs of Portugal and throw his support behind Don Antonio.

While Elizabeth sent military succor to Don Antonio, Henry III, in true dissolute fashion, appeared to have no concern about the gathering storm, and indeed "retired for his amusement to St. Germain, where he remained for the week." If anything were to be done about Philip, it would be up to Elizabeth and Anjou to act, and neither shied away from the task.

The Elizabethan spy network was in full flow by the early summer, providing intelligence on Philip's anticipated movements. Anjou himself had sent messengers, men, and money to Don Antonio, and Catherine de' Medici was secretly providing support as well.

By the beginning of July, Philip's army was on the march and had crossed Portugal to Lisbon within twelve days. On July 15, 1580, a comprehensive report was prepared by Don Rodrigo de Mendoza, one of Elizabeth's spies, who wrote:

> Don Antonio has very few men of account about him. . . . It is said he bestows what he has very liberally on those that follow him, and has raised divers base persons to the degree of knighthood. . . . Don Antonio is very sad and heavy, which is not to be marveled at since he finds himself too weak to accomplish his designs; for though he be followed by the commoners and some gentlemen, he wants both counsel and money, without which the war will go slowly forward.

By the time Queen Elizabeth received this report, Philip's army, led by the duke of Alba, had been in Portugal for several weeks and had defeated the Portuguese pretender at Setúbal. Don Antonio's forces crumbled before the might and experience of Philip's mercenary army—comprised of more than twenty-five thousand men at arms from Italy, Germany, and Spain—to Antonio's twelve thousand irregulars. The Portuguese fell back to Lisbon in disarray, while the Spanish pillaged the countryside in their wake. When Philip, still at his palace in Madrid, heard the good news of this first major encounter, he was so delighted that he tipped the messenger 100 crowns ($19,000 or £12,000 today). Don Antonio, in dire need of weapons, food, and money, skulked back to Santarém. Only a few cities continued to support him on the mainland, with the Azores alone remaining entirely loyal.

In an encrypted message dated October 1580, to Venice, the Venetian ambassador in France reported:

> News has arrived from Spain that Don Antonio had retired to the mountains with twelve thousand men. He is supported by the clergy and also by two principal maritime cities, namely Oporto and Viana, so that even if he should have abandoned his designs upon Portugal, Strozzi [a Genoese financier to the crown of France] at the instigation of Monsieur [Anjou] and the Ambassador of the Queen of England who has offered sixty thousand crowns for soldiers' pay, has nevertheless sent an individual to Portugal to learn of the state of things there.

Catherine de' Medici now threw her considerable weight behind Don Antonio, not so much to assist him, as to keep her claim alive in the hearts and minds of the nobility in Portugal. Philip's wife, Catherine's daughter Elisabeth, had recently died in childbirth, freeing the scheming queen mother from any obligation to the Spanish monarch. She had been deeply insulted by Philip's dismissiveness of her own claims to the Portuguese throne.

Then suddenly, in a fretful report from her agents in Antwerp, Elizabeth was advised that Don Antonio "has got into his hands all his predecessor's treasures, which are said to be very great." The crown jewels, including the Sancy and the Mirror of Portugal, had been stolen by the Portuguese pretender.

Don Antonio held out in his mountain stronghold and sent a message to Queen Elizabeth in person by his trusted private courier, Ruy Lopes, along with a note in the Portuguese ambassador's handwriting asking for:

1. Twelve ships well equipped with artillery, men and munitions;
2. Two thousand harquebusiers with their officers, who will all be paid in Portugal from the day of leaving England till their return;
3. As much bronze ordnance of all sorts as the Queen may be willing to direct, the realm being in great need of it;
4. A thousand quintals of gunpowder;
5. Two thousand quintals of iron balls of every sort.

6. Payment will be made in Portugal, in coin, jewels or specie as the Queen shall please.

Elizabeth waved off her attendants and gave Don Antonio's messenger a private audience, the content of which was never recorded. Did she demand his jewels in exchange for granting his demands?

It is highly likely that Don Antonio also sent a similar dire plea to Henry of France, since it was reported back to England that "Strozzi is the person employed in the matter." Strozzi was personally put in charge of the shipment of men and arms to Portugal, but they were repelled by the Spanish and returned ineffectually to Nantes. Obviously a financier would have been employed on such a mission only if there were a need to value the security for the loan.

Don Antonio's first setback in his call for international assistance to England and France came quickly. French arms and men failed to break through the Spanish blockade. By now, Don Antonio recognized that Elizabeth had greater naval and financial resources than France, and appointed two gentlemen to go to England with jewels and "other stuff of value" to sell these items to the queen in exchange for her military assistance. The queen, who was no fool, immediately understood that all was lost, yet she received Don Antonio's men in secret, much as she had done with his earlier messenger.

And then, suddenly, almost magically, Don Antonio vanished. There were various reports that he had been captured or killed, none of which could be substantiated. Philip had himself proclaimed king of Portugal at the Cortes (Parliament), promising to protect Portugal's independence within the Spanish Empire, but Antonio's supporters were rounded up and variously tortured, killed, or punished. Europe was full of rumors of Antonio's death, until the Venetian ambassador in France reported in an encrypted letter on March 2, 1581, that "Strozzi went to Tours to speak with those Portuguese gentlemen mentioned in my dispatch of February 24. They say that among them is a personage of importance. Some few insist that Don Antonio himself is in France and that he has with him in gold and jewels about two millions of money, that he has written to Monsieur [Anjou] to support his cause with the King. If his presence be true it cannot remain hid for long."

By April 1, there was a great buzz at court in Tours that the Portuguese gentlemen were acting on behalf of Don Antonio, who would not "disclose himself" until he had come to an understanding with the king or even Anjou. Antonio was in mortal fear of his life—not only from the Spanish threat, but also from those who might rob him of his immense fortune in jewels. It is probable that this tremendous and rational fear of reprisal meant that to limit the risk of losing, or indeed pawning, everything he had all at once, Don Antonio logically buried, or otherwise hid, a substantial portion of the jewels for use at a later date. His primary destination remained England, but having not had any vessels at his disposal, the only route available to him was through France, which meant dealing with the intricacies, intrigues, and political factions surrounding the French crown.

One of the French king's financial and military advisers, and a connoisseur of diamonds and other jewels, Nicholas Harlay de Sancy, secretly met and entertained Don Antonio near La Rochelle to dissuade him from crossing to England and to demonstrate the merits of pawning the gems in France under his own auspices. But the Portuguese king would not be deterred.

By July 1581, the dethroned king had finally made his way to the English Channel and crossed to relative safety under Elizabeth's protection. Don Antonio was keen to seek out Elizabeth's favorite admiral, Drake, who had returned from his three-year circumnavigation of the globe the previous September. Although that particular accomplishment was still a secret, the damage he had inflicted on the Spanish colonies—and particularly the loot he had plundered—were reason enough for Don Antonio to enlist Drake's support to his cause. Nothing would have prevented Drake from any opportunity to continue to wreak havoc among the Spaniards, and together they approached the queen for her permission to set sail at once for Portugal.

All wars come at a cost, and the queen wanted to ensure that she could exact the financial cost required for so risky a mission. When the haggling began in earnest that summer, Don Antonio's initial promise to Elizabeth that he could draw money from the Indian fleets as they arrived in Antwerp was hardly believable, since it was highly improbable that the Portuguese Indian merchants would put their goods to sea while matters remained so unsettled at home. She needed

Queen Elizabeth I, wearing the
Mirror of Portugal as a pendant
hanging from her necklace.
Painting by Marcus Gheeraerts the
Younger, c. 1592.

security, and plenty of it. She raised the matter of the jewels, and their
value was debated at length. The queen was already giving 30,000
crowns a month to Anjou for the rebellion in Flanders against Philip,
and the thought of sinking more ready money into a risky adventure
was distinctly unappealing.

By August 4, a deal had been struck between Lord Burghley, in
his capacity as the queen's chancellor, and the Portuguese king. The
jewels that Don Antonio had with him were valued, or rather undervalued, at 30,000 crowns ($7 million or £4.4 million today), and Don
Antonio purchased two ships with the cash received. It is entirely
possible that the Sancy was among this first lot of jewels pawned to
English jewelers, but the descriptions of the stones do not allow for a
definitive identification. A letter from Lord Burghley to the queen

Is Queen Elizabeth I wearing the Sancy, or is it a poor reproduction of the Mirror of Portugal? Painting by Jan Massys, 1583.

indicates that she should repay the merchants who advanced funds for Don Antonio's largest diamond that was now in her possession. But was this the Sancy or the Mirror of Portugal? We know that the Mirror of Portugal went to the queen and was valued at only 5,000 crowns ($1.2 million or £727,000 today) and that Don Antonio received a mere 3,000 crowns for it. If the jewels Don Antonio had with him were worth millions, as claimed by the Venetian ambassador to the Doges, and the second-largest diamond in the collection—the Mirror of Portugal—was valued at only 5,000 crowns, it is difficult to imagine that the Sancy was somehow held separately from the jewels valued, particularly in view of what transpired next.

To reinvade Portugal and retake his crown, Antonio needed at least twenty more ships and an army. Elizabeth had undervalued his crown jewel collection and been slow to provide vessels and victuals. Drake's reputation had obviously attracted Antonio to England, as much as England's ability to bankroll his tilting at windmills like Don Quixote. But Elizabeth's endless stalling was wearing him down, so Don Antonio stole away to France to recover more jewels from hiding and try his luck with the French.

Strozzi visited Don Antonio near La Rochelle again with Harlay de Sancy and others to cut a deal. The king himself had no money to finance the undertaking, but both Strozzi and Harlay de Sancy were not only very wealthy but also exceedingly well connected. Still, the untrusting Portuguese king was unwilling to part with his largest—and most important—gem, since the promises of ships could be withheld and French mercenaries could be recalled, or worse, their allegiances could be bought by Philip of Spain. The negotiations continued for several weeks, and Harlay de Sancy finally succeeded in agreeing with the Portuguese king to take—as security—a large, thirty-six-carat faceted diamond, later called *Le Beau Sancy* (Little Sancy). Harlay arranged for two French ships and provisions to be pledged by the French king, and Don Antonio set to work to reconquer his kingdom through the Azores with his two English and two French vessels and a ragtag mercenary force.

The first well-defined sighting of the Sancy in these clandestine proceedings was when the diamond passed into the hands of a trusted Antwerp-based Portuguese merchant and "new Christian," Francisco Rodriguez d'Evora, either directly through the negotiations with Strozzi, Harlay de Sancy, and the other merchants at La Rochelle, or through Strozzi or even Elizabeth to Anjou, who in turn pawned the diamond to Rodriguez d'Evora to raise more money for his Flemish army to rise up against King Philip. Whatever the route it took to Rodriguez d'Evora, it is certain that he was a person whom both Don Antonio and Strozzi trusted to safeguard the magnificent diamond until it could be redeemed.

The Fugger newsletters and the Venetian ambassador reported in January 1582—only four months after Don Antonio had procured his first two ships from England and two months after the French ships were ready—that all four ships had been caught in a storm, and one had sunk. Within days Don Antonio was back in Paris incognito, attempting to sell or pawn more jewels directly to Catherine de' Medici.

According to the Spanish ambassador to England, who described the battle, Drake was good to his word, and had set sail to the Bay of Biscay, despite claiming publicly that he was en route to Peru. Antonio's forces, however, had headed off separately and were defeated by the Spaniards before they could join up with Drake. Strozzi had been killed in the skirmish. Don Antonio escaped back to France into the welcoming arms of the queen mother, who openly put the defeated king under her protection and promised him a new fleet in the following year. When Don Antonio was asked about his struggles, he said he was "most hurt to see that Spanish gold carried such weight with the Frenchmen who fought alongside the Spaniards."

Catherine de' Medici was the only person who "won" in this fraught situation. Her protection of Don Antonio from Philip was highly successful and absolute. Furthermore, Elizabeth seethed at the fact that her French rival had procured many of the Portuguese crown jewels that she had lusted after herself. This rivalry for jewels between the two queens should not be underestimated, since it was a long-standing bone of contention that Elizabeth always wore the de' Medici pearls that Catherine had given to Mary, queen of Scots, as a wedding present on the occasion of her marriage to Catherine's eldest son, François II.

Yet despite this "moral" victory over Philip and Elizabeth, Catherine also tired of Don Antonio's endless demands. He harangued the queen mother for more money to mount another campaign to invade Portugal, and Catherine replied steadfastly that "there is no more money to give." With his paranoid fears of assassination and arrogant ways he was thought by many, after four years of sponging off the royal purses of France and England, to weigh too heavily on both crowns. The Venetian ambassador reported home that "Don Antonio, whose fortunes are waning daily, has received from the queen mother a little castle in Brittany, near Vannes, and 500 ducats a month ($83,000 or £51,000). He is full of debts; and lives in hired lodgings in Paris."

Don Antonio had evidently outstayed his welcome in France, and his only hope of reprisal—and survival—was to reinvigorate Drake into action, regain his crown, and recover his jewels.

11

Three Determined Men
of Dubious Character

1584–1590

THERE IS NO FURTHER WRITTEN RECORD about the Sancy in the 1580s. There is also no comprehensive record of conversations or correspondence between Don Antonio and Sir Francis Drake in 1584, but Drake required little if any persuasion to renew his assaults against the Spaniards. His abiding hatred of the Spanish monarch stretched back some thirty years to his maiden voyage, when Philip had sunk Drake's first ship, leaving him stranded on the Spanish Main with no visible means of returning home. It was a humiliation that Drake could never forget.

Nor was it necessary to cajole Elizabeth into action in the early days of the autumn of 1584. She felt vulnerable. Antwerp had fallen again into Spanish hands, Anjou was dead, the swashbuckling Protestant Henry of Navarre was now heir presumptive to the French throne, and England could literally not afford defeat. Don Antonio, who had become a nuisance in France, was now backed by England despite being courted again by Catherine de' Medici with new promises of "real" money—6,000 crowns—and restoration of his pension if he returned at once to France. He declined the tardy if somewhat provocative offer.

At long last, Don Antonio's timing seemed perfect. In fact, the French ambassador commented on that very point when he reported

94

to Paris that "Don Antonio, on the 21st September, had embarked eight thousand infantry and two hundred English gentlemen on board sixty-two vessels and had sailed towards Portugal to try his fortune in recovering that kingdom. It surprises everyone to see how rapidly the Queen of England has made up her mind [this time] to give him such large forces."

In fact, their skepticism was well founded. Elizabeth, notorious for changing her mind, had ordered both Drake and Antonio back to shore, having thought better of the foray and the dire repercussions for England should it fail. She could not, she believed, protect the Low Countries *and* attack Philip through Portugal and be successful in both endeavors. A messenger sped from London on the fastest steed available with a letter from the queen to Drake aboard ship telling him that there had been a change of orders. His queen wished him to plunder New Spain and return with yet another fortune in booty to England. No matter how much Drake would have wanted to "singe the beard" of the king of Spain, he knew a royal order when he saw one and had to separate from Don Antonio to carry out his duty. As long as Drake was plundering the Spanish—and now Portuguese—colonies, Philip would need money and be unable to supply his armies in the Low Countries. Elizabeth reasoned that this was an effective and less risky way to achieve her goals. She and England might yet stand a chance.

Her intuition was infallible. Next to Philip's temper, money was the main commodity in extremely short supply in Europe at the time. In January 1585 the pope published a bull of the Crusade to be used against England, which effectively gave Philip over a period of five years 1.8 million crowns annually ($997 million or £623 million today) by forfeiting papal concessions to the crown of Spain. The money would be collected in special chests in the mint at Madrid for the king's use against the "heretical" state of England. Rumors of a league among the pope, Philip, the Venetian Republic, Savoy, and Tuscany against England abounded. Philip, like a man possessed, trying to rid himself of the demons that drove him wild, raised further loans of 900,000 crowns.

The duke de Guise, whom Philip regarded as his personal puppet in the fight for the crown of France on the side of the Catholic League against Henry III and Henry of Navarre, gave 50,000 ducats of his own money to Philip for "The Cause" against England. Two million Rhinish guilders in gold were squeezed from reluctant German princes. Even the Fuggers raised a half a million Rhinish guilders in gold for the king of Spain from their own coffers, and other sources unknown. These last loans were granted to Philip in retaliation for the piracy carried out by Elizabeth's merchant adventurers against their consignments from the Indies and New Spain that never reached port—thanks in no small part to Drake.

Philip was fed up, and had amassed a war chest of unimaginable magnitude. Whatever men he could muster, or press into service, were called up to end "that English woman's" interference.

At the same time, Henry III was fighting for his political existence. The religious war had escalated into a political one in what would be known as the "War of the Three Henrys" among Henry III, Henry de Guise, and Henry of Navarre. Henry III needed money he did not have to win, and needed it very badly. In the ten years since he had come to the throne, he had already pawned or sold all of the crown jewels and taxed his disgruntled and oppressed people as much as he dared. Anyone with a measure of personal wealth could overcome the influence of the minions and carve out a dominant position at court. A clever man with personal wealth and a military mind could make himself invaluable—and create an even greater fortune through the spoils of war. Nicholas de Harlay, seigneur de Sancy and baron de Maule, was just such a man.

Harlay was the colonel general of the Swiss and a gentleman of the King's Household. He was also only twenty-five years old at the time of his first meeting with Don Antonio, in 1580. He was a good friend of the French king's secretary of state, Villeroy, and his daughter would later marry Villeroy's son. Harlay was intelligent, handsome, and exceedingly full of his own importance. He bore an uncanny resemblance to Don Antonio, and like the Portuguese king was persuaded of his place in history and practiced a frequent economy with the truth. None of this mattered to Henry III, though. Harlay seemed to have great personal wealth and was prepared to put it to work in the name of the king. Harlay claimed to his many detractors that he had inherited much of that wealth, but he was a master spinner of good yarns; many of his assertions simply were not believable. Like most military commanders of his time, his riches were acquired on or near the field of battle, where few if any questions were asked and certainly no answers were given. Having trained as a lawyer at Orléans, Harlay knew more than most people about the importance of disinformation as a means of combating flimsy evidence, and he played this repeatedly to advantage.

Harlay, born a Protestant, had converted to Catholicism after the St. Bartholomew's Day Massacre in 1572 to assure his place at court. The subterfuge paid off with an appointment to the important strategic position of governor of Châlon-sur-Saône, which was deemed to be the gateway to Switzerland and the Alps, and a "gentleman of the King's Household." But Harlay's fame among his contemporaries was derived not from his meteoric rise within Henry III's household, but rather from his inexplicable possession of many diamonds of high quality—two of which were exceptionally large and perfect stones. These precious possessions appear even more extraordinary when considering the fact that Harlay returned to Paris from his mission in Switzerland and Savoy as Henry's ambassador in December 1580, heavily in debt due to the exigencies inflicted on him by a reckless monarch, harangued by his creditors, and preoccupied with the potential reversal in his political fortunes by his lack of success. Yet no one asked how, if he was so poor in December 1580, he then became so wealthy by the time he met Don Antonio in La Rochelle in 1581. Then again, how was he able to buy off the Swiss dissatisfaction with him in January 1582? We will never know the answers to these questions for certain, since Harlay was undoubtedly a master of deception and manipulation—both qualities in short supply in Henry III's royal entourage. No one was going to press Harlay too hard as to the exact state of his financial affairs as long as he continued to use his wits and his money for the king's benefit.

Harlay clearly used disinformation and cunning to deflect attention from the true state of his finances, not to mention the exact sources of this inestimable wealth. By the time he met Don Antonio in La Rochelle, Harlay was evidently able to procure cash for the dethroned monarch in exchange for diamonds, and would have made a sizable commission on the transaction himself. Whether he provided any of his own money to Don Antonio as part of that deal remains a mystery, but it is a reasonable assumption that the foundations for his claim to many larger diamonds, including the Sancy, date from this first encounter.

Harlay, when pressed by the growing faction unfriendly to him at court about his precious stones, pretended on one occasion that the diamonds had been purchased on a journey to Constantinople—a journey he never made. Years later he alleged that his son Achille had brought them back to him from Constantinople—the only problem with this explanation being that his son had not as yet been to that city, as he was a youngster at the time.

Despite or perhaps because of this subterfuge, Harlay became renowned for his diamonds. He was sailing close to the wind with his tall tales about these stones. His insatiable need to self-aggrandize, and his love of being the center of attention would, at the end of the day, be his undoing. Although Harlay did not want to divulge his source of the diamond "purchases"—he was, after all, a self-confessed plunderer—he was no fool. Harlay knew that Catherine de' Medici wanted the Sancy and the smaller, thirty-six-carat stone, the Beau Sancy, for her own but could ill afford to buy them. He rightly feared the truth being leaked at court and the grueling punishment the queen mother might mete out to him for his perceived disloyalty. His healthy fear of Catherine de' Medici coupled with the fact that he came by the Sancy diamond and the other diamonds in his possession by methods that would be frowned on at court made discovery of his actions potentially a life-threatening matter. After all, he had been on official royal business for the king and the queen mother when he plotted to get hold of the gems for himself.

The high drama surrounding the acquisition and purchase of crown jewels in France—or elsewhere, for that matter—should not be underestimated. When Henry III had inherited the throne from his brother Charles IX in May 1574, one of Henry's first acts was to publish a letter patent discharging Charles's widow, Queen Elisabeth of Austria, of the crown jewels and giving them to his wife, Louise de Lorraine-Vaudemont, whom he had married the previous February. At the same time, Catherine de' Medici issued a letter patent stating that if Henry III died without a male heir, the crown jewels would go to his daughter or daughters, since she hated Henry de Navarre de Bourbon and could not bear his inheriting them as the heir apparent under Salic law. The queen mother claimed that her letter patent was to ensure the inalienability of the gems. We might have believed her if she hadn't added "and if the king dies without issue, all jewels would revert to the queen mother for her to dispose of according to her will."

One thing is certain: when Harlay was using the Sancy diamond to further his career and the king's cause in raising Henry's mercenary armies in Switzerland, it was not yet entirely Harlay's to lend or pawn. François d'O, the king's superintendent of finances, owned at least a third of the diamond until January 1588, when he ceded it to Harlay for an unspecified amount in cash. The bill of sale was registered three years later, most probably due to the delayed completion of the Sancy's purchase by Harlay, on Wednesday, June 12, 1591, at Vernon in front of a notary, just before noon, when François d'O signed the document in which he

> Leaves to Monsieur Nicolas de Harlay, seigneur de Sancy, also a counselor of the King in his Council of State and captain of fifty men at arms, one third of a great diamond weighing sixty carats, of which the two other thirds belong to the heirs of François Rodrigues, Portuguese, in the hands of which heirs the diamond should remain, such as has been declared by the gentlemen d'O and Harlay. This third of a diamond belonging to the said Monsieur d'O, and to which he has ceded all his rights, names and actions, submit to this effect the said Monsieur de Sancy in all his rights, names, reasons and actions, declaring that he has no pretensions to the said diamond, and that the said Monsieur d'O, by means of having received payment recognizes and confesses to have received from the said Monsieur de Sancy in this month of January 1588 a satisfactory payment for the diamond, of which he will demand nothing further.

The document was signed by François d'O, and Harlay with his distinctive scissors mark, as well as the notary.

But the mystery remains as to why the diamond had not remained with the heirs of Francisco Rodriguez prior to these dates, or whether Harlay had acquired his third portion before he was "lending" the

Sancy as his own property to Henry III for the king's personal use. Whether François d'O had originally spirited the diamond away from Don Antonio alone, or with Harlay de Sancy's connivance, we do not know. What we do know is that later, Harlay claimed the diamond had been in pawn since 1591 with the "Jews of Metz," when in fact the Rodriguez heirs held it in trust until such time as he could pay for the other two thirds. Granted, the Rodriguez d'Evora were originally Jews in Don Manuel's time, when the elder of the family was the king's physician, but this is as close to the truth as Harlay's claim comes.

At the end of the day it was Harlay's diamonds that most dazzled and impressed the king, and Harlay was "obliged" to loan what was still the largest white diamond in Europe, which he now called *le grand Sancy*, to King Henry to wear at the front of his toque, a velvet hat that covered the vain king's baldness. The portrait of Henry wearing the Sancy, attributed to François Quesnel, was painted circa 1585—approximately the same date of the portrait of Elizabeth I by John Bettes the Younger, where she wears the Mirror of Portugal for the first time. There is no such thing as coincidence in history, especially a coincidence of this nature. Two distinctive gems found their way into two different crowns of Europe from the same source: Don Antonio de Crato, in his desperate struggle to regain his kingdom. There is little doubt that Harlay, by fair means or foul, had Don Antonio's folly to thank for his rise to prominence.

Notwithstanding all of Nicholas Harlay de Sancy's faults—and they were many—he remained a remarkably loyal servant of Henry III, fighting against his own brother Robert, who had taken the side of Henry, duke de Guise, in the conflict that raged on in France. Harlay's military expertise staved off further incursions from the duke of Savoy and the duke de Guise into eastern territories loyal to the king, and Harlay managed to politically and financially control the troublesome Swiss mercenary forces; it was critical to keep on their side. Plunder was easy in these times, and Harlay not only took plunder but also made the Swiss pay him for receiving "favors."

While Sancy was feathering his own nest under the show of loyalty to Henry, the year 1587 would be a watershed in European history. In February the final act in a twenty-year drama was played out at the earl of Shrewsbury's castle at Fotheringhay: Mary, queen of Scots, was put on trial for the Babington Plot, which was a clear attempt to assassinate Queen Elizabeth. It had been nearly thirty years since Mary had married Henry's eldest brother, François II, and while she had failed to learn important political lessons, she would continue after her execution to be the symbol for all good Catholics to rise against the "heretic Queen Elizabeth." As the verdict was read aloud for "stubborn disobedience . . . incitement to insurrection . . . against the life and person of her sacred majesty . . . high treason . . . death," the endgame for the past forty years of intrigue between the two queens of the British Isles was finally in play. When Mary's auburn wig and head were held aloft for the executioner to speak the customary words "Long live the queen" in Elizabeth's name, Philip of Spain resolved—at long last—to prepare his Armada for the invasion. To do this, Henry de Guise would need to control France while Philip turned his impressive attention wholly to England.

By April, Philip's secret undertaking was hardly a secret—after all, Don Antonio's spies in Lisbon were reporting back on the huge preparations under way, and Antonio saw his last chance to persuade Drake to assist him. The outrage felt across Catholic Europe at Elizabeth's callous murder of Mary meant that Elizabeth could equivocate no longer against Spain, and in the end gave her final approval to Drake to make a full-scale invasion of Portugal, with Lisbon as the major target. Don Antonio would go with them, and would at last be given the opportunity to test his repeated assurances of the past six years that once he set foot in Portugal his loyal subjects would rise as one and chase the Spanish interlopers back to their homes.

Elizabeth, now fifty-four, was desperate for a victory. The preparations for the Armada's attack, the long wait for the enemy to come, and especially the prolonged mobilization by land and sea had cost her more money than she cared to spend. To neutralize French outrage over Mary, queen of Scots, Elizabeth at last relented and made Mary's Calvinist son James VI of Scotland her heir. Henry was placated, especially since he was in no position to object, being threatened daily alternatively by Henry, duke de Guise, and Henry of Navarre.

The queen knew Philip well by now, and knew that he was her match for stubbornness. While she was a past master at waging peace as if it were a war, a war that would regretfully take place on English soil, or in English waters, was a matter that would at least bestir her people's patriotism, not to mention the abiding xenophobia of her island nation. It was a situation she had hoped to avoid, but her only chance to stop the inevitable was for Drake and Antonio to succeed. An overjoyed Philip received an encrypted report that:

> The Queen of England is thoroughly alarmed for her own life and for the safety of her kingdom, both on account of the conspiracies which are constantly coming to light, and on account of the great preparations of war which rumor pictures as being made in Spain. In order to secure the support of France, she has offered to give his Most Christian Majesty [Henry III] strong places in Holland and Zealand; Drake, however, encourages her, assuring her that the Spanish noises are only salvos of blank cartridge which make rumpus but break no bones.

Philip was spending 10,500 reals per day for his officers' commissions. Like Elizabeth, he loathed spending money unnecessarily, especially if it was money he did not as yet have. Despite the vast sums he had already raised to arm his mighty Armada, another 3 million reals in gold were urgently needed.

As the favorable winds of late spring blew, Drake's ships were sighted off the coast of Spain. For reasons that remain a mystery, Drake and Don Antonio, having reached the Rock of Lisbon, decided that Cadiz would be their first objective. Some believe it was because the English admiral had heard about Philip's armada, while others assert it was because he sniffed the booty in the air.

As his sails came into view at Cadiz Harbor, cries of "El Draco!" were raised, and the people fled for their lives into the old castle; they were hastily shut in by the captain of the guard. In the overcrowded fortress packed with panicked townspeople, hysteria broke out, and twenty-five women and children were trampled to death. Drake attempted to seize the sixty ships at anchor as their defenders panicked and fled. By morning, Drake had sunk a 700-ton ship full of cochineal, logwood, hides, and wool bound for Genoa; plundered all that was worth taking from the vicinity of the quayside; and marked the other vessels in the harbor for destruction. Drake himself estimated that he had sunk, burned, or captured thirty-seven vessels in Cadiz Harbor. King Philip knew the real cost—twenty-four ships worth 172,000 ducats—and admitted that "the daring of the attempt was very great indeed."

Drake, having singed the king's beard, knew that the incursion was only a pinprick and wrote to Walsingham that:

> The like preparation was never heard of nor known as the King of Spain hath and daily maketh to invade England . . . which if they be not impeached before they join will be very perilous. . . . This service, which by God's sufferance we have done will breed some alterations but all possible preparations for defense are very expedient. . . . I dare not almost write of the great forces we hear the King of Spain hath. Prepare in England strongly and most by sea!

Drake sailed north again along the Portuguese coast and landed unopposed, but not unobserved, at Lagos. Columns of horsemen shadowed the invaders and opened fire, and the English made a dash to Sagres Castle—a third-class fort guarding a fishing village against Moorish raids from the Barbary Coast—and captured it. Drake probably never knew that it was the castle of Henry the Navigator, the first royal to understand the importance of exploration by sea. But importantly, the popular uprising so long promised by Don Antonio did not take place. Antonio professed to be amazed, and promised a better reception at Lisbon.

Five days later, the English fleet was off the coast of a heavily fortified Lisbon, and Drake was convinced that the Portuguese knew he had brought "their king" back home. When the popular uprising still did not come, Drake declared that he "had come to Lisbon just for a look at the state of things," and a distraught Don Antonio watched the Portuguese coast disappear over the horizon as Drake set sail for the final ports of call on the adventure: Cape St. Vincent and the Azores. Don Antonio had pawned the Sancy along with the most valuable crown jewel collection of its day for an uprising that never happened.

Drake wrote in his ship's log that day, "continuing to the end yields the true glory"—a phrase that could easily have been uttered to Don Antonio in his desperation. At Cape St. Vincent Drake spied the carrack *San Felipe,* homeward-bound from Goa with its annual cargo of spices, jewels, and other oriental goods that were fruits of Portugal's eastern empire. Drake easily seized the ship, since her gun ports were so jammed with precious cargo that she was unable to use them against him. The carrack was stuffed with pepper, cinnamon, cloves, calicoes, silks, ivories, gold, silver, and dozens of caskets of jewels. The total value was £114,000 ($27.6 million or £17.3 million today) and three times the value of all thirty-seven ships seized in Cadiz Bay. Considering that his ship, the *Elizabeth Bonaventure,* could be provisioned for £175 a month, and £40,000 could put an entire army in the field, this was a mammoth booty—even for Drake.

It also meant that the pirate admiral would have to set sail immediately for England to save his prize, and end any illusions that Don Antonio may have continued to entertain about seizing his throne. The queen's share of the booty would help with the battle against Philip's Armada that lay ahead, and he had to warn the queen of what he had seen. Don Antonio, despite his vociferous protestations, could jump overboard as far as Drake was concerned.

When Philip's fleet attacked the English in the English Channel in July 1588, they were defeated, but not so much by the smaller, swifter, more technologically advanced English ships as by the notorious English weather. The Armada of 134 ships limped back to Spain thoroughly defeated, and Philip's dream of a Catholic Europe was all but shattered. His only remaining hope was that his puppet Henry, duke de Guise, would win in France. If the Protestant Henry de Navarre de Bourbon became king of France, Elizabeth of England would be triumphant.

But Philip had not reckoned on Henry III making the one decisive resolution of his entire reign: to assassinate Guise. When Guise's bloodied body was searched, an unfinished letter to Philip was found that began "to keep up the civil war in France will cost 700,000 livres a month."

Harlay, and François d'O as superintendent of finance, were the prime movers and shakers in Henry III's France in 1588 and put Henry up to having Guise murdered. The civil war was too costly, and neither Harlay nor d'O had the means at their disposal—nor the empire— that Philip of Spain did. Killing Guise was their only option, so they recommended Guise's assassination in their capacities as the king's moneymen in charge of Henry III's depleted war chest. The now ailing Philip consoled himself with the thought that he probably would not have been able to "rule" the duke de Guise if he had taken the throne of France. The pope, when he heard of the duke's murder, nodded and said, "so the king of Spain has lost yet another captain."

Seven months later, Henry III himself was assassinated, bringing the House of Valois to an end and placing Henry of Navarre and the House of Bourbon on the French throne. The scramble was on for Harlay de Sancy to ensure his future as a Catholic servant to an exceedingly clever Protestant king. There was little doubt that his diamonds would be needed, and even if they were not, he would see to it that Henry IV would think that they were.

12

The Man Who "Sweated Lies from Every Pore"

January 1591–August 1596

WHEN HENRY OF NAVARRE BECAME Henry IV of France in 1588, he was literally the "last man standing" of the three Henrys vying for the crown. An eighth-generation descendant of St. Louis of the Capetian dynasty, Henry became the founding father of the French Bourbon dynasty that would last uninterrupted until 1792. His rule, however, remained under challenge. While the other two Henrys were now dead, the duke de Mayenne, a cousin of the beheaded Mary, queen of Scots, and other formidable nobles fought on for the Catholic League (French Catholic nobles who were set against Henry IV and the Protestants) in the hope of ridding the country of its Protestant king.

Henry was a vibrant, handsome, and intelligent man of tremendous courage and daring, and a notoriously rampant sexuality. Few criticized his wife of some fifteen years, Marguerite of Valois, for having failed to deliver him an heir, since he spent all of his time at court with his many mistresses. Where Henry III had been indecisive and weak, Henry IV was single-minded and stopped at nothing to achieve his aims. To rebuild France, he had to defeat the Catholic League and Mayenne decisively. But wars took money, and Henry was as broke as his predecessor from years of fighting for his crown. He and his mother had long ago pawned the last of their own crown jewel collection to Queen Elizabeth for a mere £20,000 ($5.8 million or £3.6 million today), despite the fact that the collection had been valued at three times that sum.

The French treasury, too, was empty. To aggravate the situation, the civil war was by no means over. There were enemies at the gate in the form of Philip of Spain, the pope, German princes, and the Swiss. Not only did Henry suffer from the insuperable crime of being a Protestant, but also he had to defend France and outsmart his Catholic population and neighbors to maintain power. France was like a weak and wounded animal dangerously suffering from two decades of religious civil war, and the only certainty was the unpredictability of the situation.

Since the tried and tested means of raising money—pawning the royal crown jewel collection—was no longer available, the only way the king could hope to survive was to instill a patriotic fervor among his followers and to surround himself with men of wealth willing to put their riches at risk for "the glory of France" and the crown. The most notable of these men was Nicolas Harlay de Sancy. Harlay shouldered his way to the front of the line by dashing off to cajole the Lutheran princes of southern Germany, pleading in Henry IV's name for them to lay down their arms. As the soldier-ambassador of France in Switzerland, he was less successful than in southern Germany, and was vilified by the Swiss. His many critics had already nicknamed him the "Machiavelli with small feet," "an adventurer without scruple," and "a man who sweated lies from every pore." His bitterest enemy and fellow traveler in Henry IV's entourage, Theodore Agrippa d'Aubigné, would eventually become so outraged with Harlay's half truths and arrogance that he would write a diatribe that would rob Harlay of his place in history.

As colonel of the Swiss mercenary troops, Harlay was in a remarkable position to make the most of land shipments between Philip II's dependent realms: the duchy of Milan and the Low Countries. In September 1590 he attacked a shipment of cash and arms from Milan destined for the duke of Parma, governor of the Low Countries. The cash amounted to some 56,000 ecus ($10.4 million or £6.5 million today), which in Harlay's own words he "converted to his own profit."

As Drake had done for England, Harlay reasoned that any plunder he could take from the king of Spain would make Philip's task of attacking France more difficult. Like Drake, Harlay quickly gained a reputation at court—and in Spain—as a plunderer, and many deeds of theft and pillaging were wrongly attributed to him.

It had been questioned by those like Theodore Agrippa d'Aubigné whether Harlay's amazing diamonds had been acquired by foul means. His sudden, fabulous wealth in diamonds and other gems had become a source of tremendous jealousy among the other noblemen in both Henry III's and Henry IV's courts. The two largest diamonds in his possession—the Grand Sancy, reputed to be sixty carats, including its setting, and the Beau Sancy, weighing thirty-six carats—had been acquired, as we have seen, by Harlay in vague and mysterious circumstances. He never alluded to the fact that he had "purchased" these gems from his dealings with the Portuguese pretender Don Antonio. In fact, Harlay gave not one or two but several different explanations as to how he had acquired the stones—ranging from their being a gift, or purchasing them on a journey to Constantinople, to having bought them from a "merchant" of unknown nationality or having had the diamonds in his possession for some time. By naming the diamonds after himself, he perpetuated the myth of long-standing ownership. Owners of such fabulous gems were well within their rights to hide the fact that they held these stones to avoid theft or even murder, but in Harlay's case he flaunted his ownership, using them for the crown and his own advancement, all the while actively hiding how and when he came by them. The only logical explanation is that by revealing the source and date of acquisition, he would have exposed some disloyalty to the king.

By 1590 Harlay had used the Sancy on several occasions to raise cash for mercenary armies among the Swiss; and on one occasion, when it was to be pawned to get 50,000 ecus to pay his mercenary army, Harlay sent the diamond with a faithful servant to the pawnbroker. In the Jura Mountains region, the servant was set upon by a band of brigands and mortally wounded. Word quickly reached Harlay that his servant lay dying. Panic-stricken, Harlay rushed to the inn where the man had been taken. Sweaty and filthy from the journey on horseback, with his cloak billowing behind him, Harlay raced through the crowded tavern to the back room where the servant's body had been taken and demanded to be alone with the dead man. According to Harlay himself, he pulled back the blood-soaked burlap covering, revealing multiple stab wounds, and hung his head. If the diamond was lost, he would be, too. Then Harlay's desperate arrogance suddenly took over from his panic. It struck him that the servant would never have betrayed him. Surely the man would have heard the brigands chasing after him, he reasoned. Surely he would have done something to hide the diamond to save his master. Without hesitation, Harlay delved into the man's open abdomen, searching for the stone, but none could be found. With blood-stained hands he pried the man's jaw open with as much force as he could muster, and found the diamond at the back of his throat. The relief that Harlay felt can only be imagined. If he had failed to deliver the diamond for money, his usefulness to the king would have ended, and his competitive edge over the other nobles would have been lost for good. The diamond was pawned within days, probably to Henry Balbani, a Luccan merchant residing in Geneva, and Harlay's career was saved. He wrote in his *Discours* many years later that "As I had already spent the fifty thousand ecus that I had taken from the enemy and another fifty thousand from Henry Balbani that he had loaned me against the security of my diamond rings, we were forced to return to camp since we no longer had any money."

The money had been borrowed in the name of Henry IV, loaned by the citizens of Bern, and underwritten by Balbani to be spent on the war against the duke of Savoy. Balbani, for his part, needed to guarantee that Calvinist Geneva would be assured of religious freedom against its Catholic neighbors like the duke of Savoy, but never would have been tempted to lend any sums without adequate collateral. The Sancy diamond thus found its way—very temporarily—into his hands.

But even with these vast loans, the capital required to keep the Swiss mercenaries satisfied and at arms was inadequate. According to Harlay, "The fifty companies each took one hundred fifty ecus in pay each week, which only amounted to one third of their wages, and they no longer had the means with which to continue the fight. There were many who refused to serve if they did not receive what was their due. . . . We do not have the money to even do this without the sale of some domains in Navarre."

Henry did indeed sell some of his lands in Navarre to keep his Calvinist Swiss soldiers in arms. Paradoxically, the king trusted the foreign Protestant troops more than he did his own Frenchmen, since many of them were Catholics. By the end of the day, the Swiss defeated the duke of Savoy, and Harlay was hailed as a hero by the king.

Philip II could not ignore the situation any longer. He had retreated since the Armada's defeat to the Escurial monastery, and his health was failing. Nevertheless, his rabid hatred of the Protestants had not abated, and the Venetian ambassador to Madrid recorded in cipher in March 1591:

> His Majesty is continually asked by the members of the League in France to furnish help; the Duke of Joyeuse asks for men to make head against Montmorency; the Duke of Mercure implores the dispatch of a Spanish garrison to Brittany; the Duke of Mayenne demands money to pay his troops; the Duke of Parma seeks to secure the money which will pacify his mutineers. All receive kind words and promises; and it would seem that there is a desire to oblige them up to a certain point. Money is being raised, partly on the security of the eight millions voted by the Cortes, partly by the sale of part of the royal revenue in Naples, partly by prolonging the life interests in the Indies.

Within two weeks, urgent demands for money had come from the duke of Parma in Flanders, and Philip was obliged to raise a loan of 800,000 crowns from the Fuggers. The king's finances were in as appalling a state as ever, and the Fuggers demanded security in gems for the 300,000 crowns ($142.4 million or £89 million today) previously advanced.

With the knowledge that Philip was gearing up for war, Henry needed to somehow drag Elizabeth into battle on the French side. After Nicholas Harlay's eventual successes in Switzerland in April 1591, Henry decided that he would be the man to accomplish this task. It would be Harlay's most important diplomatic mission to date, and in October of the same year he was sent as Henry's ambassador to Queen

Elizabeth to ask for more money and men to fight the Spanish. Harlay was to prey on the fear that the Spanish would make incursions into France from the Low Countries—a fear that Elizabeth often shared. Henry wanted five thousand armed soldiers to join his own forces in Picardy.

It was in the interest of Queen Elizabeth as well as of the other Protestant rulers to support Henry IV and prevent the spread of Philip's sphere of influence. After all, Philip's daughter descended directly from Henry II of France, and the pope clearly preferred her claim to the throne as a Catholic princess to Henry IV's as a Protestant prince. Yet it was widely expected that Elizabeth would only give succor to Henry in driving the Spaniards out of the maritime provinces of Brittany, Normandy, and Picardy, which were the nearest to England and therefore of the most consequence to her. Henry wanted to expel his enemies from the heart of his kingdom before he thought of attacking them on the borders. It was Harlay's task to reconcile the two.

Queen Elizabeth, now nearing what was then the remarkable age of sixty, had become—if anything—more hardened in her cantankerous, vain, and vacillating ways. The defeat of the Armada had only served to strengthen her loathing of war, its messiness, uncertainty, and above all its enormous cost to the privy purse. Yet Harlay in his arrogance describes his visit as a simple mission, "having obtained from the queen of England in two weeks all that he had demanded." The request ran counter to Elizabeth's forty-year rule of waging the peace. It is true that Colonel Norris was sent with five thousand men, but the real reason why Elizabeth agreed so readily to help the French in the north was her vain hope that she could recapture Calais for the English. It was, after all, her sister Mary who had lost Calais, and thereby her reputation as a queen who could protect her realm. Elizabeth had never relented in her desire to regain the English toehold on the Continent for her country's security and to prove her superiority as monarch over her sister. So Harlay's boasting to the king and court about his easy victory over the queen of England was an inconceivably myopic view. Fortunately for both Harlay and the queen, the campaign was a success, and the Spanish were repelled.

Since Elizabeth prided herself on her spy network through the ubiquitous Walsingham, she would surely have known about Harlay's great diamonds. Even if Walsingham's spies had failed her, Elizabeth had learned of the Sancy's whereabouts through Don Antonio's escapades and made it known that she expected to receive the famous gem as a guarantee. Harlay's failure to provide the diamond—at least as security for the soldiers—was a wise move if he ever wanted to see his precious gems again, but it also was a tremendous slight of the aged queen that she would not easily forget.

In his defense, Harlay had sailed close to the wind on more than one occasion and had seen his material fortune wane substantially at the hands of the French crown. Don Antonio's death in Paris in January 1592—as a pauper residing in rented accommodations—would have underlined his own fears about losing his wealth for a crown that was not his. Having seen his precious gems and personal fortune flushed down an apparent black hole in fighting off Henry's enemies, Harlay began to champion a brilliant scheme to neutralize the French nobles and keep his fortune intact. The king could simply abjure his Protestant faith and become a Catholic. Not surprisingly, at first Harlay met with considerable resistance. But he received repeated assurances from the warring Catholic factions that they would put down their swords if Henry and his ministers converted. Even François d'O, who had been rather outspoken against the proposal, was slowly won over. This single recommendation brought Harlay de Sancy into the heart of French power and made him a trusted adviser of the king. François d'O was sidelined as superintendent of finance, and Harlay took his place.

By the time of Henry's conversion on July 25, 1593, against the better judgment of François d'O and Gabrielle d'Estrées, Henry's much-beloved mistress, Harlay de Sancy was thoroughly ensconced at the king's side. Though the cost of this influential position was incredibly high, Harlay had at last gained what he had craved for so long: power. One by one, Harlay picked off Henry's opponents. With each nobleman who withered under his pressure and coercion, the king became more and more entranced with Harlay's persuasiveness. No other adviser, or secretary of state, held the same sway over the king—or had the king's ear as much as Harlay de Sancy. Even Sully, who would later replace Harlay in the king's affections as minister of finance, admitted that in 1593 Harlay "held all credit with the King in the affairs with the Catholic League."

In his memoirs, *Oeconomies Royales,* Sully reflected later on Harlay and his incredible accomplishments at the time:

> Mr. de Sancy—as much as he had given to the service of both Henry III and Henry IV, in truth, and his journeys and negotiations with the Swiss and Germans, he was of a lively and entrepreneurial spirit and often gave advice to the King for bad administration of the country's finances, which his treasurers and financiers by wit, tolerance or the nonchalance of François d'O followed, and since the advice was not eventually to the liking of His Majesty, he gave him [Harlay] a thousand beautiful little hopes, whether by keeping him near during the games, festivals or other little outings—so that he imagined that he could displace Monsieur d'O and gain the same power and authority that he had in these matters as well as finance.

From 1593 to 1594 Harlay became supreme in France. When François d'O died a ruined man in 1594, Harlay at last replaced his rival—and one-third seller of the Sancy diamond—as superintendent of finance. But with power came the elation of invincibility, and Harlay became reckless. He had the temerity to openly criticize Gabrielle d'Estrées, who had recently given birth to Henry IV's son Cesar. Gabrielle, desirous of becoming queen of France, responded by putting Harlay's enemy Theodore Agrippa d'Aubigné in charge of the child's education. The question of Henry divorcing Marguerite of Valois was rumored at court, and Harlay spoke out violently against it, likening the harm that could be done to Henry's throne to the English Henry VIII's abandonment of Catherine of Aragon for Anne Boleyn. As Henry IV had newly changed religions to Catholicism, he could hardly abandon his wife of twenty years for his mistress, the mother of his child. Complications relating to the succession were pointed out to Henry, and for the time being, Harlay appeared to have won the day.

But the real chink in Harlay's armor was the fact that he was a soldier-ambassador, not an administrator of finance. Hardly surprisingly, he was openly critical of his deceased predecessor, yet was unable to manage the nation's economy. Harlay promoted the relatively obscure but incredibly competent Sully as the day-to-day administrator of the new Conseil de Finances.

After much criticism from Henry IV and other nobles, Harlay's lack of success in managing the nation's finances brought into sharp focus the nagging question of his personal wealth. Despite later claims that his rings were still in pawn throughout this period, he somehow managed to be repaid from the depleted French treasury and recover his famous diamonds, the Sancy and the Beau Sancy. Harlay was living in grand style, the owner of huge mansions, and while pleading poverty during this period, lived more sumptuously than other people. As was frequently the case with Harlay, nothing was as it seemed, and the truth rarely squared with his version of facts. He may have been asset rich, but he was cash poor. Whatever the case, he resolved to change this state of affairs and sell his diamonds.

The year 1596 proved to be a watershed in Harlay's political fortunes. Once again in possession of his diamonds, he sought to undertake a "diplomatic" mission to Constantinople on behalf of the king. His bargaining position was that the Sultan Murad could act as a counterfoil in the Mediterranean to the king of Spain. Queen Elizabeth had already embarked on this course, and Harlay begged Henry to do likewise. However, Harlay's real reason for wanting to journey in person to Constantinople was to sell both diamonds to the sultan. As it was the custom to bring jewels and treasure from one's own country when visiting royalty—especially when one embarked on a diplomatic mission—it is most likely that Henry suggested to Harlay that he "give" his diamonds to the sultan as a proof of the king's esteem. It is no wonder that the urgent mission to Constantinople was abandoned and Harlay turned his gaze to the United Provinces (Holland), ostensibly to obtain Dutch troops. In fact, he wanted to make contact with the most influential international merchants to see if they could facilitate the sale of his diamonds.

Harlay's Dutch mission did nothing to endear him to the queen of England. Even the States General, who ruled over the United Provinces, begged Henry IV not to send Harlay de Sancy to them, fearing it might cause "Her Majesty jealousy." Official correspondence was sent from Burghley to Buzenval, the representative of the United Provinces, stating plainly that "the queen had much enquired after Harlay de Sancy." A letter from Harlay to Buzenval in which he approved the Dutch advice not to come to the United Provinces before first speaking with Elizabeth was shown around the English court, but Harlay did precisely the opposite. His actions inflamed Elizabeth's keen political senses. Either Harlay was planning to betray England by making a pact with the Spanish, or he was seeking to sell his diamonds to anyone except her.

Elizabeth demanded reassurances from Henry that there would be no league or other pact with the Spaniards, and was temporarily placated when Henry replied that he had no intention of entering into any peace or truce with the Spanish vermin. The Dutch eventually sent two thousand men to France, but withdrew them to Hainault, near the Dutch border, shortly after. The situation from Henry's point of view was becoming desperate: Holland could not help, and England would not. Buzenval suggested that Henry's ambassador to Holland, the duc de Bouillon, could smooth the waters and that "his presence would disperse many evil counsels, restore vigor to all the good, and restore reputation to affairs when all saw Their Majesties according for the good of this state." Bouillon engineered a triple alliance with the Dutch, the English, and the French, while Harlay busied himself with other, unspecified, affairs in Holland.

War broke out anew with the freshly funded duke of Mayenne in January 1596, and it was widely rumored that if Mayenne's forces did not slaughter Henry's army, disease would. The king had 1,000 horses, 3,000 Swiss, 1,500 *landsknechts* (mercenary foot soldiers), 4,000 ill-paid and daily deserting French, and 1,800 well-armed and disciplined French paid for by the States General. Harlay's Swiss mercenaries and *landsknechts* mutinied daily for their pay, and Harlay sprinted back to Paris to bring them 50,000 crowns from the treasury. The English ambassador wrote to Burghley that "the king was more needy of money than at any other time." Henry was adamant: there would be no surrender.

By the end of winter, the king's Swiss troops at the siege were all dead of hunger or the pains of winter rather than from the enemy's guns. Meanwhile, the Spaniards, well equipped and rested, massed on the French border at Picardy. In some considerable alarm, the governors in the province begged the king for money and means. The governor of Calais even wrote to Henry using the time-honored political blackmail card about how he was "very jealous of Her Majesty [Elizabeth] who is seeking to displace him of his government." The implied threat worked. Bouillon and Harlay were dispatched in some haste to Elizabeth with a small entourage in the hope of her providing money and men to fight off the common enemy.

Harlay de Sancy, by now referred to in most correspondence simply as "Sancy," took the initiative from Bouillon and wrote the first letter of this hugely important mission, on May 1, 1596, to William Cecil begging for an audience with the queen: "Sire, We have a letter from the King, for the Queen that he desires the signatory of this letter to have an audience today with the Queen, since Monsieur le Duc de Bouillon has fallen ill and cannot meet with her. I beg of you to recommend me if you can and remain your humble servant, Sancy."

Bouillon had already made a favorable impression with the queen in his previous negotiations with her and the United Provinces. Harlay de Sancy had irritated her and made her feel that he was untrustworthy. This letter shows little of the normal deference and etiquette that the aging queen of England would have come to expect, and much of Harlay's arrogance. It is doubtful that Harlay came bearing gifts—jeweled or otherwise—for Elizabeth, which in the courtly terms of the day was worse than being invited to stay with friends on a sumptuous estate in the country for a week and not bringing so much as a cheap bottle of wine. Elizabeth, naturally, ignored his request.

Three days later, Harlay wrote to Burghley:

Sire,

I have just received yesterday evening a dispatch from the King, and another this morning in which he gives me news that they have entered the citadel of Calais. I went to find his Majesty this morning to communicate with him. . . . (Calais is under attack and his Majesty will embark a force to defend her. . . .) It would be opportune if you could see the queen today so that I can have an answer to that which preoccupies us and that which we apprehend more and more. The Queen commanded me that she desires the King to bring about a "malheur" meaning to take promptly the upper hand and win the day. . . . the dispatch all but puts the life of the King at the pleasure of the Queen. Sancy

There was still no reply from the queen. Two more days went by and it was May 5 before Harlay sent the next letter from Boulogne to Burghley:

Sire, I beg you humbly to consider how long the time, like sands through the hour glass, glide almost within sight from my place of residence in Boulogne, which if I had known before stopping here would have never given the means to make for delay, which makes me beg you today for the good will of the Queen not to be lost. I remain your humble servant and kiss your hand, Yours Sancy

Elizabeth was toying with the man. She finally sent word that as soon as Bouillon was fit that she would meet *both* the king's ambassadors in London. The meeting, by all English accounts, was frosty, with the queen listening politely when Bouillon spoke and tapping impatiently when Harlay pleaded his master's case. Their demands were excessive, she stated: five thousand more men when they had not even repaid her for the men and arms she had loaned only five years earlier. The result was inconclusive, with Elizabeth stating flatly that she would need to consider their request and come back to them in due course.

Whether it was Bouillon or Harlay de Sancy who penned the ten-page letter signed by both, following the audience with the queen on May 10, is difficult to say. The implied threat to the queen and to England in the final paragraph is, however, unmistakable:

If your resolution is other than our wish and your words, let us hear these promptly, at least so that the fruit may be brought back to our master and each man in his service can assist him to better save what we can of our broken vessel from that which menaces it, that the King does not remain floating in incertitude, without vain nourishment of hope, and can take the road which he judges to be correct for the health of his state. And as for you, Madame, since by the judgement of your councils believe that this war belongs to the King of France against the Spanish, and that your intervention is useless; this is a belief that has frequently been held by many kings, and is one of the most menacing to hold. Your etiquette would be forever more poor, since you would have abandoned one of your friends, without necessity, to listen [to] your own council by following your own example above all other considerations. He takes care to follow the health of his state and of his people, to the detriment or advantage of his enemies.

Elizabeth had toyed with Harlay long enough. The overpowering need to stop the Spanish had to take precedence over any insult or injury. The duke of Parma had threatened Paris before, and the north of France would fall without English intervention. Cecil and Burghley reasoned with her that she could make Harlay pay for his insolence toward her in time, but for now, she had to send troops to defend the Continental side of the English Channel. Elizabeth eventually agreed, and a treaty was hammered out at Greenwich based on the letter that Bouillon and Sancy wrote on the following day to King Henry:

> We, Henry de la Tour, Duc de Bouillon, Marechal de France and Nicolas de Harlay, Sieur de Sancy, Councillor of the King and Counsel of State, deputised by the King to treat with the Queen of England for an offensive and defensive league against the King of Spain, contest that we had by the articles of the said league today treated and agreed between ourselves that the said Queen would be ready to assist the King with four thousand men of war, all the time that she would have gathered . . . as soon as the King would have signed and approved the treaty for the league, that she would also provide the King two thousand men with pay who would not be used otherwise, and who should be utilised in the towns of Montreuil and Boulogne. . . . At the same time, the Queen will make an advance of the wages for four months for the two thousand men and if the King wishes to keep them any longer that the King will pay them the twenty thousand that the Queen had already loaned him nominally.
>
> Please heed our particular cautions that twenty thousand ecus will not suffice for this occasion for four months wages and that [the] Queen will have used this effectively to have your obligation

expunged. . . . We have countered that after twelve months, your Majesty will take on the wages of the men and have said that we would address ourselves to the King, and that he would let us know if this would be agreeable so that the Queen would make such a declaration to the King as is thought fit. Bouillon and Sancy

Within the week, Elizabeth wrote directly to Henry, commending him on the work done by Bouillon, and damning Harlay with faint praise:

Greenwich, 18 May 1596
   By a thousand graces I come to you to recommend myself after your very loyal Duke who has done you proud after so many years of valuable and constant service, hoping for his good treatment and that of all your servants are of the same humour to serve you well in your hour of need. One says that the old adage of the old servants are the ones most loved is always reassuring. Believe this. I beg you to do this so that the others look on in envy in order to live less well. He [Bouillon] and Monsieur de Sancy have told you much of me, and to do less would anger you in my writing. . . . But one thing I would dare to promise to you that as the most beautiful could easily find, as a great pain of the most loyal of the entire world would show to you, as God knows, to whom I pray will guard you under his wings and give you victory against your enemies as you desire.
   Your most assured sister, Elizabeth R.

Bouillon and Harlay had beat a hasty retreat, and the queen wrote again a few days later to Henry commenting on the same and warning the king that "the best is that I hope to make this King not forget his friends nor neglect them . . . the English have made their respect for your place and their Prince known, for the object of the Queen, your own cause."

Harlay and Bouillon returned to France, claiming victory over the cantankerous queen, and later Harlay would state in his *Discours* that the queen of England "loaned me 20,000 ecus on my simple promise, which I sent the next day." The outrageous claim would be hilarious if it had not been for the gravity of France's affairs, and the indebtedness of its king. In fact, within ten days of Bouillon's and Harlay's

hasty retreat, William Cecil sent an account to Villeroy in France, list-
ing Henry IV's debts to the English crown:

Date	Debt	Sum (in British pounds sterling)	Sum (in francs)
1589	for the obligation of M de Beauvoir, Buby, Burinual	22m 3£ 5s	71,165.20
1591	Disburs. For the expense of the army under the conduct of Count d'Glise in Normandy	60m 192£ 22s	200,640
	Disburs. For the expenses of the soldiers Employed in Britanny since the month Of April 1591, until the month of Feb 1594	190m 3£ 50s 6d	634,502.46
1590	19th Nov—obligation of M de Beauvoir to the Mayor of London	2m 1£	7,000
1590	25th Sept Presented for the obligation of M de Beauvoir	10m	33,333.20
1594	Disburs. For the expenses of the navy employed by the commanders of the King at Brest	14m 1£ 73s	47,234.20
1589	Presented for the obligation of M de Beauvoir and Mr du Fresnes	15m 7£ 50s	52,500
1596	For the obligation of M de Bouillon and M de Sancy	6m	20,000
1596	9th July—Disburs. For the expense of 2000 soldiers in Picardy for the first six months	20m 2£ 51s 4d	67,505
	Total Sums:	£341,166 26s 5d	1,137,222.45

All of which expense is confirmed by the express obligation of the King or good
verification of the accounts made according to the schedules comprised in the
contracts.

IN ADDITION TO:

Date	Debt	Sum	Sum (francs)
1596	Disbursement for the intervention of 2000 soldiers for 8 other months which remained for the same reason outside of the accounts	£20,100	67,000
1589	Disbursement for the expense and transport of the soldiers in helping the King under the conduct of Baron Willoughby	£6M	20,000

1587	Disbursement by the hand of Horatio Palanicino For the delivery of the German army, conducted By Baron d'Auncan for which [sum] there is an obligation of the ambassadors of the King dated in Frankfort	£30,468	101,560
1590	Presented in 1590 for the delivery of the German army under the conduct of Prince d'Ansalt on the obligation of M. le Viscomte de Turinne	£10,000	33,333.20
	Sums in Sterling	£407,734	
	Sums in Francs		1,359,116.20
Of which it is already received:		£6,000	20,000
Therefore, which is still to be Received:		£401,734 16s 6d	1,339,116.20

It was an inescapable fact that Henry IV was bankrupt, and his money men would soon follow if peace eluded France. While Harlay returned home to marry off his daughter to Villeroy's son, Harlay plotted his next adventure for the "good of France." It was time, he felt, for Gabrielle d'Estrées to be removed from the king's affections.

13

The Curse of Blind Ambition

September 1596–March 1604

❦

BOUILLON AND SANCY RETURNED to Paris in July with a treaty that in Henry's own words "was not enough to free him from the necessities in which the advantages gained by the enemy had plunged him." Nonetheless, Henry never contemplated undoing what had been done and disavowing his servants. He ordered Harlay to do what he could to raise more troops in Germany, Switzerland, and Italy while he attempted to lull the Dutch United Provinces into a sense of security—by using the carrot of promises and the stick of threats—for them to go along with the course of action agreed between France and England.

Elizabeth sent the earl of Essex to France at the vanguard of her two-thousand-man force, accompanied by one of Harlay's entourage, the pernicious and insidious Antonio Perez. Perez was Philip II's former secretary of state who had been sentenced to death in Spain but had escaped to England some years earlier. Later, he sought refuge in Henry IV's court. Perez wrote to the queen, "his return to France was like going to his death, unless he could think of returning to England as a hope of resurrection." This sentiment, initially taken as flattery, was an omen of things to come.

Harlay, meanwhile, having procured what mercenary troops he could in Switzerland, Germany, and Italy with the queen of England's 20,000 crowns, returned to Paris to argue for the ratification of the

Treaty of Greenwich, recently negotiated with Elizabeth by the Estates General (Parliament). Fortunately, it passed, but by a slender majority. However, when the treaty was published, a number of key terms were kept secret—most notably that the French king would ask for only two thousand foot soldiers for six months and that an "equal" number of French soldiers must be provided; if the king failed to repay the queen in full for all her expenses for the two thousand foot soldiers, she would no longer be bound by the treaty to provide more aid in the future; and that Bouillon and Harlay de Sancy would repay the 20,000 crowns within four months of May 7 (the date of their promise) and not twelve, as originally agreed. The total estimated sum of £15,655 4s ($3.2 million or £2 million today) for the English queen's intervention also was kept secret.

Bouillon returned to England on August 24 with the ratified treaty and a new ambassador, de Reaux, whose appointment was so sudden that he had to beg leave of Her Majesty to return to France for six weeks to sort out his own affairs. No explanation was given to Elizabeth for the change of ambassador; indeed, none was required. The queen of England had made her feelings about Nicholas Harlay well known in the intervening period to King Henry by her own military ambassador and confidant, Essex. To make matters worse, Bouillon's mission with de Reaux was blighted by the mysterious fact that Elizabeth's Privy Council believed the ratified treaty with Henry IV's seals was a forgery and demanded that the queen send her own ambassadors to France to meet with Henry to clear up the matter at once.

Bouillon's problems continued when he discovered that Harlay had not made the first repayment of the 20,000 crowns to Queen Elizabeth. Elizabeth was threatening to delay the first shipment of men and arms to Picardy by a month until she received her installment. Yet as proof of her belief in Bouillon, she sent a gift to him, which Bouillon thanked her for in writing but claimed that "it would be better to do nothing for the servant and more for his master." This had the desired effect on Elizabeth, and she replied that she would instantly fulfill all the conditions of the league with France but that "it behooved Bouillon and Harlay de Sancy in the beginning to provide for due performance of all things contracted at the conclusion of the league so that small neglects in the beginning should not cause Her Majesty to expect worse in the ending."

At the same time, Elizabeth's archenemy Philip II, who was very ill, faced another bankruptcy. Years of war against England and the insurrection in the Low Countries had drained his resources despite shipments of gold and silver from the Americas and gems and spices from the East. Drake had enriched England beyond all reckoning with Spanish gold. More than half of Spain's shipments were lost to piracy or poor weather. The seven Dutch United Provinces had forsworn allegiance to Philip and Spain in 1581, and Amsterdam was rapidly eclipsing Antwerp as the center of the luxury trade, since Antwerp was still in the Spanish-held Netherlands. Antwerp had been sacked in 1585 by the Spanish and had become suspect. Draconian Catholic laws were instituted in Antwerp and Philip, yet again, suspended payments to his Antwerp merchant-creditors.

Philip declared that his suspension of payments was not due to bankruptcy but was rather "due to intelligence that some of the merchants had promised the king of France a million and a half of gold." Philip most probably believed that in paying his Antwerp merchant bankers he would be financing war against himself. He may well have been right.

This affront to the Dutch and Flemish merchants stepped up hostilities between England and Spain again. Cadiz was selected as a target because it had offered Philip 30 million malaverdes in gold payable over twenty years, which the king had had the temerity to refuse, hoping instead to never have to repay the sum. According to a Madrid "intelligence report" sent to an Italian merchant at Rouen, the city's clergy and ecclesiastical confederates had instead granted 20 million malaverdes payable over twenty years for the sole purpose of "making wars against Her Majesty and her estate of England." Elizabeth acted swiftly and ordered the sacking of Cadiz by her fleet, commanded by the earl of Essex. Within a day, he had taken Cadiz Castle and 40,000 ducats that the paymaster of the king of Spain's navy was holding for the soldiers. There was also a great deal of silver and jewels belonging to individuals of the city that were taken as booty and returned to England with Essex. It was a pinprick, but one that helped the English war effort and would hinder Philip for some months to come.

Meanwhile, apparently out of touch with this side of international affairs, Harlay bestowed a sizable dowry of 40,000 ecus on his daughter Jacqueline for her marriage to the baron d'Alincourt, Villeroy's eldest son, while again pleading poverty to all. He also openly lamented the fact that the reason for the parlous state of his affairs was due to his unstinting loyalty to the king, and the use of his entire personal fortune for the good of France. And to make matters worse, now the king was repaying him—and other loyal servants—by talking of marriage to his young and beautiful mistress in an affair that, in Harlay's opinion, would risk Henry's crown.

By the time of his daughter's wedding, Harlay had begun a whispering campaign in earnest against Gabrielle d'Estrées within his court entourage. He was utterly unguarded in his criticism of how the royal liaison undermined the stability of the crown, since Henry had no children by Marguerite de Valois, and Gabrielle d'Estrées had recently given birth to her second child by Henry. According to Harlay, the situation had become untenable. Other ministers nodded sagely, but none voiced his own opinion of the affair. Harlay mistook their nods for concurrence, and stepped up his campaign against the beautiful courtesan when the marquise de Montceaux, as Gabrielle was known at the time, acted as Henry's queen during the embassy of Lord Shrewsbury to Henry at Rouen. Harlay's criticism became rabid and merciless. He ranted that Gabrielle d'Estrées sought to become queen of France at the expense of Henry's own crown. Harlay claimed that she was ambitious, greedy, and had besotted the king. After all, had the king not taken back the private jewel collection of Henry III's widow, Louise de Vaudremont, only to place most of the dowager queen's jewels on Gabrielle d'Estrées? Even the Venetian ambassador noted that the king had "placed on her finger the table-cut diamond ring that he received at his coronation ceremony: truly sacrilegious."

Harlay, certain of his invincibility and blinded by ambition as so many of the Sancy Diamond's owners before him, seemed oblivious to the consequences of his vitriol against Gabrielle and her matrimonial designs. Gabrielle, on the other hand, was well aware of Harlay's disfavor, and ensured that Henry would hear of it indirectly through Harlay's Protestant enemy and her unlikely ally Agrippa d'Aubigné. Almost imperceptibly at first, Harlay was kept at a distance from the king. Sully was consulted directly on matters of finance, and Harlay's key role as an ambassador to England was at an end, too. As the peace broke out gradually between 1597 and 1598, his importance as money-lender for the king waned. At last, even *he* was forced to admit that he had been perhaps too outspoken on the subject of Gabrielle d'Estrées and that his "disgrace could only have been caused by this affair."

But why did Henry not simply tell his minister to hold his tongue? After all, Harlay de Sancy had been his favorite minister, one of the authors of his conversion to Catholicism and of the Edict of Nantes of 1598, granting free worship to the Protestant Huguenots. Harlay also was the mastermind behind the submission of the duke de Mercure in Brittany, thus ending the Catholic League's activities there. It seems likely that Henry knew that *this* minister would not be silenced. Further, he also knew that Harlay had not merely criticized the king's mistress and mother of his children but also had betrayed him and France.

But whom would Henry have trusted enough to lose a major financier such as Harlay? The answer is Elizabeth I.

Elizabeth had made Henry aware in no uncertain terms that she was displeased with his minister. It was a displeasure that the king could ill afford, since Elizabeth was his major "nation creditor" and could withdraw her soldiers from France and demand repayment for her trouble at her rather notorious whim. Still, more importantly, during Harlay's embassy to England, he committed a grave "impru-dence," which was mysteriously reported as a "great secret" in official documents. His crime was that he had plotted with the perfidious Antonio Perez. Perez, who had sympathized with Don Antonio, was reviled at court in England, and his unctuous and insinuating nature made him the object of tremendous ridicule and disdain.

Yet Harlay de Sancy liked Perez and even admired his audacity, and had struck up a close friendship with the exiled Spaniard. A con-fidential letter from 1596, written by Lord Naunton, who was the earl of Essex's man in France, stated:

> In the negotiations for the peace at Vervins, Henry IV insisted
> strongly on Perez's pardon: but the Spaniards alleged, that, he hav-

ing fled from the Inquisition, the King could not pardon him; nor, if he returned to Spain, hinder that Court from seizing him. In several of his letters Perez speaks of Henry IV's having promised not to restore the Duke d'Aumale at the insistence of Spain, until his wife, children and estate were restored to him; and of that King's having persisted in that resolution, until this difficulty, concerning the Inquisition was started by the Spaniards.

Nicholas de Harlay, Baron de Sancy, who was sent over by the King into England in 1596, had formerly been Master of the Requests, and had engaged his whole fortune, in order to raise a body of Swiss troops for the service of Henry III in 1588; and was afterwards Intendant of the Finances, in which post he was succeeded by Monsieur de Rosny, afterwards Duke de Sully. Mr de Perefixe, in his Histoire de Henri IV, part III, says, "he was a man of great intrepidity, and feared no person, when he acted for his Master's service; but was somewhat rough and free in his language towards him [the king]."

Harlay saw Perez as a kindred spirit and despite later claims that he was seduced by Perez's guile, was more than a willing partner in the plot that followed against Gabrielle d'Estrées and even the king. The sorry saga began while Harlay was at Greenwich negotiating on behalf of Henry. Harlay let it be known in the right circles—or the circles that would relay the information to Queen Elizabeth—that Gabrielle d'Estrées and her son Cesar would be given the city of Calais in the event of Essex liberating the beleaguered town. In light of Elizabeth's fixation on regaining Calais, Harlay's hatred of Gabrielle, and the fact that Perez and Harlay had revealed this politically sensitive information to Elizabeth to thwart the king's plan, it is incredible that Harlay did not lose more than his preeminence at court. Perez thought nothing of double-crossing Harlay on his return to France when confronted by Henry.

But this was not the limit of Harlay's blind ambition. While on a mission to raise a new mercenary army in Italy, he opened negotiations for the sale of the Sancy and Beau Sancy diamonds with the duke of Mantua. Harlay admired the duke's lifestyle and opulence and saw an opportunity in creating something of a similar nature for himself. The Duchy of Milan, still loyal to Spain, represented the greatest danger from the Italian Peninsula, and this new mercenary army would, he hoped, prevent the Spaniards from penetrating into France from there. Surely, Harlay reasoned, if the king would not repay him what was his "due," then Harlay and his Swiss, German, and Italian soldiers could occupy Milan for their own account.

Harlay's anger at the situation in which he found himself was imparted personally to Lord Naunton, who in turn wrote in November 1596 to the earl of Essex:

> Sancy takes a quite contrary course to all the rest, to encounter his anger with anger. Why? Had he not his pension duly paid him? Is he not made Counsellor of State for his reputation? And where else will he go? Or were he absent from here, where could he betake himself more advisedly than here [Paris], to be either comprehended in this peace, if it go forward; or to live at ease upon his pension, if war continues? This nettles him more than all the rest. He has written to this his chastiser [Perez] a very round letter above all the rest. And in this heat he has imparted to me that deep secret, which he has often glanced at heretofore, but would never elucidate it till now. I am bold to convey it to your Lordship . . . for which I account myself more beholding to his present anger, than I could be all his former kindnesses.

Surely it had been Harlay's plan to blame Perez for any plots against Henry and the betrayal to the English? Essex, as Elizabeth's favorite, was certain to pass the information on to the queen—who had already made Harlay personally aware of her displeasure against him for various crimes of etiquette. Still, it seems inconceivable that he somehow believed that Perez, and Perez alone, would be blamed for the plot to take over Milan. Harlay's colossal ego and vainglorious ambition must have outweighed any modicum of reason. Naunton, transfixed by the sheer gall of the man, related the gory details to Essex, from the origins of Harlay's wealth to the preposterous scheme to overrun Milan:

> Sancy at length being great . . . delivered himself into this midwife's hands of a vain ostentation of his own estate and wealth, that he had gained such and such a huge mass of treasure by gaming and

play: That he had furnished many of the King's greatest necessities of himself alone, what by the loan of his own stock unto him, and what by the pawning of a great value of rich jewels into Germany for his use: That he made account the King would have finished all his wars here in France within a year or two at most; and that then he [the king] had promised to repay him the first of all the debts he owed, and to lend him underhand, being Superintendent of his Finances, some 150,000 crowns for two years. Now that with this means, and by the intelligences, obligations, and assistances of his many friends, which he had treasured up in Swiss, and those confines, he would, at his pleasure, without any difficulty at all make his entrance into the State of Milan, take the Town itself, and possess himself of the Duchy. Yea, he was so ready in laying out all this expedition in maps, which he had ready-drawn, and limned out by him, as Perez could not but amuse himself at the blindness of his ambition. Had he not been alike free in committing unto him diverse other secrets of consequence as of the King's late capital spleen against the Duke of Bouillon; of his like diffidence and exceptions against your Lordship; of his new-entertained design touching this new found succession etc a man might have imagined, that this had been but a feigned confidence, devised to make trial of Perez, either of his judgment in believing or of his secrecy in keeping such an enterprise to himself.

Perez had two or three times wondered at Sancy's so much engaging himself and all his estate so deeply in the King's affairs, as he did. "Certainly, said he, either he loves your Majesty more than one man can love another; or else he has some high design in his head answerable to this deep obligation he seeks to fasten on your Majesty." The King answered him briefly that all the reason of Sancy's undertaking for him was "what this brute would do for my love." This great insinuation of the King to Sancy, Perez would interpret for a suspicious surmise of the King's own head. . . . And he infers here upon that either Sancy had opened this affectation in a like manner to some other body, that may have betrayed it to the King; or else that the King of himself has some such plot in apprehension. . . . For myself, he neither bad me nor forbad me to communicate it to your Lordship. If Sancy, in his ostentative humour has opened this his own aspiring unto any other, it may be that the detection hereof has been one of the principal causes, among others, of his late disgrace with the King.

Henry may have felt that he was perhaps not in a position to act strongly against Harlay at the time he found out about the betrayal, and decided that the just punishment would be to cold-shoulder Harlay out of court.

Rather than let the thaw take its normal course over time, Harlay reacted with his predictable venom. He ranted about how he had made innumerable contributions to the good of the country, how he had impoverished himself for the king's crown, how he had put his entire fortune at the disposal of France, and how his treatment by the king was unfounded and unfathomable. In Harlay's *Discours* he went so far as to intimate that he and his fortune were responsible for France's freedom. This disloyal assertion was offensive to Henry, damnable to Queen Elizabeth, and perfidious to the de' Medici, who had given far more than Harlay to ensure France's independence. The more Harlay bitterly complained, the more the king became deaf. And with the king's deafness, Harlay's toying with the idea of selling his famous diamonds became an absolute necessity. Henry IV had borrowed them on several occasions and had wanted them to be "given" to him as king for the crown jewel collection. Harlay tentatively negotiated with Henry, but would never sell or give them to the king as long as there was the remotest possibility that they could end up worn by Gabrielle d'Estrées—and as long as the king did not make good on his debts.

When his antics came to no avail at court, Harlay changed tack, and thought he could advance his place at court by becoming a Catholic again—as he had done under Henry III. Naunton speculates with amazing foresight on this ploy to Essex when writing:

> It may be again, that this affection [the Milan affair] was not the least cause of his late change in religion whereby seeking to make him more capable of the end of his designs it seems he has defeated himself of the means, whereby to come to do it. I doubt he is now so far off from borrowing any such great sums of money out of the King's coffers, as he will hardly ever recover his lending.

Indeed, Henry had no intention of repaying one penny to his former confidant. With the passage of time, the fullness of his minister's betrayal became evident and his usefulness to the king more dispensable. Harlay would be frozen out of court and die a pauper, as he deserved—a trial and death were too good for him. But Harlay's massive ego also would be crushed. His brother Louis would be Henry's new ambassador to Elizabeth's court and showered with favors and accolades.

Harlay was now desperate. He had assets—in his two diamonds and other gemstones—but no cash. His creditors were following hard on his heels, having heard the wild accusations of his disfavor at court. A controlled panic set in, and Harlay made a more serious offer of the diamonds to Vincent, duke of Mantua. Vincent was reputed for his remarkable physical beauty and ardent partaking of pleasurable pursuits. The duke lived the sumptuous lifestyle of kings, believed in chivalry, and had an inquisitive mind. He was the patron of the artists Peter Paul Rubens and Porbus, and adored beauty in all its forms. For Harlay, the duke represented a worthy owner of his diamonds—and an answer to his political and financial woes. Milan may yet come to him with Mantua's help. Harlay offered the Sancy and the Beau Sancy for 100,000 ecus ($6.2 million or £3.9 million today). The duke replied with an offer of castles in lieu of cash. There was a rapid exchange of correspondence, and with each letter, the price offered for the Sancy and the Beau Sancy dropped. It was an utterly deplorable situation for a man who could no longer pay his creditors.

There were other sources of cash—other wealthy rulers in Europe and Asia. But Harlay was adamant that Queen Elizabeth, despite the fact that she had never hidden her desire to own the Sancy, should never possess it.

Harlay renewed his efforts with Sultan Murad, and even went as far as to have a crystal replica made to show him the perfection of the stones. But unbeknownst to Harlay, his man in Constantinople named Brèves also represented Henry, to whom his true loyalties lay. On January 28, 1597, Brèves wrote to the king with the details of the proposed transaction, stating that Harlay had sent him the crystal of the two diamonds as well as a crystal of a large ruby. What Harlay did not expect was that Brèves informed Sultan Murad that:

> Sire, These large diamonds were the property of the dead emperor and belonged to the subjects of His Majesty, Henry IV of France.

That a gentleman of His Majesty's court is proposing to send to his
Highness a large diamond as represented in the crystal in the hope
that his Highness the Sultan would find agreeable, I have recommended that his Highness the Sultan makes his excuses and not
acquire the diamonds. . . . Your very humble and very obeying and
loyal servant and subject, Brèves

At the same time, the Venetian ambassador reported to the Doges
that "the Queen has heard that Mr de Sancy wants to sell his diamonds
and she is anxious to buy them." Elizabeth was ready to explode.
Again, she had not been offered the stones. She sent her ambassador
to the sultan with jeweled gifts, and confirmed her support for him
and his new first vizier. The message to the Sultan was unmistakable:
don't touch the diamonds.

Elizabeth also made certain that Henry learned the details of all
Harlay's transgressions. Essex was sent to impart the news in person,
based on Naunton's correspondence and the queen's own experiences.
Harlay's fate was sealed.

Over the next fifteen months, though Harlay had been thwarted
in Constantinople, he continued to visit various rulers in Europe—
even approaching the crown prince of Russia—in search of a cash
buyer. He approached every ruler imaginable, save Queen Elizabeth,
who was, at the end of the day, probably the only buyer who would
have been able or willing to pay what Harlay wanted for the Sancy
and the Beau Sancy. The omission of including Elizabeth on his pros-
pective purchaser's list speaks volumes. Like Gabrielle d'Estrées, Harlay viewed Elizabeth as his nemesis, and she would have the Sancy
diamond "over his dead body."

While Harlay turned to solving his financial woes, the king had
set in motion his divorce proceedings against Marguerite de Valois.
The pope had been approached, and it was reported in France that
Henry had made all the necessary arrangements to make his children
by Gabrielle d'Estrées legitimate, and heirs to the crown.

Then, on April 10, 1599, something completely unexpected and
mysterious happened: the young and beautiful Gabrielle d'Estrées was
taken ill during a party, adjourned upstairs to a comfortable bedroom,
and died. Henry IV was devastated and wept inconsolably for days,

granting her as much of a state funeral as decorum would allow. The Venetian ambassador reported that:

> The effigy of the Duchess of Beaufort (Gabrielle d'Estrées) has been shown to the public for four days continuously. It was made of plaster, is life-size, and was placed in one of the rooms of her house in a large bed to which one mounts by three steps. The figure appeared to be sitting up, and had a ducal coronet on its head and a golden mantle lined with ermine; there was a baldachino overhead, also of cloth of gold. The room was hung with the magnificent arras belonging to the King. The archers of the royal guard were on duty, as also the masters of the ceremonies, the gentlemen-in-waiting, and other officers of the household.

Then the ambassador added in cipher: "The King is well; he has taken a purge and been bled. He declares openly that he intends to marry again, and has shown some inclination towards the Princess Maria [de' Medici], niece of the Grand Duke of Tuscany."

Agrippa d'Aubigné started a rumor that was never substantiated: that Harlay—who happened to be in the house at the time Gabrielle took to her bed—had poisoned her, as he was reputed to have done to the cardinal of Plaisance. Harlay's reaction to her death led many to believe that Agrippa d'Aubigné's allegations were true, since he simply could not hide his delight. No charges were ever brought against the disgraced minister, yet the rumor persisted until long after his own death.

Contrary to Harlay's assertions, much of Henry IV's successes and triumph over the Catholic League in France were due to de' Medici money, and it may well have been in the cards for him to marry the reigning duke of Tuscany's niece, even if Gabrielle d'Estrées had lived. Henry was no fool; he knew that his kingdom needed the influence, cash, and power that the de' Medicis could give. He also needed heirs whose legitimacy would be above reproach.

Eighteen months after Gabrielle d'Estrées's death, the marriage between Henry IV and Maria de' Medici took place by proxy, in the cathedral in Florence on October 5, 1600. A breathtaking banquet was given at the Palazzo Vecchio, where each lavishly shaped and decorated dish formed part of an extraordinary allegory upon the martial brilliance of the French king and the dazzling virtues of the House of Medici into which he had so wisely married. There were horse races and tournaments; processions and pageants; fireworks displays and water festivals; and live performances at the Uffizi with settings by Buontalenti of *L'Euridice* by Jacopo Peri, the composer of the first opera ever performed there. This ceremony would become the inspiration for many of the fetes at Versailles given for the pleasure of Henry's and Maria's grandson Louis XIV.

At last Harlay de Sancy saw an opportunity to mend his fences. The new queen, Maria, had a reputation as a diamond-lover. If he could interest her in his most precious gems, he might be able to regain the king's favor and also get the arrears he believed Henry owed him. Still, the king would not be persuaded to purchase anything—let alone diamonds he felt already belonged to the crown—from the disgraced courtier. Queen Maria, on the other hand, was relentless. It was not enough that Henry lavished her with jewels and diamonds on every conceivable occasion—the birth of children, national and religious holidays, New Year's Day, anniversaries, banquets, and pageants. She was determined to have Harlay's diamonds, which were still the largest in Europe, and she mercilessly hounded her husband. Yet Henry would not budge.

Then fortune seemed to smile on the renegade Harlay. In March 1603 Queen Elizabeth became weak and yet refused to take to her bed to rest. The lord admiral was sent for, and she was forcibly taken to her bedchamber. She was seventy years old, and everyone knew there was no hope of her recovery. The queen refused all remedies and became unable to speak on the morning of Wednesday, March 23. She died the following day.

James VI of Scotland was proclaimed James I of England, and Harlay sent word to his brother Louis, still the French ambassador to England, to offer the Sancy diamond to the new monarch. After nearly a year of negotiations following Elizabeth's death, Louis, baron de Monglat, finally succeeded in March 1604 to sell the Sancy diamond to James I of England for 60,000 ecus, or £20,000 ($4.2 million or £2.6 million today). James ordered the Exchequer to pay a third of the amount on receipt of the gem, with the two other payments to take place over the following two years.

Harlay took advantage of the sale of the Sancy in a final attempt to persuade the king to forgive him. He thought he was using his customary guile, which had long ago eluded him, to successfully complete the sale of the Beau Sancy to Queen Maria, but as Henry's letter authorizing Sully to buy the stone for his wife clearly shows, the king was not amused by his former favorite's antics: "I will be most at ease, to recover them [the gems] more than to allow them to go outside my realm in order to be sold to strangers, as if I buy them, then no one else but I will own them."

Maria had her diamond, the Beau Sancy, mounted on top of her crown, and had Porbus paint her portrait wearing it. James had the Sancy diamond mounted in an extravagant hatpin with the Mirror of Portugal and also ensured that his portrait wearing this most historic diamond would be painted twice.

As for Nicolas Harlay de Sancy, his son was killed at the siege of Ostend, and his health and finances continued to deteriorate inexorably. After the sale of the Beau Sancy to the queen, she ensured that Harlay would be named *chevalier de l'Ordre du Roi,* or gentleman of the Order of the King, effectively as recognition of his past services to the crown. Harlay was seething at the emptiness of the symbolic gesture: he wanted real recognition; renewed power; and, above all, his money.

Henry and Maria threw themselves body and soul into the establishment of a crown jewel collection to rival that of any kingdom in Europe, recruiting some of the most talented jewelsmiths for their *garde-robe* or royal wardrobe. Henry IV installed twenty-seven residences and five large workshops for the best artisans in diamond cutting and jewelry making on the ground floor of the Royal Palace of the Louvre in 1608. This innovation allowed the foreign professionals, exiled from Flanders due to religious persecution, to work in freedom from the guilds' interference for the glory of the crown.

Maria gave birth to six children by Henry (who had had nine illegitimate children by the time of his death), but the king had steadfastly refused to allow her to have a coronation as his queen. Prior to his marriage, an old soothsayer had predicted that if he allowed his wife to have an official coronation ceremony, he would be killed violently. After ten long years of haranguing and plotting by Maria, he finally relented. Within two hours of Maria's coronation, Henry IV was assassinated and Cardinal Richelieu was proclaimed regent with the queen, for the young Louis XIII.

The day after, Nicolas Harlay de Sancy, with impeccable timing, published his *Discours sur l'occurrence de ses affaires* (Discussion on the Conduct of His Affairs) for the queen and some select ministers to explain that France owed him its security—and a fortune in unpaid debts. In his own words, "no one can doubt that I loaned during the wars, when the affairs of state were in such disarray, that which all of France must thank me for in order to exercise freely its will."

The cardinal and the queen largely ignored his pleas, and on October 17, 1629, he died. On his death, a royal order was found in his pocket to prevent him from being imprisoned for fabricating counterfeit money—a "get out of jail free card" that he had used to taunt the local police on numerous occasions while flaunting the counterfeit cash. Folklore claims that the local constables would drag Harlay off to prison, and at the gates, he would fish into his coat pocket and produce his royal order and be released until the next time. The truth of the matter—like so much surrounding the disgraced minister—may never be revealed.

14

Inalienable in Untrustworthy Hands

1603–1620

IN THE GRAY HOURS of Thursday, March 24, 1603, the Tudor England that Elizabeth I had so patiently constructed came to an end. On her deathbed, Elizabeth communicated by signs and called for her Privy Council. They called out the names of possible successors to the queen, and when the king of Scots name was uttered, she touched her hand to her head so they all would know that he was the man she desired should reign after her. The late queen had made this remarkable decision long ago, when she begged forgiveness of James Stuart in writing to him of her betrayal and innocence in the execution of his mother, Mary, on February 14, 1586.

By daybreak, two horsemen galloped furiously on the northern road to Holyrood Palace in Edinburgh to pay homage to the new ruler of the British Isles. At ten in the morning, at Whitehall Gate in London, James VI of Scotland—the only son of Mary, queen of Scots—was proclaimed King James I of England and Wales. The nation feared revolution, and men began to gather arms in preparation. Then Robert Cecil, the late queen's personification of her achievements for both church and state, spoke, and the lords and Council agreed that they should accept Elizabeth's wishes, and civil war was averted.

Puritan sailors who had taken out their ships to guard against the "popish" invasion from the Flemish coast put back to port; and the guards of the northern English castle turrets learned from their predominantly Catholic masters that since England and Scotland now had one king, the Scottish skyline no longer represented the territory of the foe. The reconciliation work of Elizabeth had stood its first test of consent, and the English people invited the royal line of Scotland to fill her place.

James I had become king of a country that was both different and richer than Scotland. He had been king of Scotland practically from birth, and had learned about kingship in the rough school of Scottish politics. Scotland, however, was a backwater compared to England. Although the English population was only 2.5 million to 5 million people, the majority of whom lived in the countryside, the English had played an important role in European politics since the time of Henry VIII. Country society was not a closed caste, as in Scotland, and frequently a poor country gentleman could save his estate by finding girls with hefty dowries for their sons to marry. Where Henry IV's French court encouraged the French nobility to assert its place by living in Paris or Versailles, James and his heirs regarded the status of "country squire" as a profession in itself. The military barbarism of the moated castle was a thing of the past, and the Renaissance civilization introduced at the Elizabethan court had penetrated the countryside.

Estate lines had been drawn, and prosperity began to spread. These were the halcyon days of pride in new prosperity, and the final success of Elizabeth Tudor's rule. Ostensibly, James had inherited all of Elizabeth's glories, but in reality these were a mere mirage and a flawed legacy.

The cities contained a small part of the English population and were frequently victim of the plague and squalid conditions. Basic hygiene was unheard of, and disease and infant mortality prevented population increase. Medicine was formulated on superstition rather than science, personal habits were filthy among rich and poor alike, and the standard of public decency would not stand up to Western twenty-first-century scrutiny.

Despite the natural English tendency to remain insular and mistrustful of foreigners, the English had fallen under the spell of the

Dutch, and under Elizabeth, lessons about the Dutch way of life—as England's friend and enemy—had already been drawn. The Dutch supremacy of the seas; their ability to keep the small country free from war and destruction as a prosperous oasis in the wilderness of devastation raging in religious strife throughout the rest of Europe; their newfound humanist philosophy; and their advances in the sciences, philosophy and the arts, agriculture, gardening, finance, and trade became a utopian vision for England in the final years of Elizabeth's reign. Much like most countries today, Elizabeth's England saw the advantages that advancement of technology could bring. Harnessing technology had created a more efficient war machine, as was seen in the defeat of the Spanish Armada.

Catholics were tolerated, as long as they practiced their religion in secret, as recusants. Still, by today's standards, English humanity was low. Their treatment of other races was no better than that of the Dutch or French, with the exception of the Spanish or Portuguese Inquisitions. The scandalous practice of "witch-finding" had remained under control, unlike in the rest of Europe—largely due to Elizabeth's steadfast refusal to yield to fiercer laws "not suffering a witch to live." With James's accession to the throne, this all changed, and a virulent outburst of witch-mania gripped the nation, as it had done under James in Scotland.

The new king was intelligent if somewhat prickly; a good horseman; devoted to the hunt, theology, and handsome young men; endowed with a pithy wit; and in the prime of his life at thirty-eight. He had grossly coarse manners, belching and breaking wind in public. He adored his drink but was never overcome by drunkenness. He had an authoritative temper in politics, was easily flattered, disliked public appearances, and believed in the divine right of kings.

Though Elizabeth had long held a semidivine status, she never claimed nor proclaimed it. James I, in sharp contrast, stated in both his writings and public speeches that kings were God's lieutenants on earth. He would lecture Parliament and even his people about it, and as a result discarded Elizabeth's former sobriety at court. He was determined to have a more magnificent court than Elizabeth's and to create an entirely new class of nobility. On his month-long progress south from Berwick to London he "made up two hundred thirty-seven knights," according to the Calendar of State Papers. James's court would become a byword for extravagance and corruption as the king showered offices, titles, lands, and money on his favorites.

James intended to keep Robert Cecil in place; outwit the pope; manage the new king of Spain, Philip III; convert the English Catholics by proclamations; and guide his subjects on the path of unity. He viewed himself as the "Restorer of perpetual peace in Church and Commonwealth." Still there was one major hurdle to overcome: he knew nothing of the laws and liberties of England—either in the spirit or the letter—and had ordered a thief who preyed on the crowd who greeted him at Newark in Nottinghamshire to be hung without trial. He would be near the end of his reign before he would come to grips with these "tiresome anomalies" of constitutional custom and parliamentary procedure—too late to make amends.

Though pedantic, he was human. He was instinctively warm to his people, except when annoyed, yet had an uncanny ability to unconsciously vacillate and was rabid in his criticism of anyone or anything he disliked. He was also essentially homosexual, and the male favorites he chose often had the innate will to exercise evil power over good, often with monstrous effects for the nation. James's greatest fault was that he was incapable of telling a good man from a rogue, or a wise man from a fool. He shunned excellence, and he chose his advisers based on his personal love relationships with Robert Carr and George Villiers, the future duke of Buckingham.

James had married Anne of Denmark some years earlier. She had borne him a daughter and two sons—the eldest being Prince Henry, the younger, Prince Charles. When James made his way south to take possession of the crown of England, he wrote a loving letter to his son and heir, Prince Henry:

> Let not this news make you proud, or insolent, for a King's son and heir was as before, and no more than that. The augmentation that is hereby like to fall unto you, carries a heavy burden. . . . Look upon all English men that shall come to visit you as upon your loving subjects not with that ceremony as towards strangers and yet with such heartiness as at this time they deserve. Be diligent and earnest in your studies, that at your meeting with me, I may praise

you for your progress in learning. . . . Farewell, your loving Father, James R.

James began his reign with an opulence that indicated how he intended it to continue. He bound this letter and the sonnet he wrote at the end of it in purple velvet, adorned on one side with the Arms of Scotland on a plate of gold, crowned and surrounded by the collar and jewel of St. Andrew, and with the motto IN MY DEFENCE GOD ME DEFEND. The borders of the cover were adorned with thistles, the symbol of Scotland, in gold.

James was mindful that first impressions counted, and that his progress toward London should be arrayed with the richest finery—not only for himself, but also for his wife. Elizabeth had refined fashion into an essential expression of her power, and James's queen would not be outdone by fond memories in the people's minds of the old queen. Within days of writing his letter to Henry, and while still in the far north of England, he wrote to the lord keeper and other ministers on April 15 about jewels for Queen Anne, making it clear that:

> Touching the jewels to be sent for our Wife, our meaning is not to have any of the principal jewels of State to be sent so soon nor so far off . . . we have thought good to put you in mind that it shall be convenient that besides jewels you send some of the ladies of all degrees who were about the Queen, as soon as the funeral is past, or some others, whom you shall think would be appropriate and most willing to serve and be able to abide work, to meet her as far as they can at her entry into the Realm, or soon after; for that we must be mindful of her honour.

When James arrived in London, the French ambassador, Louis de Harlay, baron de Monglat, knew that his proposal on behalf of his brother for the purchase of the Sancy diamond would be well received. Not only was the Sancy seductive for its historic importance, but also de Monglat's sales pitch would have included the tantalizing truth that despite Queen Elizabeth's best efforts, the gem had eluded her grasp. The Sancy would become the symbol of James's pinnacle of power—the "jewel in the crown" of England. James was hooked on the idea that the English crown jewels would become the most fabulous in Christendom—and he instructed his ministers to complete the purchase.

The English crown jewel collection had grown tremendously under Elizabeth, through fair means and foul. She had accepted any number of jewels from various rulers in Europe as "surety" for her loans of men and artillery to fight in Continental wars, sometimes returning the gems, sometimes not. As the merchants who lent money to Don Antonio de Crato of Portugal found to their cost in 1582, the queen of England could not necessarily be relied on to pay against security received, and William Cecil, Lord Burghley, wrote to her on more than one occasion to treat these gentlemen fairly:

> May it please your Majesty
>
> My Lord of Leicester coming to me, has moved me in your Majesty's house to know my opinion of your Great Diamond [the Mirror of Portugal], and how it came in his custody for the money which certain merchants of London lent to Don Antonio for your Majesty. These same merchants do duly call for payment, and in my opinion consideration of your Majesty rather of your jewel is so great and royal, and that this payment is only due to your Majesty, for which you have but a bond. . . . I think your Majesty might be taken of your Jewel into your hands for pride safely, and should pay for it of your own money and of your princely good relieve your merchants who for their loyal duty to your Majesty, for no other did come to hide your fame, and for your Majesty might have a better say, than you have for many as sure to you and though I like not to hide your money in sending the repayments so slowly yet by this act, your Majesty has in policy to pay for it yourself, in such sort as by your silver ready money, or bullion that lie in store. Thus if I am bold to scribble to your Majesty, for yet my Lord Leister so told me to do so. Your most humble and pure servant W Burghley.

The English crown jewel collection undoubtedly owed much of its preeminence to the dubious transactions of its monarchs. The oldest gem in the collection, the table-cut diamond the Mirror of Naples, had belonged to King Louis XII of France in about 1500. Three months after the death of his wife, Anne of Brittany, in 1514, he remarried

Henry VIII's sister Mary and gave the jewel to her. Louis died on New Year's Day the following year and Mary returned to England, having already secretly married the duke of Suffolk. Henry was apoplectic and confiscated his sister's treasury, including the Mirror of Naples, which had been valued at 60,000 crowns. Anne Boleyn's diamond, a large, teardrop-shaped stone resembling a spearhead, weighed approximately twenty carats and was a gift from François I of France. The diamond had been confiscated from baron de Samblançay, François's superintendent of finance, when the baron had been found guilty of embezzlement in 1527 and was sentenced to death. Anne received the gift at the meeting of the Cloth of Gold in 1532, and this stone became the first diamond in Europe that was said to have been cursed, since its first two owners had been hanged and beheaded, respectively.

With James I's accession to the throne came the crown jewels of Scotland, including the Great Harry, also known as the Stone of the Letter H of Scotland. This jewel had belonged to Mary Stuart as early as her 1561 jewel inventory, which had been compiled after the death of her first husband, François II of France. When Queen Elizabeth had offered Mary "asylum" after she fled Scotland when James was one year old, she also wheedled away all of Mary's jewels.

Still, it was the Sancy that James lusted after. On March 10, 1604, the deal for the 55.232-carat stone was at last concluded. It sold for only 60,000 ecus, instead of the 100,000 ecus that Harlay de Sancy had demanded eight years earlier from the duke of Mantua. At the eleventh hour, the king agreed to pay 30,000 ecus on delivery (10,000 more than originally stipulated), with the remainder to be paid over the next two years.

James was radiant with pride at the acquisition of the most important diamond in Europe and made it known to his jeweler that he wanted the Sancy to be set for his coronation procession in March 1605.

The Sancy was set in a famous hat ornament known as the Mirror of Great Britain, and was suspended from a large sparkling lozenge made from four large diamonds set edge to edge, giving the appearance of one huge single diamond. Two of the other stones used in the jewel were estimated at thirty-six carats each, with a flat-backed twelve-carat rhombus diamond and the twenty-carat Great Harry. James also

James I of England and VI of Scotland, with the Sancy as part of a hat ornament known as the Mirror of Great Britain (on table at right). Painting by Daniel Mytens, 1621.

had other hat ornaments made, including one described in the Royal Schedule of 1606 as "a fair jewel, like a feather of gold, containing a fair table-diamond in the midst and five and twenty diamonds of divers forms made of sundry other jewels." The king's other most favored hat ornament was the Three Brothers—which after 126 years was finally reunited with the Sancy.

Yet none of these jewels was part of the larger crown jewel collection of Scotland and England, nor did they form part of the royal coronation regalia, which had been used in the official coronation ceremonies in England since the eighth century. In light of the checkered history of pawning, pillaging, and otherwise decimating the crown's jewelry collection over the centuries, James, on March 29, 1605, authorized the lord treasurer to make a new inventory of the crown jewels in the Tower of London. Unlike today, these jewels were not exhibited to the public, and there was little to prevent any future monarch

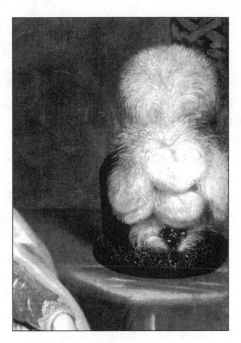

Close-up of the Sancy
as part of the Mirror
of Great Britain hat
ornament.

from continuing to trade in these priceless gems as part of his or her personal treasury. James was anxious to secure *his* collection—as the most fabulous in the world—for future generations, and on completion of the inventory declared all the crown jewels inalienable—including the Sancy and other gems he had acquired or would purchase.

James's and Anne's lust for jewels nurtured the royal goldsmith and lapidary industry that had mushroomed during Tudor times. Prince Henry and Prince Charles were lavished with diamonds and other jewels befitting their rank, and portraits of Henry wearing jewels indicative of his enthusiasm for learning and maritime and military exploits were painted. One of the three large diamond brooches in the hat of his 1604 Garter portrait is crowned with a ship; another has an armillary sphere at the base.

Jacobean courtiers caught "jewel fever" and patronized royal jewelers, spending heavily, often beyond their means. After years of deprivation as king of the impoverished Scottish nation, James was determined to enjoy the many creature comforts that fortune had bestowed on him. For James, England was the promised land. The only problem was that Elizabeth's apparent glories had been gained against the backdrop of many years of disharmony with Catholic Europe, rising inflation, and the cost of modernizing England's navy. James had, in fact, inherited debts, not cash, and had little visible means to support the lifestyle to which he believed he should become accustomed.

His single greatest problem was how to pay to run the government. The costs of the kingdom had become increasingly expensive, and the king was expected to live "of his own"—that is, on the revenues from crown lands and other dues settled hundreds of years before, in the feudal ages. Parliament, which James refused to convene for ten years, could only be asked for money in the event of declaring war. One way to get money was to knight men who would pay their dues of fealty. Perhaps this was why James ennobled more men than any other monarch ever. Another method at his disposal was to attempt to tax the landed gentry during times of peace for the daily running of government, but this was naturally highly unpopular. The third alternative was to dispense with Parliament—a move that would have been in tune with what was happening throughout the Continent at the time—and thereafter develop the full extent of the royal divine right to impose all sorts of taxes and dues. All these methods of raising money had been used in the past, so both Parliament and the king could equally claim right on their side. James would set in motion a number of events that would result in a progressive erosion of trust between the monarchy and the people and that would culminate in disaster for both.

In 1603, James opened his reign by making peace with Spain at long last, creating a huge surge of economic activity. In the same year, James summoned a theological conference at Hampton Court for the Puritans to voice their demands for a further reformation of the Church of England. Although the conference was an utter failure, James had wanted to maintain the concept of a truly national church, as Elizabeth had done. As a Calvinist, James understood the basis of the Puritan movement in England and the fact that its "godly ministers" practiced faith in action. But the Catholics, despite having received assurances from James while he was still in Scotland assuring their freedom of worship, remained disgruntled. Fines levied under Elizabeth, but never collected, for "recusancy" were now enforced in exchange for allowing public Mass. Catholics would be required to transfer their loyalty from the pope to the king, and while Puritans and Anglicans alike applauded the measures, Catholics were now alarmed.

In November 1605 a plot known as the Gunpowder Plot, to assassinate the entire royal family and all members of Parliament and hatched by the Catholic Robert Catesby, was foiled. If it had succeeded it would have been the single greatest catastrophe to hit the political, economic, and social infrastructure of any Western society. Catesby and his coplotters were no fanatics—they were desperate men, fighting for their very existence—and save for the fact that they felt that assassination of the entire English establishment was the only means to achieve that end, their courage and self-sacrifice are to be admired and their plight pitied.

All of the plotters were "gentlemen of name and blood." Guido "Guy" Fawkes, a professional soldier whom the plotters had brought back from Flanders from the English Catholic legion fighting for Spain, had enlisted in the service of Spain after selling his Yorkshire property. He had learned the art of war from the Dutch and Spanish and showed his coconspirators how to drive a tunnel safely through the cellar of a building into the foundation wall of the Houses of Parliament. Thirty-six barrels of gunpowder, strewn with huge iron bars to shatter through the roof of the undercroft, were stored for six months until the opening day of James's first Parliament, on November 5, 1605. The plotters were discovered as a result of a carefully composed letter sent to Lord Monteagle, the brother-in-law of the plotter called Tresham, which read:

> I would advise you as you tender your life, to devise some excuse to shirk your attendance at this Parliament; for God and man hath concurred to punish the wickedness of this time. And think not slightly of this advertisement but retire yourself into the country, where you may expect the event in safety, for though there be no appearance of any stir, yet I say they shall receive a terrible blow this Parliament, and they shall not see who hurts them.

Robert Cecil, recently elevated to the title of Lord Salisbury, was given the letter by Monteagle, who feared being implicated in the plot. Yet Cecil had no idea who to look for or, for that matter, where to look. Cecil sent out word to men he could trust to discreetly search the Houses of Parliament. On the afternoon of November 4, the earl of Suffolk walked past a solitary watchman in the undercroft of Parliament and asked him to whom the iron bars and wood stacked in the shadows belonged. The watchman was Fawkes, who replied honestly that they belonged to Lord Percy—omitting, of course, that Percy was one of the Catholic plotters. By eleven o'clock that evening, Fawkes was dragged away, bound and struggling, to the Tower of London.

Catesby and many of the other conspirators were tracked down and killed at Holbeche House in Staffordshire. The few remaining plotters were carried off back to London, bleeding from mortal wounds, to face trial and certain death. The fact that the conspiracy was betrayed by a Catholic peer is indicative that the scheme did not have the broad support of the Catholic community, which itself was divided into smaller factions.

Bonfires were lit and prayers of thanksgiving said in churches throughout the realm. James himself believed that the Sancy and his other precious stones had brought him luck—and perhaps invincibility—and that he could only go from strength to strength. James decreed that "Guy Fawkes Night" would be commemorated throughout the land every November 5, with a special service of thanksgiving said at all the parish churches. Catholics were made to swear an Oath of Supremacy to the king over the pope. After a brief period of terror in which Catholics were imprisoned or fined, James hatched a plan to heal the religious wounds. He would marry his son and heir, Prince Henry, to a Catholic princess, and his son Charles to a Protestant one. By December 1605, an embassy was sent to Spain to initiate discussions with Philip III for the hand of his daughter, the infanta Maria, for Prince Henry.

Meanwhile, Salisbury hit upon import duties as the best means of supporting the royal family. Duties were imposed for the regulation of commerce and were part of foreign policy—and anything to do with foreign policy pertained to the royal prerogative. James had found his safety valve.

Then disaster struck. In 1612 the talented and loyal Salisbury died, followed shortly thereafter by James's heir, Prince Henry. Henry was a young man of exceptional promise and was only eighteen when he contracted typhoid fever. James had put all of his energies into Henry's succession, having completely ignored the younger and sickly son, Charles. The king was simply devastated. All his plans and hopes were transferred to the uninspiring Prince Charles, and James spun steadily into a downhill spiral.

His court became increasingly tarnished with scandal, such as the poisoning of Sir Thomas Overbury for his resistance to the divorce of Frances Howard to wed James's current favorite, Robert Carr, now the earl of Rochester. The sordid saga of their affair, wedding, and Overbury's murder was laid before the House of Lords, and their henchmen were hanged. James intervened to save Carr and his new wife, and they were allowed to live out their existence in seclusion, but the scandal exposed his court for its active perversion of justice. Other courtiers knew that the only way to the king's heart was to inspire him with love for another man, and found the impoverished younger son of a Leicestershire gentleman, George Villiers.

Villiers was believed to be the handsomest man of his age and was groomed to attract the king's eye. James fell head over heels in love, making Villiers a viscount in 1616 and duke of Buckingham in 1623. But Buckingham would prove more dangerous than Carr or any other of his predecessors. He combined blind ambition, political aspirations, and total ineptitude, and as James grew older and more besotted with his "dog" (James's nickname for Buckingham), the duke would bring the nation to the brink of disaster.

15

The Wooing of the
Spanish Infanta

1618–1624

BUCKINGHAM, UNRESTRAINED BY REASON and motivated by self-aggrandizement, supported a scheme in 1618 that would herald a disastrous return to war with Spain, and set in train events that risked the loss of the Sancy for the English crown. He and other ministers close to the king, known as the war party, thought England could better secure her own colonies in the Americas by letting loose Walter Raleigh upon Spanish America with some ostensibly innocuous mission in search of gold for England. The alleged peaceful purpose to Raleigh's release was nothing short of a harbinger of war. Raleigh, after twelve years in prison on trumped-up charges, was utterly desperate to prove himself, and had known only treachery and hatred since his return to England. America meant his salvation. But the only mariners he was able to enlist to his fleet were the "scum of men," since the enterprise seemed to experienced sailors to be no more than a piracy operation. At the end of the day, Raleigh found no gold mine, fought the Spanish fleet on the Orinoco, and lost his son in the battle. He sailed home to meet his fate, knowing that returning empty-handed to James would mean his execution as a traitor under the old sentence passed a dozen years back. Buckingham, who had instigated the disastrous campaign, had already done an about-face before Raleigh had sailed. Instead of attacking Spain, Buckingham now advised the king to marry his surviving son, Prince Charles, to the Spanish infanta.

James did not grasp that such a match would abandon all of the Protestant reforms of the previous sixty years, nor that it would be anathema to his people. He had not noticed that Maria de' Medici, on the death of Henry IV, had ruined the Protestant cause in France, and that the sway she had held over her children as devout Catholics presented a problem for that nation. Continental Protestants were clamoring for James's aid, but he was too busy empire-building in America to note the source of their distress. The king had lost the sound council of his young son Prince Henry, who, when James proposed that he marry a French Catholic princess, replied that "the two religions shall not lie side by side in my bed." But Prince Henry was dead, and Charles was not cut of the same cloth.

The Spanish match became the main objective of James's foreign policy for the next several years. Tolerance at home would need to extend to Catholics to prove the king's resolve, and the misery of forced allegiance to the king over the pope would become a thing of the past. Unwilling judges were commanded to release Catholics from every prison in England, and the recusancy fines dwindled to a trickle. Persecution of Catholics continued only in the remotest parts of the country, where local justices of the peace were hostile to the influence of the central government.

The proposed match was presented to the English people as a favor to Spain. The Spanish ambassador to England, Gondomar, was pandered to in an extravagant way by king and court, and acquired, next to Buckingham, the most powerful voice in English affairs between 1618 and 1621. Gondomar was a knight in shining armor to English recusants, with the faithful waiting upon him in the anterooms of the Spanish embassy. The French ambassador, who saw his role as protecting the Catholic faithful in England, jealously complained that he had been neglected by the English Catholics. Non-Catholics felt threatened, and caricatures, lampoons, and sermons directed against the Spanish were punished rigorously by the Privy Council at Gondomar's instigation. Since James had been ruling for the previous ten years (1611–1621) without calling Parliament, they could not vent their frustration and fear in any other way.

In the next two years the project to marry Prince Charles to the Spanish infanta—to which James had sacrificed the fortunes of his country and the love of his subjects—proved to be a diplomatic absurdity and a very costly mistake. What was to follow was something out of a bad "B" movie and included a lovesick prince; a reluctant bride; villains with twirling mustaches; and bounders and brigands, and would end in war.

The ultimate folly began when two young men sporting false beards and calling themselves John and Thomas Smith left New Hall in Essex by horseback on the frosty morning of February 18, 1623, bound for the southeastern coastal port of Dover. The taller, handsome "Smith" was carrying in his breast pocket a fortune in diamonds that he hoped to sell to Charles, the prince of Wales. The first quizzical looks were cast in their direction at the Thames crossing southeast of London at Gravesend, where they had so wildly overtipped the ferryman that he immediately presumed they were suspicious characters. He quickly alerted the local justices, who caught up with the two "Smiths" some fifty miles later, at Canterbury. When confronted, the taller Smith removed his beard and revealed himself as George Villiers, the newly knighted duke of Buckingham—the king's favorite man, "bedfellow," and chief minister. The ever-charming Buckingham claimed that he was traveling incognito to "take a secret view of the forwardness of His Majesty's fleet." The justices humbly apologized, and the two gentlemen were allowed to resume their journey. What Buckingham did not disclose was that his small, nondescript companion was the twenty-two-year-old Charles, prince of Wales.

Buckingham also had lied about their purpose. This was the inauspicious beginning of their foolhardy quest for Prince Charles to personally woo the Spanish infanta. The entire episode became infamous in English circles and would earn Buckingham and Charles the titles of "The Knights of Adventure" in the English press for several months.

On this journey, Buckingham, who always had an eye to the main chance, had taken a fortune in diamonds in his breast pocket, having agreed previously with a wealthy merchant, Sir Paul Pindar, that he would bring Pindar's great diamonds along, to discuss their purchase with Charles. The young prince would be away from court and all paternal influences, and Buckingham assumed Charles could be easily beguiled into the acquisition. One of the diamonds was an exceptional 36-carat gem called the Great Diamond (later called the Pindar, and valued at £35,000 the following year) that the king often borrowed to wear at state occasions. The once-humble Buckingham was not above—or beneath—a little commerce and earning a personal commission while engaged on official royal business. He, like all of the Jacobean court, suffered from diamond fever, and knew how to profit personally from the Stuart lust for these gemstones.

Buckingham's sales pitch to the impressionable young prince stressed that the diamonds could be used to dazzle the Spanish infanta, and with English wealth, he would win her heart. After all, James I had already reset the Mirror of Portugal, stolen from the Portuguese crown by Don Antonio on Philip II's invasion, to astound the princess. But Charles resisted Buckingham's charm offensive for the time being, and told him he would only buy the Pindar once he became king.

In a stormy six-hour voyage across the English Channel they were hideously seasick, and on landing in France could not find refuge in an inn until the second evening after their crossing. Not wishing to be unmasked again, and in far riskier circumstances now that they were on foreign soil, Buckingham took the added precaution of buying them large wigs to "better veil their faces" while they visited the French court.

When the pair finally arrived at the French court, they hovered amid the throng who had come to take part in the public court rituals, which included dining with the king and queen mother. Buckingham then plucked up the nerve to ask the queen's chamberlain to admit them with a bevy of other spectators to watch the queen, Princess Henrietta Maria, and "other fair dancing ladies" rehearsing for the masque to be performed before the king. Since Buckingham and Charles appeared to be well mannered and well groomed, if curious foreign gentlemen in large wigs, the queen's chamberlain saw no harm in Buckingham's request and obliged him willingly.

It was thought that the young Princess Henrietta Maria held some considerable fascination for Charles, since she was the sister of Elisabeth of France, mother of the Spanish infanta, Maria. But this could not have been more remote from the truth. For some uncanny reason—most probably spurred on by the swashbuckling Buckingham—Charles had deluded himself into believing that he was madly in love with the infanta, shutting himself away for hours, mooning over her portrait. He often wrote her love letters, too—all of which remained unanswered. In fact, Charles had agreed to undertake the whole insane voyage through France to Spain, again at Buckingham's suggestion, to personally romance her and to bring the infanta back to England with him as his bride.

Early the next morning, Buckingham and Charles set out for Spain without making further contact with the French court. They were, however, recognized en route to the Spanish frontier. This time they were ordered by the English ambassador, Lord Herbert, to "make all the haste out of France and take care not to do anything which might annoy the authorities on the way." The Knights of Adventure, duly chastised, agreed, and reached Spain without further incident.

When Charles was at last admitted to the Spanish court, he realized that his task would be more difficult than he had been led to believe by Buckingham. The Spanish court at the Escurial was truly splendid, strewn with all the riches the Spanish—and Portuguese—colonies could offer. Charles felt ashamed of his few baubles, and with Buckingham dashed off a note to James on April 22, 1623:

> Sir,
>   I confess that you have sent more jewels than at my departure I thought I had use of; but, since my coming, seeing the many jewels worn here, and that my bravery can consist of nothing else, besides that sum of them which you have appointed me to give to the Infanta, in Steenie's [a nickname for Buckingham] opinion and mine, are not fit to be given to her; therefore I have taken this boldness to entreat your Majesty to send more for my own wearing, and for giving to my Mistress: in which I think Your Majesty shall not do amiss to take Carlisle's advice. So humbly craving your blessing, I rest
>   Your Majesty's humble and obedient son and servant, Charles.

A hastily added postscript from the ubiquitous Buckingham states: "I your Dog, say you have many jewels neither fit for your one, your son's, nor your daughter's wearing, but very fit to bestow of those here

who must necessarily have presents; and this way will be least charge-
able to your Majesty in my poor opinion."

Naturally, in Charles's mind, there was no question of giving the
infanta any of the crown jewels—including the Sancy—but in the
scribble from the immensely cheeky duke penned three days later to
King James on the same subject, it was clear that the Sancy's power
was required to persuade the Spanish that the Jacobean court meant
business:

> Dear Dad, Gossip, and Steward,
>   Though your baby himself has sent word what needs he has of
> more jewels. . . . I give my poor and saucy opinion what will be
> most fit to send. . . . Sir, he has neither chain nor hatband; and I
> beseech you consider first how rich they are in jewels here, then in
> what a poor equipage he came in, how he has no other means to
> appear like a King's son, how jewels are useful at such a time as this,
> when they may do yourself, your son and the nation honor, and
> lastly how it will neither cause nor hazard you any thing. . . . I hope,
> since you have ventured already your chiefest jewel to your Son,
> will serve to persuade you to let loose these more for him: first your
> best hatband—the Portugal diamond; the rest of the pendant dia-
> monds, to make up a necklace to give to his Mistress; and the best
> rope of pearls, with a rich chain or two for himself to wear, or else
> your Dog must want a collar; which is the ready way to put him
> into it. There are many other jewels which are of so mean a quality
> as they deserve not that name, but will save much in your purse and
> serve very well for presents.
>   Your Majesty's most humble slave and Dog, Steenie.

It was a clear plea for the king's hat ornament Mirror of Great
Britain, which included the Sancy and the Mirror of Portugal. The
jewels that had long been used for war and diplomacy were now
needed in the art of love. But James refused to release his "lucky" diamond, the Sancy. Instead he sent "a collar of gold containing thirty
pieces whereof fifteen are roses in each a great pointed diamond and
fifteen crown ciphers of the King and Queen's names having in each
of them a table diamond" to the lovestruck prince along with "The
Three Brethren [the Three Brothers] that you know full well, but newly
set and the Mirror of France, the fellow of the Portugal diamond which

I would wish you to wear alone in your hat with a little black feather." The king also thought of his favorite, Buckingham, and sent him a table diamond for his hat.

Newly empowered by his magnificent gems, Charles made an utter idiot of himself by climbing up the palace walls to glimpse a view of the infanta, or smuggling himself, more than once, into her presence for a private talk. Now, having actually seen her, he believed himself completely head over heels in love at first sight. Spanish etiquette, however, dictated that the prince never address the infanta directly, and certainly not in her bedchamber. When the queen heard what had transpired, she demanded to see him in a private audience and gave him a royal chastisement. He had served no purpose, she told him, other than to embarrass himself and his country. Charles promised that if she could get her daughter to change her mind that he would make every concession to English Catholics—repeal all of the Penal Laws—and allow his and her children to be raised as Catholics. His pleas only served to debase him further. The queen confirmed in the bluntest terms that his cause was hopeless. The infanta made no secret of her revulsion at the prospect of any marriage to a Protestant heretic.

Buckingham erupted, provoking a personal and public quarrel with the Spanish nation. He exclaimed in full earshot of the Spanish court that "we would rather put the infanta headlong into a well than into the prince's hands." Charles joined in the fun, mocking their rulers, their barren land, the beggarly population, and the tumbledown inns they had seen on their journey to Madrid. The priceless historic gems were wrested from the Spanish court, and the two adventurers made for home. When Londoners learned that the prince had safely returned and that he was still a Protestant—*and* a bachelor—the city, and later the nation, broke out in rejoicing that could not have been more heartfelt than if he had brought back the entire Spanish fleet as a prize of war.

The young prince's unrequited love and embarrassment had turned to hatred, and the adventurer Buckingham stoked the fires of shame whenever he could to serve his own self-interest. The romantic interlude had been nothing more than a Quixotic illusion, with Charles tilting at the windmills of matrimony without a damsel to save. The pity is that this Spanish folly was the one and only romantic gesture of Charles's life, and one that brought England to the brink of war.

What James I of England had regarded as a marriage of political necessity, Charles had crazily believed was a match made in heaven. Yet he, unlike Prince Henry, had not been educated to power. His father, who had neglected or alternatively berated Charles for his stammer and lack of physical stature, changed neither his views about his surviving son nor Charles's preparation to become king. Incredibly, neither James nor Charles saw that Charles's proposed betrothal to a Catholic princess was a diplomatic hot potato that would have serious repercussions. Europe continued to divide itself along Protestant and Catholic battle lines, as James already knew to his personal cost. Several years earlier, in 1619, James's daughter, Elizabeth, and his Protestant son-in-law, Frederick Elector of the Rhineland Palatinate, had made the catastrophic decision of accepting the crown of the kingdom of Bohemia after the Lutheran nobility revolted against their Catholic Habsburg overlords. The Austrian Habsburgs retaliated, ousting Frederick, his English wife, and their numerous progeny from Bohemia and his Rhineland territories, thereby igniting the Thirty Years' War, which virtually engulfed all of the European powers at one point.

James had plotted and connived for more than twenty years to retain absolute personal power over his three kingdoms (England and Wales were one, then Scotland, then Ireland) and was not prepared to allow his heir, Charles, or his daughter to be "insulted by Catholic upstarts"—even if their name was Habsburg. But James could not afford his saber rattling, let alone a war. Although the crown was apparently the wealthiest in Europe, James simply had no cash to maintain his regal lifestyle, and wars were notoriously expensive. By making the crown jewels inalienable—"inviolate and inseparable" by his decree of 1605—they no longer afforded a means of raising capital. He had refused to call Parliament for more than ten years, yet he needed Parliament to levy taxes. The only apparent remedy to the Catholic problem created by the Stuart dynasty therefore remained for Parliament to tax the nation to build up a war chest.

But that would not be enough. Wars needed allies, and Continental wars needed powerful friends. James's dilemma could only be resolved by bamboozling a Continental ally to weigh in heavily on his side. But who? There can be no doubt that James also was envious that the three great families on the Continent at that time—the de' Medici, Bourbon, and Habsburg—were united through marriage, and James desperately wanted to add the Stuart name to the 'A' list of Continental royals.

Charles's failed wooing of the infanta had given James a rude awakening. He discerned, at last, that the Spanish Habsburgs' prevarications over the past three years meant that there had never been any real intention of allowing the marriage to go ahead. So the unstoppable king cast his eyes to France, and in January 1624 opened negotiations with King Louis XIII to marry the hapless Charles to Princess Henrietta Maria.

16

In the Crown of
Henrietta Maria, the French
Queen of England

1624–1628

❦

IN SPITE OF THE SANCY'S INALIENABILITY, it would soon be given
to England's future queen by Charles. The French, for their part,
brushed off any qualms that they were a stalking horse in case the
Spanish marriage deal fell through, and sent a French envoy to London with a gift of twelve falcons, and twelve huntsmen and twelve
horses with trappings to match, as a gesture of goodwill. James sent
the experienced "wooing ambassador" Viscount Kensington to the
Louvre, the royal palace at that time, in February to clinch the deal.
On February 24 Kensington wrote to Buckingham to transmit to the
king, "Sir, you will find a lady of as much loveliness and sweetness to
deserve your affection as any creature under heaven can do, but her
growth is very little short of her age; and her wisdom infinitely beyond
it." Basically, Henrietta Maria was tiny—barely four feet tall—but ener-
getic and clever.

In May, Kensington had reinforcements sent in the person of the
earl of Carlisle, the experienced diplomat in the Spanish affair, who
arrived with the official proposal of marriage. The negotiations on the
thorny issues of the marriage contract and the political alliance with

159

France had begun in earnest. Buckingham, with his unique blend of arrogance and political incompetence, insisted on linking the marriage to the political alliance to save James's unfortunate daughter and son-in-law, whereas Kensington advised the king that the two matters should be separate. James, of course, listened to Buckingham.

Cardinal Richelieu and Queen Maria were prepared to give in if something could be done about the plight of the English Catholics. On this point Buckingham intervened personally with Cardinal Richelieu. Although Richelieu disliked Buckingham intensely, the cardinal remained pragmatic, and knew through his comprehensive spy network that the duke wielded great power. A compromise was reached, and on September 13 the Venetian ambassador in Paris reported that the religious issues holding up the match had been settled. "The king and Prince of Wales promise in a separate written document, which the Secretary of State will also sign, that the Catholics of the kingdom shall enjoy the same privileges and exemptions at the instance of the Most Christian [king of France] as were conceded to the Catholic [king of Spain] in negotiations with him. They shall be allowed to live in the profession of their faith, without molestation, and shall not be persecuted or compelled in any matter of conscience." The Venetian ambassador was using a euphemism of the day when he described the promise as "a separate written document." It was an *escrit particulier*—better known today as a secret treaty.

It was now the autumn of 1624. James had virtually made over the government to Buckingham and Charles. The king's health was deteriorating rapidly and the Habsburgs—both Austrian and Spanish—remained the firm targets for his personal vendetta in the petty dynastic conflict he had resolved to fight. The war on the Continent had contributed to a slump in the export of English textiles. Failed harvests were followed by famine. Amazingly, despite Buckingham's incompetence and Charles's inexperience, they bamboozled the newly reconvened Parliament into voting £300,000 ($45.9 million or £28.7 million today) toward a joint land and sea attack on Spain with the Dutch, on the condition that the Spanish marriage negotiations were broken off for good and that war be declared *only* against Spain. James, who had not kept Parliament apprised of the debacle in the Spanish marriage negotiations, promised that he would abide by their conditions, but on Buckingham's advice, spent the money instead on subsidizing foreign armies in the Rhineland, hoping that they would reestablish Frederick and Elizabeth in the Palatinate. On November 23, two days before Henrietta Maria's fifteenth birthday, the marriage contract was signed by the French. With King Louis's solemn undertaking to finance the mercenary army, as proof of good faith, King James and Charles signed the marriage contract at Cambridge on December 12. The Sancy diamond would be given to Henrietta Maria as the central gemstone to mount in her gold crown as queen.

An allowance of £40,000 ($6.1 million or £3.8 million today) was given to the ever-greedy Buckingham for his expenses in representing Charles at the proxy wedding, to take place at the Louvre Palace. The sumptuousness of this personal allowance can readily be set into context against the £300,000 that James had raised five months earlier to fight a war.

What had escaped the attention of both James and Charles was the fact that the English people felt little support for any marriage with France. Even English Catholics were against the French marriage, since they had heard about the Spanish protestations on their behalf, and wrongly felt that the French did not care about their persecution. The Puritans were outraged that Henrietta Maria had been given every right to practice her religion, with properly ornamented Catholic chapels provided in all royal residences. Furthermore, the future English queen's private royal household would comprise only French Catholics chosen by the king of France. Any children of the marriage were to be brought up by their mother until they were twelve years old, and if she became a widow, she would be free to return to France if she so wished, taking all her goods and personal jewels, though not the English crown jewels, with her. It would have seemed likely that the teenage bride already counted the Sancy among her personal jewels, though this was not the case, as it had already been declared inalienable by James.

James was fifty-eight, bad-tempered, constantly slobbering, belching, scratching himself in public, and suffering from a variety of unpleasant ailments he did little to disguise, ranging from indigestion and flatulence to diarrhea. Still, when the end came, it seemed to surprise everyone, and James, according to *Birch's Historical Review*, died within a week of his "distressing condition worsening" on March 27, 1625.

The first act of the new King Charles I was to confirm all his father's ministers in their offices. The second was to agree to a wedding date within a month of his father's funeral. Ever confident, Buckingham was certain he would be needed at home to advise Charles, so Sir George Goring went instead to France to represent the king at the proxy wedding. The duke had already spent £20,000 on a lavish wardrobe he had intended to wear as the proxy bridegroom, which included a suit of purple satin embroidered all over with Oriental pearls. It never saw the light of day.

On May 11, 1625, Charles Stuart was married by proxy to Henrietta Maria de Bourbon in front of the Cathedral of Notre-Dame in Paris. The diminutive bride wore a gown of gold and silver encrusted with diamonds and gold fleurs-de-lys and a train so heavy that the three ladies responsible for carrying it corraled a spare gentleman to walk underneath, to take some of its weight on his head. Everyone present glowed and sparkled with gold and silver, diamonds, and other precious stones. King Louis looked like "the glorious sun outshining the other stars." The wedding ceremony was followed by celebrations that continued for several days with firework displays, illuminations, lavish entertainment at the Luxembourg Palace and cannon salvos, all provided by the triumphant queen mother, Maria de' Medici.

When Henrietta Maria said her good-byes to her mother on June 16, Maria, true to form, tried to fire her up with an inspirational religious sermon about how Henrietta Maria was the guardian angel and crusader for all English Catholics. All indications are that the new child queen remained unmoved, since her conspiratorial mother had done little to endear herself to Henrietta Maria during her childhood. Neither her mother nor the English knew what Henrietta Maria had in store for them.

The Venetian ambassador's report from London in July 1626 put it rather succinctly: "The queen is thoroughly French, both in her sentiments and habits. The marriage has not changed her one whit . . . and does not seem likely to do so by a long way." That was the kindest remark made about the stormy three years that followed.

Whereas Charles stuttered and was awkward in manner and un-remarkable in appearance, Henrietta Maria was nimble and quick-witted. Whereas he was excessively orderly—compartmentalizing his days into rigid timetables devoted to prayer, exercise, business, eating, and sleeping—she loved frivolity, diversity, music, and laughter. He was slow and plodding; she, mercurial. She was a bubbly brunette with large black eyes, but only reached to her short husband's shoulder. Her only unfortunate feature was her teeth, which were described by her niece, the duchess of Hanover, as "guns pointing out from a fortress," though these were never depicted accurately in royal portraits. The only character trait that the new royal couple shared was an uncompromising nature.

In celebration of his wedding, Charles had finally bought the Pindar diamond that Buckingham had first tried to sell him during the Spanish misadventure. It weighed some 36 carats, and Charles bought it for a reduced price of £18,000 ($2.8 million or £1.7 million today) on a deferred-payment plan. The king did not present the Great Diamond, as it was called at the time, to Henrietta Maria, but characteristically and unromantically added it to the state crown jewel collection instead. He did, however, present Henrietta Maria with her very own gold crown, with the Sancy mounted at the center. Their first meeting as husband and wife was understandably gauche, especially when Charles made his disappointment known by asking his diminutive and sensitive child bride if she were wearing high heels.

From the moment Henrietta Maria stepped foot on English soil, she sought to surround herself with anyone and anything French. She obstinately felt that it was her right—and it was, as written in the marriage contract. As time marched on—peppered by public rows between Henrietta Maria and Charles, his indiscreet complaints that "all was not as it should be in the bedchamber," and Henrietta Maria's adolescent temper tantrums—an acrimonious atmosphere prevailed at court. Charles took to hunting and sleeping at different royal palaces where his queen was not in residence. The news of the royal rift spread, and Londoners, who had not seen much of Henrietta Maria, felt confirmed in their worst suspicions of their Catholic queen.

To compound matters, she made absolutely no attempt to learn English and seemingly felt that there was no reason why she should have to—ever. The French supported her in this view, especially since the English had not fulfilled their obligations under the secret treaty. English Catholics were still subject to the recusant laws that made Henrietta's devout Catholic practices even more shocking to her English people.

Buckingham rode to the rescue on a tide of his own egotism as royal marriage counselor. He warned the queen that the king would no longer put up with her coldness to him and that if she did not mend her ways she would become "the unhappiest woman in the world," a term used by Henry VIII for Anne Boleyn. He then went farther and urged Henrietta Maria to accept English ladies in her household and suggested that his wife, sister, and niece would do rather nicely. A major international incident was now brewing, and Henrietta Maria had been in England for only six months.

Despite the growing discontent on Charles's side, it is fair to say that Henrietta Maria did not as yet consider herself to be unhappy. She had not been brought up with the expectation of love or even romance, as we are today. Charles was exceedingly dull and undemonstrative but not cruel. He did not keep a string of mistresses whom he showered with diamonds and precious stones to challenge her position, as her father, Henry IV, had done. Nor was Charles essentially homosexual, as James I had been. Her main threat was Buckingham, whom Charles idolized as a younger, awkward brother would his handsome and clever older sibling. As long as she remained propped up by her sumptuous French household of three hundred servants, she could manage just fine and not think too much about the future. She was, after all, only sixteen.

Henrietta Maria's first six months in England also were marred by a severe outbreak of the plague. By New Year's 1626 the disease had killed some sixty thousand English subjects. As a consequence, their coronation as king and queen had been delayed and was now set for Candlemas Day, February 2, 1626, but would be held without the usual magnificence characteristic of a royal coronation. In fact, the royal decree for the coronation stated, "it being resolved, from motives of economy, to save [the] three hundred thousand crowns which it would have cost and to use the money for other important and needful purpose." This was no mere austerity drive by Parliament. It was a humiliating admission by Charles that he was effectively broke.

The truth was stark. James had tried, but failed, to build on the Tudor aura through the official creation of the crown jewel collection, leaving Charles with new Jacobean debts due to irresponsible spending and lack of fiscal reform. By January 1626 Charles, forever lacking in foresight and bereft of wise counsel, made the most incredible blunder any monarch of the day could possibly make: he announced to Parliament that he was compelled to pawn all of the crown jewels to Jewish merchants in Amsterdam, since Parliament would not vote him funds to fight the Spanish. For the most part, the Jews of Amsterdam were, of course, refugee descendants of Spanish Jewry exiled since the Spanish Inquisition, and had become expert diamond brokers in an activity that complemented diamond cutting, also dominated by Jews, in Antwerp. Diamond brokerage remained a quasi-banking activity, and one of few professions open to Jews at the time. It was the Jews' very expertise that a century earlier had usurped the positions of Florence and Venice as places to pawn gemstones, and transformed the commercial histories of Antwerp and Amsterdam.

Pawning the crown jewels was an act of expediency by a young, arrogant monarch uneducated to power. It also was a direct contravention of James's 1605 decree stipulating that "the crown's most beautiful jewels were to be part of a collection that was to be indivisible and inseparate, forever hereafter annexed to the Kingdom of this realm." The pawning came as an utter shock to Parliament, where Sir John Eliot lamented: "O! Those jewels! The pride and glory of this realm! Which have made it so far shining above all others! Would they were here, within the compass of these walls, to be viewed and seen by us and to be examined in this place. Their very name and memory have transported me!"

The pawning is even more extraordinary when we consider that at the time, jewels were so essential to the concept of royalty and the essence of royal splendor that to be without them was to be less of a monarch. The jewels themselves were still imbued with various powers—from the healing powers of toadstone to the diamond's ability to make its owner invincible. The settings continued to evoke devotional,

Charles I, King of England. Painting by Daniel Mytens, 1631, during the time when the crown jewels were in pawn.

magical, classical, natural, or heraldic themes and symbols, with the type of jewelry (garter, collar, ring, hat ornament, etc.) denoting further symbolic importance. For Charles to have parted with all these jewels—and especially the Sancy and the rest of his "invincible" diamonds—at a time of war was an act of sheer arrogance, and was the first tangible evidence that he felt he was answerable only to God. Henrietta Maria's crown was thus stripped of the Sancy, and the diamond, with the rest of the crown jewels, was sent to Holland.

Thanks to the inventory of jewels that James undertook in preparation for Charles's aborted marriage to the Spanish infanta in July 1623, we can understand just how spectacular these were.

All the jewels set in James's hat ornament known as the "Feather," which had previously included the Sancy and the Mirror of Great Britain, were pledged. Literally hundreds of gold chains, Henry VIII's splendid gold and jeweled collars, ninety-nine diamond rings, pearls, and the Three Brothers were all shipped off to Holland. Anne Boleyn's diamond, too, was in the collection. Elizabeth I's most significant acknowledged acquisition from the Portuguese crown jewels, the Mirror of Portugal—the long, rectangular, 26.07-carat table-cut diamond obtained from Don Antonio—was also among the pawned jewels. The Great Harry from Mary Stuart's 1561 jewel inventory was pledged as well. The Pindar, purchased only months earlier in exchange for a knighthood for Nicolas Ghysbertij, also was gone. Ghysbertij was the father-in-law of Thomas Cletscher, whose famous *Sketchbook* illustrates the pawned jewels. Cletscher acted as facilitator for the pawning, and also was the crown jeweler to Frederick Henry, prince of Orange.

The Mirror of France, a "great table diamond set in gold" that had previously been pawned by the French in Italy before 1589, then sold to the English crown before it could be redeemed, was pledged again. Also gone was the incredibly historic Mirror of Naples, a fabulous diamond valued at 60,000 crowns by Henry VIII.

The Anchor, a large, twenty-carat table-cut diamond suspending an anchor made up of an odd stone with lozenge-shaped cut and broad parallel facets, a long saddle-shaped baguette, and a briolette with a round cross section, was pledged, too. The first ever briolette-cut diamond, known as the City, which had been given to James I by financiers of the City of London and weighing twenty-two carats, also had been pawned. Thousands of large rubies, pearls, and cameos were pledged as well. All awaited redemption at some unknown date by some unknown means in the Netherlands.

With the jewels pawned from January 1626, and the coronation scheduled for early February, Charles would have recognized that his coronation would be less resplendent, since he would have shown himself to his people without the jewels' invincible aura in his first official ceremony as king. Further, there is little doubt that a portion of the proceeds went toward this ceremony. The very real threat of the plague came as a blessed relief to Charles and helped preserve his self-image. As to the crowning of Henrietta Maria, with Charles alienated from his wife, he controversially agreed with Archbishop Laud that Henrietta Maria should not be crowned in a Catholic ceremony in his Anglican church. The insistence on the Catholic ceremony was entirely hers, and it proved to be the first of many gross errors of judgment she would make. Since she obstinately refused any compromise, Charles proceeded with his own coronation without her. In any event, Henrietta Maria was never crowned officially, and did not even attend the ceremony at Westminster Abbey for her husband's coronation. The people, and Parliament, took her rejection of the coronation ceremony as a cruel insult, inflaming public opinion against her. Parliament also blamed the dreaded Buckingham for failing to exert his absolute power over the king in the affair and criticized the duke again for his costly and terrible military advice in the futile war. Henrietta Maria was humiliated, stripped of her position and "glory" without a crown or the Sancy she had been promised.

Buckingham, as always, ignored the critics. He saw Henrietta Maria's refusal as a good excuse to turn up the heat under her Catholic entourage and bring the queen to heel. He began a whispering campaign against the queen and pointed out to Charles that if his own wife would not obey him, he could hardly expect to assert his authority over a rambunctious Parliament. The king readily agreed, and charged Buckingham with handling her. Buckingham seized the day and told the queen's senior adviser, de Blainville, that he was a pernicious influence, was not welcomed at court, and was barred from the queen's household. When de Blainville tried to see the king, he was refused an audience. Naturally, Henrietta Maria threw a royal temper tantrum and informed her husband that they were no longer on speaking terms. Charles advised her, naturally through the ubiquitous Buckingham, that he would not see her until she apologized for her behavior. Weeks passed, and in the end, Henrietta Maria asked what she had done to vex her husband so much. He hesitantly replied that when he had "advised the queen that it had been raining, she had replied that it had not." The allusion was lost on her, but she apologized nonetheless.

Buckingham's influence on the king seemed boundless after this series of confrontations with Henrietta Maria. He chipped away at her Catholic household, sending back to France all who displeased him and putting his own cronies in place, until finally he persuaded the king to remove the queen's household entirely. While Buckingham used their venomous influence on the queen in making her love all things French and dislike all things English as an excuse, the real reason for this slash was that the king's well-known financial problems were greatly exacerbated by the frivolous queen's three-hundred-person entourage. Charles sent an ambassador to the French court with the glad tidings, giving rise to further speculation that the king's straitened circumstances were so bad that he now needed the other half of the queen's dowry of £161,000 ($23.4 million or £14.6 million today). Once the ambassador had left Dover, Charles ordered all ports closed and confronted Henrietta Maria with his decision that for her own good, and the good of the country, he was shipping her entire household back to France immediately. While the king was unveiling the plan to Henrietta Maria personally, Charles's secretary of state told the defiant senior members of the French household that they were about to be deported.

Now Henrietta Maria truly flew into an adolescent temper tantrum. She burst into floods of tears, alternatively praying, then groveling on her knees at Charles's feet for him to change his mind. When that did not work, she screamed so loudly that her cries, according to Charles, would have "split rocks." Seeing that Charles remained unmoved, she raced over to the windows and smashed the glass with her fists, grabbing hold of the bars and screaming in French to the English royal household in the courtyard below to help deliver her from this evil. Charles was appalled by this shameful display and dragged her away. Her hair was disheveled, her dress was torn, and her hands were cut and bleeding.

While Charles's publicly stated purpose of this ruthless act was to gain control over his teenage wife, the financial aspects of the exercise cannot be underestimated. After only one year in power, his spending had spiraled out of control. He had pawned the greatest symbols of his royal wealth and power, and drastic cutbacks were essential. Yet getting rid of the entire French household, just as getting rid of any workforce today, did not come cheaply. There were unpaid bills—from the £1,500 for the French bishop's "unholy water," as the English called it, to £4,000 for "the necessaries of the queen" and some £22,000 in cash and jewelry ($3.2 million or £2 million today) by way of back salary and gifts. By the time the French had left the royal residence at Somerset House, the queen's wardrobe had been extensively pillaged, leaving her "but one gown and two smocks" to wear. When the king's men ordered the "French freebooters" to return Her Majesty's clothing and accused them of outright theft, Mamie St. Georges, the longest-serving servant to the queen, declared that if they had been thieves it would not have served them very well, since the English were too poor to be worth robbing.

Mamie St. Georges was right. By this time Charles had begun to sell his personal jewels as well. On November 17, 1626, the king issued a royal warrant for the sale of a gold collar set with diamonds to the earl of Holland (formerly Viscount Kensington) for £5,800. Between 1626 and 1628 there are several such warrants for the sale of jewels to other lords, including Buckingham and Lord Carleton, but no other sales were for so much money.

Henrietta Maria lamented that she was now *tout à fait prisonnière* with the king, even following her to the close-stool (toilet). There is no doubt that Henrietta was overly dramatic, but now her situation was mightily uncomfortable indeed. Charles had, at a stroke, torn up the marriage contract. He had been deeply offended by her refusing him conjugal rights and had become cold and unloving. She rightly felt threatened by her husband's favorite, Buckingham, who had gone to great pains to remind her that there had been queens of England who had lost their heads for less in the recent past. She was even surrounded by Buckingham's family as her new English ladies-in-waiting. When the English ambassador appeared at the French court and eloquently explained how Henrietta Maria, taking bad advice from her French bishops, had misbehaved to king and country, both Louis and Cardinal Richelieu agreed that Charles had not been unreasonable to try to bring her under a semblance of control. They also agreed that the brutality of his actions required rebuke. Protracted negotiations took place to allow Henrietta Maria some of her French clergy, subject to the "king's pleasure."

Nonetheless, tensions mounted between the two countries, and Charles, egged on by Buckingham, wanted to go to war against France while continuing the war against Spain. After all, Charles had some money now, since the Sancy and other pawned crown jewels had, in part, financed the war effort.

The French insisted that Charles make good on his promises contained in the *escrit particulier* of the marriage contract, granting English Catholics freedom of worship. Charles was not prepared to do anything of the kind, since it would have meant political suicide with the powerful Puritan faction of Parliament and his vision for a Protestant England. What the king did not grasp was that his vision included seminal changes to the Protestant Anglican Church services that reflected some of the most hated Catholic pomp and ceremony. Charles was already treading in perilous waters.

When Charles asked for funds to declare war against France, Parliament refused, so the king dissolved it. The ever-arrogant Charles resorted instead to a back-door form of taxation called the "forced loan," which was raised in exactly the means implied by its name. It met with widespread resistance, but as the king threatened to imprison those who withheld payment under a contempt charge, some £300,000 was finally raised to beef up the run-down and mutinous navy. The appalling state of the navy was the direct responsibility of its lord admiral—none other than the duke of Buckingham.

While Buckingham was away at war, Henrietta Maria's attitude to Charles changed markedly. She was now seventeen and had matured somewhat. Charles had allowed back a dozen well-vetted Catholic priests from France and was no longer being poisoned against her daily by his idol, Buckingham. Henrietta Maria, while still very young, was intelligent enough to know that she had to make good use of the time she had without Buckingham whispering against her in the king's ear if she were to have any chance at happiness. So the queen began to learn English and take a greater interest in her new country. Her attitude toward her husband became sweet and subservient. Her obvious efforts to please impressed Charles, and she was finally allowed to get close to him. Charles appeared to be incapable of having more than one favorite at a time, and with Buckingham at a safe distance, Henrietta was the person to whom he now turned for close human contact. In a letter dated August 13 to Buckingham, Charles added this postscript: "I cannot omit to tell you, that my wife and I were never on better terms; she, upon this action of yours, showing herself so loving to me, by her discretion on all occasions, that it makes us all wonder at and esteem her."

On the surface, it seems odd that when her husband went to war against her own country—where her brother was king—Henrietta

Maria should warm to her husband. It is less peculiar if we think of Henrietta Maria's change of heart within the context of her not having to compete for her husband's affections with Buckingham, and that she was using Buckingham's absence as the very opportunity to endear herself to Charles. Further, she had been married for nearly two years and had not fulfilled her primary function of "brood mare" for the crown. More than anything else, she wanted to produce an heir.

BY THE BEGINNING OF 1627 the French had made real inroads into the merchant trade through their naval victories, and Londoners were frantic. Charles felt that this time he could at last ask Parliament for money with impunity. What he had forgotten was that Parliament was wary of him after its last rapid dissolution, in 1626, when it criticized him for pawning the crown jewels, and Buckingham for his questionable military policies. On March 17, 1627, Charles addressed this untrusting Parliament and typically decided not to launch a charm offensive. For starters, he lectured members that the sole purpose for which they had been summoned was to provide him with the means to wage war. Most members ignored their king's appeals to not waste time in "tedious consultations." By May, Parliament delivered its first written ultimatum to the king: the Petition of Right. This document demanded that the monarch cease his extraparliamentary taxation policies, arbitrary arrest warrants, compulsory billeting of the military in private homes, and issuance of orders of martial law. Buckingham, newly returned from battle, enflamed the situation by going on the attack in defense of his king, and Parliament's patience boiled over. There was a vitriolic exchange with a member of Parliament, lawyer Edward Coke, who stated publicly that "The Duke of Bucks [Buckingham] is the cause of all our miseries. That man is the grievance of all grievances." It was a view shared by nearly everyone.

With Parliament raging for Buckingham to be dismissed, Charles gave way in early June, probably to save Buckingham's position, and accepted their petition limiting his royal prerogative. But emotions were running high, and within days Buckingham's doctor was hacked to death by an angry London mob. Wild rumors raced through the

Queen Henrietta Maria. Painting by
unknown artist, background by Hendrik
van Steenwyck, c. 1635.

streets of London of alleged Buckingham plots to overthrow the monarchy. Posters were nailed in the streets bearing the words *"Who rules
the kingdom? The king. Who rules the king? The duke. Who rules the duke?
The devil."*

What made these protests macabre were the superstitious portents
of doom. The duke suffered a violent nosebleed. His portrait fell from
the wall of the high commission in the London borough of Lambeth.
Buckingham's father's ghost had been seen walking the corridors at
Windsor Castle warning that Buckingham would die. But neither the
duke nor Henrietta Maria and Charles took any notice of the public
unrest or the bad omens.

Throughout this time, Henrietta Maria's need for money seemed
to be unquenchable. In July 1628 the Venetian ambassador reported
an interesting anecdote that the queen asked the king for £2 to give

to a poor person. When the king asked her who this person was, she replied "I, sire, am the penniless pauper." Charles, however, was not amused because he had recently instructed the lord treasurer to ensure that the queen's income would equal that of his mother, the late Queen Anne, who was given £28,000 annually.

In August the final disaster struck down Buckingham at Portsmouth. When he was coming out of an inn to meet the king, one of his own men, a Lieutenant Felton, killed him with a dagger. Felton made no attempt to escape, and when questioned said that he killed Buckingham "only partly" because he had been due £80 in back pay and had been unfairly passed over for a promotion. His main reason was that "in committing the Act of killing the Duke, he should do his Country great good service." The king, on hearing the news, locked himself away in a private passionate grief and remained incommunicado for two days. When he emerged, he engaged in a flurry of activity, doing more work in two weeks than he had done in the previous three months with the assistance of his beloved Buckingham.

Henrietta Maria, who had been at Wellingborough taking the waters in the hope of becoming pregnant, rushed to her husband's side when she heard the news. While the loss of Buckingham was certainly a blessing to her personally, she made no attempt to show this to Charles. On the contrary, by all reports at court, her behavior was that of a dutiful and sorrowful wife. Charles, deprived forever of his dear "Steenie," now turned irrevocably to his wife not only for solace but also for counsel. Through Henrietta Maria's concerted efforts to endear herself to her husband, her position was at last assured. From this dubious turning point she would become Charles's most trusted adviser, friend, and coauthor of disasters yet to come.

17

Redeemed and Cursed as the Ultimate Symbol of Power

September 1628–1645

DESPITE THE PARLOUS STATE of the king's financial affairs, Charles set aside £60,000 ($8.7 million or £5.5 million today) on a state funeral for Buckingham in September. Considering that the people had been held back by the king's men from lighting bonfires rejoicing at Buckingham's assassination, it was act of folly. Buckingham's murderer had become a popular hero. The public's mood was black, and in the end, Buckingham's body had to be smuggled into Westminster Abbey for a quick funeral due to fears of a popular uprising.

But this was only the beginning of Charles's cursed descent. The Amsterdam merchants were militating to sell the English jewels, and had claimed that the pawned collection had at least two cursed jewels—the historic Sancy diamond, and Henry VIII's great collar. A month later, the English were routed at La Rochelle, and thousands of Huguenots were murdered within full view of the English fleet. The penniless king was forced to sue for peace, first with the French, then with the Spanish, and treaties were signed with each in 1629 and 1630, respectively. Charles was bereft of money and military might.

Some superstitious merchants were already claiming that the Sancy's curse existed and that the king's use of the gem as a blood diamond would bring about his eventual destruction—just as it had done for the Burgundian dukes Antonio de Crato and Nicolas Harlay de Sancy. Yet Charles and Henrietta Maria remained oblivious to the dangers that lay ahead.

With the nation at peace, Charles was forced to set his finances in order. When he had pawned the crown jewels in 1626, he also had been impelled to sell extensive crown lands. The Duchies of Cornwall and Lancaster remained in his possession, but much of the remaining lands to the north and east were fens (marshes). Essentially, where he had previously earned his money from the land, he was now obliged to look at more creative and innovative ways of generating income. The king concentrated on trade as a way of reducing his £2 million deficit ($290.9 million or £181.8 million today).

Charles embarked on a momentous policy in his personal quest for power that, for once, would have good as well as long-remembered devastating effects. Five years at war against Spain, then France, had made the situation dire. If Charles had not levied taxes on shipping tonnage as well as the dreaded Ship Money, a type of fiscal feudalism imposed to defend the ports and expand the merchant fleet, government would have ceased to function.

By 1629 the royal household was in such a dilapidated state that Henrietta Maria purportedly received the French duchess of Tremouille in the dark. Given Henrietta's penchant for melodrama, this episode should not be taken too seriously, as she later remarked to the duchess that "they make the most miserable economies even in things that show the most."

In 1629 Charles appointed as his lord treasurer the able Lord Weston, who set about reducing royal expenditures while looking at new ways to generate income. Weston, however, was frequently at loggerheads with the tempestuous Henrietta Maria, whose diehard, absolute monarchist approach brokered no compromise. If Charles refused Weston's advice, the crown jewels would be at risk of being sold on the open market by the Dutch pawnbrokers.

Weston devised all sorts of "royal projects" in an attempt to meet the crown's needs, including draining the fens; manufacture of a "new" royal soap; making salt from seawater, reviving copper mining in the king's Duchy of Cornwall; manufacturing turf out of moorland waste; soft iron; clay pipes; and even white writing paper. Most of the projects ended in scandal, lining the pockets of the merchants to whom the licenses were granted, with the result that by 1639 the Privy Council revoked many of the commissions and licenses. This act made Charles some important enemies, the most ruthless of whom was the Puritan evangelist Oliver Cromwell, nicknamed "defender of the fens."

The unpopular taxation overcame the commercial failures and spiraling royal household expenditure despite the birth of several royal children. By 1635 the king's improved fiscal position, as stated on the royal "balance sheet," looked something like this:

Item	Credits (£)	Debits (£)
HM Customs & Excise (new taxes), of which £29,000 from import of tobacco and alum	358,000	
Crown lands	90,696	
Duchies of Cornwall and Lancaster	25,735	
Purveyance	30,330	
Wardship (forestry fines)	54,000	
Fines on Catholic recusants	13,000	
Other projects, commissions, and interest from patents	46,618	
Household Expenses*		
Maintenance of king and queen, prince, and other royals		135,000
Pensions		139,099
Wardrobe		26,000
Treasurer of navy		40,000
Royal masques		1,310
Fees to ambassadors, judges, secretaries, officials		179,499
Debt repayments		54,000
Interest		20,000†
Fees		41,628
	618,379	636,536

* This includes the king's and queen's households; payments to the royal children; payments to Charles's sister Elizabeth, queen of Bohemia; and expenses for wardrobe, chamber, jewel house, guard, ordnance, castles and garrisons, keepers of the royal horses (security services), and amenities.
† Interest of £20,000 was a repayment of monies advanced by the international merchant banker Filippo Burlomachi against Henrietta Maria's second half of her dowry (£161,000), which does not appear in these accounts.

The Sancy in Queen Henrietta Maria's crown. Undated drawing by Thomas Cletscher, Dutch court jeweler.

This small deficit at the end of 1635 was transformed into a cash surplus the following spring. In 1636 Charles recovered all the pawned crown jewels, which were brought back to London and housed in the secret jewel house at the Tower of London for safekeeping—rekindling his own, and the nation's, passion for them. The Sancy was remounted into Queen Henrietta Maria's crown, and her perceived power was restored. Charles's decision to redeem the jewels clearly puts their importance above the cash solvency of the crown.

By 1640 all the Jacobean debts had been repaid and the Exchequer showed a tiny surplus for the first time in more than forty years. Despite this fiscal miracle, royal expenses kept soaring, through the royal children's own "requirements" for royal palaces and servants, and Charles's extravagant vision of his own absolute power.

Charles had rashly pawned the crown jewels, and now had to reverse the perception of being a bankrupt king. Gems were the essence of the monarchy for Tudor kings and queens as well as for James, and it remained at the heart of Charles's ability to reign. Although Charles

The Sancy with the Beau Sancy and the Florentine diamonds.
Undated drawing by Thomas Cletscher, Dutch court jeweler.

is not remembered for having bought many jewels, and indeed gave many away and sold others early in his reign, the reinstatement of the crown jewels to the monarchy and their resetting in a more modern fashion were critical to how he considered his personal rule.

Another linchpin to Charles's rule was his flair for collecting art. Despite an impoverished first seven years as king, Charles was to become the greatest patron of the arts who ever sat upon the English throne. The Italian Renaissance had long before spread throughout Europe, but had stalled at the English Channel due to Henry VIII's Reformation. The passionate revival for antiquity in Charles's reign would leave its indelible footprint on the landscape of England. England's own Renaissance man Inigo Jones created much of the classical architecture that survives today in London, such as Whitehall's Banqueting House, the Queen's House, Greenwich, the portico for St. Paul's Cathedral, and the piazza at Covent Garden, to name a few.

Supported by the crown, sculpture, painting, and theater also exploded onto the English cultural landscape. Painters of international renown were brought to England to work. Peter Paul Rubens was commissioned to decorate the ceiling of the royal palace of Whitehall's Banqueting House with canvases glorifying James I. Anthony van Dyck, a pupil of Rubens's, immortalized the royal family through a series of idealized portraits.

But the king's patronage was not entirely philanthropic. It reflected Charles's egocentric vision for his personal rule on canvas, onstage, through jewels, and in stone. Charles's patronage of the arts, combined with the increased grandeur he was to reintroduce into court during these years, became the symbols of his power. He simply wanted to have the grandest court of Europe.

Charles set the trend for what was to become the power currency of all kings. All of his taste and knowledge would be reflected in every room of each palace with paintings, antiques, sculptures, miniatures, and all types of masterpieces. Jewels would adorn the king and queen, and the queen's clothing would have precious jewels sewn on as decorations. All who craved power would need to emulate him.

This is precisely what the aristocracy did. They revitalized English towns, estates, houses, theaters, painting, and sculpture, and literally changed the way the country would look forever. They, too, commissioned fabulous artworks and jewelry and financially backed artists, poets, diarists, and playwrights. The popular theaters of the Globe and the Rose, which had overflowed by popular demand to the plays of Shakespeare and Marlowe under Elizabeth I, were now replicated in the main towns and cities outside of the capital. The great English country house, the most magnificent addition to the landscape, flourished. Their neoclassical designs shook off the heavier (but regarded today as "fairy tale") Elizabethan medieval rooflines sprinkled with chimneys and parapets, for mathematical precision and deliberate restrained order, both inside and out. It was no accident that the adopted architecture of the day should so mirror the king's obsession for order.

But this paradise in which Charles lived with his family was about to self-destruct. The church, as with his predecessors, was at the heart of his troubles. Charles had decided to take what appeared to him as merely another step in consolidating his power base by decreeing that the English Book of Common Prayer (or as Henrietta Maria called it, "that fatal book") be the sole prayer book in the Scottish kirk (church).

At the kirk, the hub of all social as well as religious activity, news was read aloud to a largely illiterate congregation, and gossip was exchanged. It was the coffeehouse of seventeenth-century Scotland. By striking at the fundamental core of Calvinist life there, Charles forced the Scots into an open revolt in July 1637. His decree was condemned by a Calvinist fury of fire and brimstone, with hundreds of thousands of Scots eventually signing the celebrated National Covenant, some in their own blood.

Faced with the first serious challenge to his authority, Charles prepared for war in the summer of 1638. Henrietta Maria added to the boiling religious cauldron by asking her Catholic lords to contribute cash in support of the king's army, inciting a public relations campaign against Charles with her "popish" collusion against the Scots. Henrietta Maria's Catholicism, always barely tolerated, now became an open wound. A truce was agreed when the armies finally faced off at the Scottish border.

Yet within a month, new Scottish demands were made, and Charles knew that he would have to summon Parliament to raise money to put down the Covenanters' rebellion for good. The king had not yet understood that the gamble initiated by Henry VIII to create an invincible aura of power around the crown had failed, and that now it was, according to Lord Weston, "he who had the most money to buy the best army" who would win the day.

Charles made a terse thirty-second demand for money in Parliament. Parliament, led by John Pym, a formidably intelligent, tenacious man possessing an unparalleled knowledge of inscrutable parliamentary procedures, ran rings around the king. No matter how Charles tried, Pym's Parliament remained intractable. So Charles dissolved it.

Public animosity toward the king stirred up Ireland, in a phantom plot allegedly led by the king's close friend the earl of Strafford. While an Irish "threat" was an illusion at this stage, the Scots were camped out on the English border again, and Charles had no money to fight them. Reluctantly, he called his last Parliament in November 1640.

Now the witch hunt began in earnest. Parliament sensed its power and immediately issued an arrest warrant for Charles's friend Strafford, for the plot with the Irish, and he was sent to the Tower of London. Archbishop Laud, who was behind the prayer book debacle, was imprisoned in the Tower, too. By December 1640 the queen was told that she must dismiss the English Catholics in her service. In the midst of this furor, the royal couple's three-year-old daughter, Princess Anne, died.

Henrietta Maria turned to Catholic Europe for help, but it was Protestant Holland that would offer a solution. Frederick Henry, prince of Orange, wished to marry his son Prince William to Charles and Henrietta Maria's eldest daughter, the nine-year-old Princess Mary. This would give the English royal coffers a desperate injection of cash. On May 2, 1641, the wedding took place in a very low-key family affair in the chapel at Whitehall Palace.

A week later, mass hysteria gripped London with wild rumors raging of a French alliance, an invading Spanish army, and even the Irish being on the move. A Bill of Attainder, an obscure law whereby Parliament can convict an accused person of treason, was issued to execute Strafford, but it required Charles's signature. Mobs gathered outside court, baying for blood. After hesitating for forty-eight hours, Charles betrayed his closest ally and signed his friend's death warrant.

By June Parliament had turned its heavy guns onto Queen Henrietta Maria. Her role in urging her Catholic friends to save Strafford from execution and her plan to secure the port of Portsmouth for a royal getaway to France had been reported to Parliament. Henrietta Maria, fearful of being trapped by a mob, wanted to accompany her daughter to Holland. Parliament discovered Henrietta Maria's intention to take all her jewels and plate with her, and Pym urgently petitioned the king to change her mind, stating that he "would make every effort for her security." The king had used the crown jewels once before to raise money to fight a war, and Pym was taking no chances.

Two months later, Henrietta Maria wrote to her sister Christine, queen of Naples, "From the highest point of happiness I have fallen into despair. . . . Imagine what I feel to see the king's power taken from him, the Catholics persecuted, the priests hanged, the people faithful to us sent away and pursued for their lives because they served the king. As for myself, I am kept like a prisoner . . . with no one in the world to whom I can confide my troubles."

But the royal descent into hell was not yet complete. Henrietta Maria wrote to all her Catholic supporters for help, but when Ireland broke out in open rebellion in November 1641, brutally killing and drowning Protestants, Parliament deduced that the queen's entreaties were the cause of the "Irish butchery." The Irish rebellion gave Pym and his supporters the excuse they needed to mount their next campaign against the king, who had just made peace with the Scots.

Pym forced Charles into signing the unprecedented document called the Grand Remonstrance, which was a comprehensive litany of all Parliament's grievances against the crown. It demanded that in the future the king could only employ the services of advisers approved by Parliament. This was a direct assault on Henrietta Maria, who as Charles's most trusted adviser, did not understand that Parliament, the Scots, or the Puritans might have a valid point of view. For Henrietta Maria, the situation could not have been simpler: whoever went against the king's authority was a rogue and a traitor. Charles, fearing that Parliament would attempt to seize the royal family, tried to arrest Pym, but, in Charles's words, "the birds had flown the nest." Fearing for his family's lives, he hastily removed them to safety at Hampton Court, thereby relinquishing control of the capital, and the crown, to Parliament. Charles and Henrietta Maria slept with all their family in the same bed that night, where they agreed that Henrietta Maria must urgently seek help on the Continent.

Henrietta Maria quickly inveigled the prince of Orange's personal envoy to make an official request for Princess Mary to join him in Holland, accompanied by the queen. Charles, of course, agreed. This time Pym made no objection, believing that Charles would be more malleable without his strong-minded wife at his side. But Parliament was unaware that Henrietta Maria was to perform the crucial function in financing the brewing war. As the royal family made its way through London to Greenwich to set sail, the queen and her entourage stopped for a few days at Greenwich Palace. On her way there, the queen made her way to the Secret Jewel House at the Tower, where she collected all her own personal jewels as well as those of the king. It was later reported to Parliament by the Tower guards that she also "made off" with the Sancy, the Mirror of Portugal, and several gold collars set with gems, including one set with rubies and pearls belonging to Henry VIII. She told the Venetian ambassador who had come to pay her a farewell visit at Greenwich that "to settle affairs it would be necessary to unsettle them first"—a clear allusion to her purpose and planned military resistance to Parliament through the pawning or sale of the crown jewels.

When the queen embarked from Greenwich, Charles and she embraced, then wept and clung to each other until Charles finally tore himself away. His intrepid queen carried the hopes of her king and the royalist cause with her—hopes based on raising a foreign army to invade England.

The queen and king had agreed to write one another in code while they were separated, and she reminded him to "take good care, I beg you and put nothing which is not in my cipher. Once again I remind you to take good care of your pocket, and let not your cipher be stolen." Throughout their separation, her letters constantly prodded Charles into action, providing him with money and military solutions, and trying to give him more backbone for the fight ahead.

It was against this background that Henrietta Maria began her crusade to raise money by pawning her own, her husband's, and the crown's jewelry. Whereas the first pawning of the crown jewels was expedient, this time it was a matter of absolute survival for the crown. In May 1642 the prince of Orange took Henrietta to Jews in Amsterdam to lend her money against the jewels. By then a rumor had reached Holland—probably spread by the English Parliament—that the queen had carried off all her jewels and those of the crown against the king's wishes, and only a few merchants were prepared to lend her money until she received a power of attorney signed by Charles.

Most merchants did not believe that she had authority to part with the royal couple's most personal possessions, such as the king's pearl buttons. Still, when the power of attorney arrived, they were only too happy to buy these outright. She wrote to Charles, "You cannot imagine how handsome the buttons were, when they were out of the gold and strung into a chain. . . . I assure you I gave them up with no small regret. Nobody would take them in pledge but only buy them. You may judge now that they know that we want money, how they keep their foot on our throat! I could only get half of what they are worth."

By June Henrietta Maria had managed to send the king his first European weapons financed with blood gems: six cannons, one hundred barrels of gunpowder, and two hundred pistols and rifles just as the king's attempt to secure the weapons store in the northern English city of Hull failed. A month later she had raised thirty thousand guilders from the prince of Orange, one thousand saddles, five hundred rifles, two hundred firelocks, and ten loads of gunpowder. But parliamentary blockades were up, and many of the weapons cargoes bound for England were captured or sunk.

Henrietta Maria struggled on, writing to Charles that "there is nothing in the world, no trouble, which shall hinder me from serving you and loving you above everything in the world. . . . Justice suffers with us. Always take care that we have her on our side: she is a good army."

Still, no matter how she cajoled, no one would touch Henry VIII's great collar, the Mirrors of Portugal and Naples, and especially the Sancy. Henrietta Maria herself had become convinced that there was a malediction on them. By February 1643 she had raised all the monies she could in Holland by the sale of the jewels—except the "cursed" ones—and she resolved to set sail to rejoin her husband in his new royal capital and stronghold at Oxford.

Parliament tried to keep Henrietta Maria from reaching England, and the queen was attacked by parliamentary forces in the Channel. She escaped at the head of her own small but determined mercenary army and marched to join Charles at Oxford. When Parliament heard that king and queen were reunited, Pym gave up all hope of a negotiated peace, as "she may by her influence do considerable mischief in the successful conduct of affairs."

Henrietta Maria's ordeal in support of Charles had lasted fifteen months. Their court at the new capital, Oxford, completely disrupted university life. Scholars were forced to abandon their studies, and many enlisted in the army. Food was stored at the Law and Logic Schools, Magdalen College had become an artillery store, and New College was the ammunition magazine. Military uniforms were stitched by tailors at the Music and Astronomy Schools, and the new royal mint was churning out royal currency at New Inn Hall. All the other colleges were hijacked as accommodations for the court's lords, ladies, and officials, army commanders, royal servants, and hangers-on.

The queen's return was the beginning of a year-long mock resumption of courtly life, including masques, tennis playing, and entertaining dinner parties, with Charles leading sporadic forays against the parliamentary forces under the devil-may-care guidance of his nephew Prince Rupert. Meanwhile, behind the scenes, Henrietta Maria hammered home her message by letter to the new power in charge of France—Cardinal Jules Mazarin, prime minister and godfather to the five-year-old King Louis XIV, who also was Henrietta Maria's nephew. Both Cardinal Richelieu and his lifelong mortal enemy Maria de' Medici had died in 1642, and the power-hungry Italian-born cardinal regent had every intention of building an even greater and more powerful France for his child king than Richelieu had done for Louis XIII. Mazarin saw himself as, and indeed became, the most important power broker of the day. His greed was legendary, and with his power and greed came the imperative need to acquire diamonds.

It is clear from Henrietta Maria's earliest entreaties to Mazarin from Oxford that the plan to possess the Sancy (as well as the other gems sold in Holland) hatched in Mazarin's mind. These plans, however, were left to simmer while he consolidated his political position. Mazarin reasoned that as long as the parliamentarians controlled the navy and London, which were the country's nerve centers of power and trade, France would side with Parliament.

In December 1644 Henrietta Maria knew that she was again pregnant and could no longer take as active a role as adviser until her child was born. Her mental attitude became phobic, fearing an attack by "the mobs," and she wanted to flee Oxford when Charles left for battles in the north. The queen still possessed the "cursed" jewels, including, of course, the Sancy, and focused on their various maledictions, worrying excessively about her own health and that of her unborn child.

On April 17, 1645, she finally fled Oxford and headed south "to safety in France." But the queen was forced to stop at Exeter when she fell ill. Parliament agreed to allow her doctor to go to her from London. They could not afford a rise in public sympathy for the queen, should she die or lose her baby due to their callousness. Nonetheless, Parliament and Mazarin hoped that she would die: the English queen now represented the greatest political threat to both countries. She hardened Charles's will for absolute power. If she fled to France, where Mazarin would be forced to grant her asylum, she would wreak havoc with the aristocracy in support of her husband.

Henrietta Maria's baby girl was born on June 16, but the queen's health worsened, with Henrietta Maria complaining of "a paralysis of the legs and a constriction around the heart." In response to her doctor's pleas for help, Parliament made the threatening reply "the air of London would be healthy for Her Majesty" (implicitly suggesting a sojourn in the city's infamous Tower), leading Henrietta back to her phobia of being "shut up in a siege." Two days later—paralysis or not—she set out for the Cornwall port of Falmouth with what remained of the jewels and plate. There, on July 9, she wrote her final farewell to Charles: "I am giving you the strongest proof of love that I can give: I am hazarding my life that I may not incommode your affairs. Adieu, my dear heart. If I die, believe that you are losing a person who has never been other than entirely yours."

Henrietta Maria set sail with the Flemish fleet, and despite being fired on with "a hundred cannon shot," only one hit was successful. It was reported to Parliament that she had "no other courtesy from England but cannonballs to convey her to France." Henrietta Maria, queen of England, reached the shores of Brittany by climbing up over rocks onto a steep cliff, more reminiscent of a windswept romantic heroine than royalty of the time.

Cardinal Mazarin's worst nightmare was about to begin, but as a consummate plotter, he had prepared for this moment.

18

The Exiled Queen and the Cardinal Thief

1645–1649

THE BEDRAGGLED QUEEN OF ENGLAND reached sanctuary at her nephew's court in Paris two weeks later. The French royal family, led by Anne of Austria, Louis XIII's widow and the queen regent, showed the pitiable and frail Henrietta Maria great affection and gave her royal apartments at the Louvre. These would be her home for the next eight years.

As soon as she had recovered her health, Henrietta Maria resolved to continue to broker jewels for arms on behalf of her husband, and her first call was on the ubiquitous Mazarin. She had escaped to France with the Sancy and the Mirror of Portugal as well as Henry VIII's great collar, but was loath to pledge them for arms. Surely Mazarin would see her dire situation and help the English royal family, who was related by blood to France. But Mazarin politely abstained from any involvement. Henrietta Maria had failed to appreciate that England's civil war gave a green light to France—and thereby Mazarin—to act unimpeded in its own European ambitions. Mazarin told the English queen, "France itself did not have a single soldier to spare," but hinted that the duke of Lorraine may have an entire army for hire. He was setting a Machiavellian trap for Henrietta Maria, since

Lorraine had promised his army to Spain. If she succeeded, Mazarin would have neutralized Lorraine and Spain at a stroke. If she failed, England would be sidelined in its civil war, and France would still have free rein on the Continent.

Henrietta Maria also had not bargained on Charles's long-standing enemy the defender of the fens and early opponent of the king's policy to drain them, Oliver Cromwell. In 1645 the evangelical Cromwell created the elite crack military force (trained, promptly paid, and uniformed) called the New Model Army. It was born out of the same religious fervor that has inspired soldiers from the time of the Crusades through to the Taliban. Charles had made a mortal enemy in Cromwell, who believed the king to be the embodiment of all that was evil in England. The king believed absolutely that his personal power *was* England when, in fact, the notion of the nation-state had emerged in the hearts and minds of his people, and they were demanding their say in the country's affairs.

Then disaster *really* struck. Not only had Charles and Rupert been disastrously defeated at Naseby in June 1645, with one thousand royalist troops killed and four thousand to five thousand prisoners taken, but also Charles's and Henrietta's letters and their codebook were seized with the king's lost baggage on the battlefield. It revealed all their plots and plans since 1643. A month later, Parliament published these under the title *The King's Cabinet Opened*, providing conclusive proof against the crown of foreign plots with papist Ireland and France.

On April 27, after spending the evening in front of a well-stoked hearth burning incriminating documents, Charles stole away from Oxford in the middle of the night. Two days later he surrendered to the Scots in the hope that he could cut a deal with them. In June the prince of Wales escaped to France and was granted asylum by a reluctant Mazarin. Four other royal children—the duke of Gloucester, the duke of York, Princess Elizabeth, and baby Princess Henriette—were all under house arrest in England. In January 1647, when the Scots could not agree on terms of settlement with the intransigent Charles, he was handed over to Parliament for £400,000 ($55.4 million or £34.6 million today) in ransom money. Charles said it was "cheap at the price." When the king refused to sign the army's proposals for his reinstatement—for now Cromwell's Puritan army effectively ruled Parliament—Charles officially became their prisoner.

Henrietta Maria tried to have Charles rescued by the pope; the Irish; the prince of Orange; and Anne of Austria, who naturally referred her sister-in-law to Mazarin. All attempts failed. Her only hope remained that Parliament and the various army factions might fall out with one another, leading to Charles's reinstatement.

By June 1648 the queen was treated by everyone as an evangelical fund-raiser whose letters or visits were received with dread. She was constantly complaining about her extreme poverty, claiming, "I had not another piece of gold or coin" other than a gold drinking cup. This was not exactly true. Henrietta Maria still possessed Henry VIII's great collar, the Sancy, and the Mirror of Portugal, all of which she steadfastly refused to sell to Mazarin at a drastically reduced price. Once those pieces went under the hammer, she would have nothing left with which to bargain.

Cromwell multiplied his victories while Henrietta Maria was embroiled in Mazarin's snare, believing the duke of Lorraine would deliver ten thousand mercenary troops to England for the fight. The prince of Orange now ignored her pleas for ships to carry them as well as three thousand more soldiers. The heir to the throne, Charles, prince of Wales, and two of his siblings along with Henrietta Maria tried to broker a marriage between them and any nation that might give succor to Charles.

In desperation, she turned to Mazarin, who advised that should she find troops, they could not set sail from any French port. Charles, in the meantime, had secretly negotiated with the Irish. Both king and queen ignored the fact that the English would view their activities as treasonable acts leading to foreign invasion. The sole concern of the royal couple was money for mercenaries and arms, and they would get it by fair means or foul.

Mazarin tightened his grip around Henrietta Maria's slender throat by loaning her cash for her subsistence at court for herself and her children, while steadfastly refusing to help with armaments. His constant denial to the queen is extraordinary, since he had been making a vast fortune in arms trafficking since 1642, and regularly traded in gunpowder, cannons, copper, and lead. In fact, Mazarin was personally profiting from any military action—including France's arms sales—as an intermediary between merchants and governments, adding his hefty commissions on the sale of all components in Europe's seventeenth-century war machine. A small testament to his arms dealing was found on his death in 1661, when some six thousand rusted swords and armaments were discovered at the home of one of his banking henchmen, Cenami, in Lyon.

But how had Mazarin risen to such absolute control? When he arrived in France in 1639 as the unknown diplomat Guilio Mazzarini on behalf of Pope Urban VIII, he had caught the eye of Louis XIII's minister Cardinal Richelieu. Mazarin was a hungry thirty-seven-year-old diplomat with a burning ambition, and still unknown in the prime of his life. Richelieu spotted his talent as a negotiator and admired his thirst for power. He schooled Mazarin as his protégé, making him a cardinal in 1641. Mazarin's rapid elevation as a prince of the church is even more incredible when we consider that he had never been a priest.

On Richelieu's death in 1642, the architect of Louis XIII's France was purported to have said with his dying breath, "I believe I have acquitted myself of all my good work due to your Majesty in leaving you Mazarin." Richelieu had acted as the invisible hand of God and loathsome screen between king and country. Mazarin's rule would prove even more unpopular during the reign of the infant Louis XIV.

But what gave Mazarin his ultimate power was the well-oiled machine that fed his greed. His agents, in place since 1641, were mainly Italians from Lucca and included the king's banker, Thomas Cantarini; Cantarini's brother-in-law Pierre Serantoni; and Vincent Cenami. Barthélemy Hervart, originally from Augsburg, would join the group a few years later and would take up a position in the administration of the crown's finances. These men literally held the fortunes of France in their hands. Catarini, for example, "invested" 31 million livres ($242.7 million or £151.7 million today) of crown money between 1643 and 1648. During this same period Mazarin held two accounts with the Cantarini family: one in his name, the other in the name of Abbé Mondin, the man in charge of Mazarin's illicit transactions.

As long as Anne of Austria remained Mazarin's supporter, there was no other royal authority to check his power. The cardinal pandered to the queen regent, and allayed any fears his cohorts may have had while they collectively raped not only France of her riches, but much of the Continent as well. The cardinal was entirely free to begin his personal quest of making himself the wealthiest man in Europe. His political quest—to put an end to rivalry among the Catholic nations of Europe—was well under way, too. And now the queen of England had become critical to that plan.

Henrietta Maria had possessions of tremendous value—unrivaled beauty, and power that the cardinal wanted—and unwittingly had become a hapless fly in the spiderweb of Mazarin's design. The cardinal was holding out hope, and dashing it, for a purpose—the Mirror of Portugal and the Sancy. Yet the more he intimated that he would be able to help Henrietta Maria by the purchase of the diamonds, the more the intrepid queen dug in her heels.

He *needed* these most important gems. It was integral to his self-image as a voracious diamond-lover and collector of all things of great beauty. He wanted to be the man who restored peace to Christendom while wearing the largest white diamond in Europe. The parallels in his personal Christian goals and his political ones are easy to see. Diamonds still represented invincibility and power, and he simply would not have second best. They also represented the most readily transportable form of wealth—and for the scheming cardinal, one that might well come in handy.

Mazarin's thirst for diamonds and other personal wealth was covered up in Byzantine transactions, with ownership being, at the best of times, a moving feast. Sometimes jewels were means to an end—as in the case of the pearl necklace he bought for Henrietta Maria's daughter Mary, princess of Orange, in his manipulation of her mother.

The diamonds he bought in the name of Anne of Austria were another case in point. Between 1641 and 1648, when La Fronde (a bloody civil war brought on by Mazarin's and the royal family's excesses) broke out, the cardinal had already acquired 714,868 livres ($1.8 billion or £1.1 billion today) in gems. He claimed that half that amount was spent on jewels for Anne of Austria or other royal houses of Europe. The other half, naturally, were for Mazarin himself. This does not explain, however, how two diamond crosses—the smaller one belonging to Anne of Austria—had been in the cardinal's private collection at the time his Paris palace was raided. His own larger cross was valued at 120,000 livres ($294.2 million or £183.9 million today) and was only one of thousands of pieces of jewelry commissioned by the cardinal. When the parliamentary representatives put both pieces in pawn to feed the nation, Mazarin was openly accused of trafficking in diamonds and other gemstones.

While Henrietta Maria had flailed around France and Holland looking for salvation for her beloved Charles, Mazarin was buying huge quantities of diamonds in Portugal from 1647 to 1648 through Abbé Mondin. The abbé had been in charge of the purchase of precious stones for the court of Savoy and was a gifted amateur in the selection of good stones. He also knew how to launder money, and was an essential player in the cardinal's criminal network. In addition, the abbé lent his name to several false bank accounts for Mazarin, and held a secret account for the cardinal at Cantarini's bank that Parlement investigated during La Fronde.

But before the civil war would take hold, Mazarin would have nearly two years in which to garner wealth beyond even his most extravagant imaginings. Mazarin wrote to Mondin about his diamond purchases:

> There is a large quantity of diamonds in Lisbon that you must absolutely acquire. . . . Be careful to keep the purchase secret. . . . But especially, you mustn't lose any time to send for more money should you need it, you and Mr. Cantarini only know of this and you two alone can keep others from gaining the slightest knowledge of this purchase. . . . It would be good if you could apply yourself to purchase the largest stones rather than things of little value.

Once Mondin purchased the rough stones, they were brought back to France (without duty paid or importation license granted), where they were cut and polished by Italian artisans. The stones would then be sold or reexported via Antwerp or Amsterdam. The profits from these operations were astronomical.

Whether Henrietta Maria knew about Mazarin's trafficking in gems we do not know, but we do know that by March 1648, the queen had no other alternative but to pawn both the Mirror of Portugal and the Sancy to Mazarin's cohort Bernard de Nogaret, the second duke d'Epérnon (1592–1661), who would soon be exiled in England. With the funds advanced by Epérnon, Henrietta Maria remitted 36,000 crowns to Charles. The queen had nothing left to give, but Charles still saw fit to rebuke her for the money "as assistance that is little enough." Then again, anything short of a national treasury and a full-blown military miracle would have been too little.

La Fronde was in full flow at the end of 1648. The state was effectively bankrupt—owing more than 100 million livres to Mazarin's banker friends, largely for the Thirty Years' War—with civil servants remaining unpaid, tenants ruined, and food in short supply. In Parlement, the advocate-general, Omer Talon, declared to the queen regent:

> It is ten years since the countryside is ruined, peasants are reduced to sleeping on straw, their furniture being sold to meet a taxation that they could never satisfy, and for these poor people to hear of the luxury of Paris, these millions of innocent souls obliged to live on a cupful of oats and who have no other protection than their powerlessness. These unfortunates possess only the goodness of their souls, since it is the one thing they cannot sell.

The dissipation of the nation's finances was remarkable. Jean-Baptiste Colbert, the cardinal's own personal assistant and able administrator, was called upon by Parlement to investigate how Mazarin had the means to buy himself a palace in Rome and build another one in Paris, where he housed a fabulous collection of tapestries, paintings, books, manuscripts, and precious objects of all sorts. But the Italian cardinal resisted xenophobic cries for his head, and thought he could ride out the wave of public anger.

Among Mazarin's collection were a huge number of paintings and tapestries collected by Queen Henrietta Maria and King Charles. During Henrietta Maria's first Continental trip to raise arms, men, and money for royalist England, Oliver Cromwell had ordered the king's collection seized from all the royal palaces and sold for the good of the nation. Of the 1,910 paintings and sculptures sold—mostly by masters like Titian, Rubens, da Vinci, Michelangelo, Van Dyck, Correggio, Breughel, Holbein, Tintoretto, and Raphael—Mazarin had amassed a staggering number. Each time Henrietta Maria went to Mazarin's

home to plead for money or arms, she would wince in shame on seeing her former wealth hanging from the cardinal's walls.

Henrietta Maria now knew that her cause was utterly hopeless. By
New Year's Day 1649, Cromwell had successfully run roughshod over
his opponents in Parliament, excluding all but fifty-six survivors who
became known as the Rump. These survivors passed an illegal ordi-
nance into law for the "Trial of Charles Stuart the Now King of
England and Man of Blood." For the first and only time, Charles
answered a public gathering without a stammer in response to these
charges when he said, "Remember I am your king, your lawful king.
. . . I am not betraying it to answer to a new unlawful authority. Therefore resolve me that you shall hear no more of me."

His eloquence came as a shock and exposed the proceedings for
the sham they were, and the members of the Rump began to waver.
Charles was taken away from the first trial amid cries of "God save
the King." At his second trial Charles again replied that Parliament
was making laws illegally and that he would not reply to the charges.
It took Cromwell two more attempts to bully his parliamentarians into
submission before he finally succeeded in obtaining the guilty verdict
he was confident God had preordained. These four trials took just one
week, and Charles was impeached as a "tyrant traitor murderer and
implacable enemy of the Commonwealth of England."

On January 29, 1649, Charles bade a heartrending good-bye to his
imprisoned children Princess Elizabeth and Henry, duke of Gloucester. In Elizabeth's words set down immediately afterward, she wrote:

> He wished me not to grieve and torment myself for him, for that it
> would be a glorious death and that he should die. . . . He told me
> that he had forgiven all his enemies and hoped God would forgive
> them also, and commanded us, and all the rest of my brothers and
> sisters to forgive them. He bid me to tell my mother that his thoughts
> had never strayed from her, and that his love should be the same to
> the last.

As she wept, Charles added, "Sweetheart, you'll forget this." He
then reminded Henry never to agree to become king, because it would
spell the death of his two elder brothers, Charles and James, and to

always remain a good Protestant. Charles then gave his two children the last of his personal jewelry.

The following day, Charles I mounted the scaffold in front of Banqueting House wearing two shirts so that he would not shiver from the cold and the crowd would think he was cowardly. His final act was to give the last of his crown jewels to Bishop Jackson, the royal diamond signet ring Insignia of the Garter, eloquently and simply saying, "Remember." He bravely put his head upon the block and made the sign for the executioner that he was ready. The king's head was severed with one blow, and England slid into eleven years of uneasy commonwealth under the dictatorial Cromwell—the only interregnum in its history.

Cromwell, wishing to eradicate the king from the national memory and the crown jewels and their perceived power from its psyche, ordered all the remaining crown jewels sold, with the gemstones stripped from their settings and gold plate melted down. If Henrietta Maria had not stolen the Sancy diamond, its history probably would have ended there.

19

Mazarin: Corrupted by Absolute Power

1650–1661

MAZARIN RESPONDED TO THE EXECUTION of King Charles with restrained horror. Henrietta Maria, now a broken woman, displayed none of her former dramatics and barely reacted at first, as if disbelieving the monstrous news. When the heinous crime sank in, she sobbed for weeks on end, and feared for her four children, who were still "prisoners" of Parliament. Mazarin inevitably played the game well: he broke off diplomatic ties with the barbaric English and agreed more readily to give assistance to the English queen, who, in a near-catatonic state, no longer felt the need.

The investigations initiated by the judicial oligarchy against the cardinal had begun in earnest, and picked up pace, with much of the nobility joining in. The cardinal's absolute power over Anne of Austria and the young king were feared by all, just as his Machiavellian ability to foresee and forestall events were admired by many of his foes. Charges were being prepared against Mazarin, yet he still believed himself to be above the law and "invincible." Like Saddam Hussein in the face of the coalition forces, Mazarin thought that something would turn up—someone would save him. In the end, in the foggy, small hours of the night of February 6, 1651, Mazarin fled into exile, leaving behind a wealth of documents including "combinations" with his bankers and a paper trail that Colbert could follow.

From his exile at Saint-Germain-en-Laye, the disgraced cardinal continued his arms and gem trafficking. While he was busying himself with new acquisitions, the Frondeurs stormed the Palais Mazarin with a parliamentary order and confiscated some 800,000 livres in fine furniture. An inventory was made titled "The Inventory of the Wonders of the World Seen in the Palace of Cardinal Mazarin." It described a scene where:

> There are shamefully nude statues . . . rare cabinets of ornate ebony . . . marble tables with carved marble flowers . . . a large room dedicated to antiquities . . . tortoiseshell cabinets . . . marble tables sculpted in the form of birds . . . an ivory bed . . . a chair, that when you sit in it, rises and falls when you pull on a cord . . . let's escape this House, fear its contents. Its passion suffocates our hearts and curiosity. We do not want to consider its riches in other than a treasure of misery, since its rarities have been bought with tainted gold and the fear of the people.

The poor of Paris could hardly understand such treasures, and they rose in rebellion. The barricades for which Paris is so famous were thrown up, and the witch hunt against the cardinal was on. Paris was in a feeding frenzy, littered with pamphlets called Mazarinades accusing the cardinal of tremendous avarice, unbridled abuse of power, and even of a secret marriage to his devoted servant Anne of Austria.

Mazarin feigned indifference, but according to his old friend Madame de Motteville, "It pains him greatly, since he loved all that he owned and particularly that which had been brought into his home from foreign lands. . . . This loss simply means that his enemies will be placated with their gains."

Madame de Motteville was right. The pillaging of Mazarin's residence led to a calming of the frenzy for the cardinal's blood, and within a year he was able to return to Paris. What was not publicly known at the time was that the cardinal and his network of bankers had hidden most of his diamonds and jewelry and all of his precious gold and silver plate, valued at some 900,000 livres ($1.9 billion or

£1.2 billion today). Cantarini and Abbé Mondin alone had "bought" precious objects for 212,950 livres, among which was the jeweled clock of Maria de' Medici. This "purchase" reverted back to the cardinal at the precise moment when Mazarin's fortunes miraculously turned.

So while the Frondeurs did their worst in Paris, those loyal to the cardinal not only helped him to hide his treasures but also actively worked to bring him new acquisitions. Jobart, another of Mazarin's business agents, delivered between May and December 1651 some four packets of diamonds via four different couriers. These were smaller "untraceable" stones, not the larger, notable ones that Mazarin had requested from Mondin three years earlier, in Lisbon. All receipts were put into the Cantarini account in the name of Mondin. The cardinal had become a merchant banker rather than a prince of the Catholic Church—and a savvy merchant banker at that.

Little by little, a picture emerged. From 1643 to 1647, Cantarini made nine loans to the young King Louis XIV. Cantarini's associate Mazarin obtained 50 percent of the profits from the transactions, which on Mazarin's death in 1661 showed that the king had been overcharged interest by 6,222 livres ($13.3 million or £8.3 million today). Some 129,305 livres in principal had been overpaid as well, and Parlement demanded restitution. Mazarin's other merchant banker, Barthélemy Hervart, also overcharged the royal purse between 1647 and 1659 by some 271,662 livres ($582.7 million or £364.2 million today).

In 1651 Colbert had a list of the cardinal's receivables compiled, showing an astronomical income—larger than that of the king (amounts in livres):

Pension of the cardinal (1641)	18,000
Appointments as counsel (1642)	6,000
Appointment as minister (1643)	20,000
Extraordinary pension (1643)	100,000
Exceptional gratuities (1639)	50,000
Superintendence of the queen's household	60,000
Superintendence of buildings (1643)	50,000
Concierge of Fontainebleau (1643)	55,000
Company of the north (1645)	30,666
Government of Auvergne (1647)	50,000

Profits from annexed domains	
In Franche Comte (1645)	100,000
From the sea (1645)	200,000
Stipend from the regiments (1642)	46,000
Auch pension	34,000
"King's rights" (1650)	20,000
Extraordinary "affairs"	
Rentals of houses and shops in Paris	12,000
Ecclesiastical benefits (1648)	200,000
Total	1,037,666

None of the cardinal's illicit income from arms trafficking, commodities trading, precious stones trafficking, art and luxury goods trading, interest due on loans, funds earned outside of France, sales of offices, and his governing in La Rochelle, Brouage, Ré, Oléron, Dunkerque, Bergues, Mardick, Toulon, or as superintendent of the education for the house of the duke of Anjou, is included in the above schedule. The best estimates are that the illicit income outstripped his legal income by more than double.

From the moment the cardinal reentered Paris after his first exile, he set about reacquiring his original riches that had been looted by the Frondeurs. Many of these vagabond precious objects were brought back from Spain, Holland, Germany, or Sweden. Those who had taken advantage of his dire circumstances were tracked down and treated without pity. Mazarin demanded full restitution from Parlement for the sacking of his palace and personal treasures—and got it. In 1655 Colbert wrote to the cardinal that there was a 12,000-livre shortfall in his compensation. It was decided that in the name of the king, this sum should be taken from the young son and heir of one of the commissioners responsible for the sale of his pillaged treasures, leaving the boy penniless.

Yet even before Paris had become safe again for His Eminence, he was instructing his minions to grab whatever they could from the executed king of England's collection, now being auctioned by England's republican Parliament. It represented a unique opportunity for Mazarin. After all, Charles's collection was reputed to be the finest and largest in Europe.

So diplomatic relations were resumed in 1653, and an ambassador, Antoine de Bordeaux, was sent to London to obtain whatever he could from the collection that had been gathered at Henrietta Maria's home, Somerset House. Daily missives were exchanged, and the cardinal ended up with a fabulous number of Van Dycks, Correggios, Titians, and Tintorettos. Most of the Flemish tapestries acquired dated back to Henry VIII's reign, and were the finest ever made. In all, by the time of Mazarin's final inventory in 1661, he owned sixteen hundred tapestries. Mazarin counseled parsimony in these acquisitions, but in de Bordeaux's letter of April 3, 1653, he makes it clear that "there is no appearance of finding anything here cheaply, if they are to be selling the Queen's furniture, as they say, at any moment."

With literally thousands of pieces of art and furniture to finance, good money still needed to be made to feed the cardinal's lust for luxury. The cardinal supplemented his substantial income by lending money to the French royal family—often confusing their funds with his own or the nation's, as well as accommodating other royals bereft of friends and money. Loans made to the French crown had the added benefit of acting as buffers for the consortium against inflation and the vagaries of international exchange, giving Mazarin and his cronies a hedge against monetary devaluation, with a sovereign guarantee from none other than Louis XIV.

Hedging international exchange rates had become a concern for the cardinal and his men as well, and de Bordeaux wrote excitedly to Mazarin in October 1653 from London that:

> I have been advised by some bankers how one could manage the exchange rate which today is 54 percent, no one wishing to conduct business with France [due to the Fronde], for fear of a rupture. They are advising me to bring here silver Louis' or Reals from Mexico where the exchange against sterling will only cost us 10 percent, and better still, if we could send silver ingots from Saint-Malo, stamped from 1580, the profit would be 15 percent at least.

The cardinal and the king's bankers had made a fine art of profiting from the misery of the nation in the hands of an adolescent king, just as they had done against the exiled queen of England and her children. By the time of his exile, Mazarin had loaned, or arranged to have loaned, to Henrietta Maria some 427,566 livres at 5 percent interest, compounded yearly. Henrietta Maria's pawning of the Sancy and her other jewels still meant that Mazarin could not get his hands on them to call his own. He pressed her to sell the gems to him in forgiveness of her debts, but she refused. Mazarin had become to Henrietta Maria the same kind of enemy that Richelieu had been to her mother.

Instead, on September 16, 1656, the aged Henrietta Maria sent a letter to her son Charles, now king of Scotland, attesting to the vast debt she owed the cardinal, Cantarini, and Serantori, and begging him to somehow repay it on her behalf:

> I, Henrietta Maria, by the grace of God, Queen of Great Britain, declare and certify to the King, Our honor to you as our son and Sovereign that our dear cousin, the Cardinal Mazarini, has procured payment and put into our hands at different times for the benefit of the dead King of our glorious memory by the bourgeois bankers of Paris, Cantarini and Serantori, the sum of five hundred ninety-seven thousand four hundred sixteen livres and thirteen sous and four deniers between 1643 and 1645, and again in 1648 and 1649. All of this money was employed to help us in our most urgent affairs. We beseech you, Our Sovereign and son, to give to our cousin the Cardinal Mazarini the recognition of this sum and the promise of your obligation and willingness to pay our cousin.

But Charles had his own problems. Scotland remained a poor nation, entrenched in its Presbyterian Calvinist principles, and having invited Charles Stuart back into the country as its king, was uncertain how to treat him. England remained a republic without monarch under Cromwell, the Lord Protector, and Charles was consumed with the hope of reclaiming his English crown. His mother's debts would simply have to wait.

When Charles declined to assist his mother "regrettably for the time being," Mazarin saw his moment. Either Henrietta Maria would sign over the Sancy and the Mirror of Portugal against her debts, or she would be forced to leave France. Henrietta Maria at last relented, but not without attempting to save face. She refused categorically to sell the Sancy and the Mirror to Mazarin directly. Instead, on May 19, 1657, a convoluted transaction between Duke d'Epernon and Barthélemy Hervart took place wherein the amount for the jewels in pawn was repaid to d'Epernon by Hervart, who in turn sold them to Mazarin. In a parallel transaction, Hervart:

> Not having any rights to the said diamonds, nor any rights to the three hundred sixty thousand livres for which the retrieved diamonds were purchased, agrees to sell the said diamonds for the specified sum to Monseigneur His Eminence Jules cardinal Mazarini, who has put the said diamonds in the hands of Monsieur Jean-Baptiste Colbert, who advanced the payment to the dame queen.

Still, this was not the end of the affair. While Mazarin had "purchased" the diamonds from his minion Epernon, the English republican Parliament naturally refused to honor the debts of the dethroned queen. Then, on February 21, 1660, the members of Parliament who had been purged by Cromwell and his army in 1648 were at last allowed to take their elected seats. Mazarin, on hearing the news, knew that it would be only days before Charles would be invited back to take his place upon the English throne. On March 5, 1660, Mazarin wrote to Charles's trusted adviser Lord Jermyn:

> The Letter Patent that Milord Jermyn brought to have signed by the King of England concerns the debt of 597,416 livres 13 sous 4 deniers of which 396,000 livres is in principal and 201,416 livres 13 sous and 4 deniers in interest (at 5 percent) was proposed to have been repaid by the end of December 1656. According to the clauses in the original agreement, payments should have been made to reduce the payments from the total of the 396,000 livres in principal.
>   But her Majesty is finding difficulties to employ this clause of the agreement. It follows at least that we must adjust the total sum of her indebtedness from 396,000 livres from the first of January 1657 until the signature of the declaration which follows in the end from the person of Marie [Henrietta Maria], which investment for three years and three months since its expiry means that there is an additional interest due of 84,150 livres which brings the total now

due to 597,416 livres 13 sous 4 deniers. The total due from her now
stands at 661,566 [sic] livres 13 sous 4 deniers in this new declaration to be recovered in its entirety on the last of March 1660. . . .
It suffices to read the accounts and observe.

The letter is signed "M" with the distinctive sweep in Mazarin's
hand. The accounts that Mazarin enclosed demonstrate his penchant
for confusing the "king's accounts" with his own, since all sums paid
for Henrietta's upkeep were costs to the French crown. The sums paid
by Cantarini were naturally from the cardinal.

Interest at 5 percent since 1st July 1643, until 31st Dec 1656, 13 years at ½
33,750 ℓ

Mémoire [IOU] for that which has been paid to the Queen of England these last years by her order of the year 1643.
In 1643 in the month of June it was paid to M. de Montaigne for the Queen of England employed one Cantarini.
50,000 ℓ

And was paid by the same Cantarini on the order of Her Majesty according to her receipt in the date of 25 August 1645
100,000 ℓ

Interest since the 1st Sept 1645, until last of December 1656, for 11 years, 4 months
56,666 ℓ 13s 4d

And was paid by the said Cantarini, on the same order of Her Majesty, following her receipt dated 14th October 1645
100,000 ℓ

Interest from first July 1648 until the last December 1656, for 8 years, and ½
42,500 ℓ

And was provided in letters of change paid in Amsterdam by Cantarini to S. Webster for the Queen of England, by the same Cantarini for her Majesty. Employed in her books in the months of July and August 1648
111,000 ℓ

Interest for 7 years
12,250 ℓ

Paid to Milord Jermyn for the voyage of the Marquise d'Ormont in February 1649
35,000 ℓ

Total 396 000 ℓ

Total interest   201,416 ℓ 13s 4d
Principal   396,000 ℓ
Total due   596,416 ℓ [sic] 13s 4d [$1.3 billion or £799.7 million today]

Charles was still in Brussels when he received Mazarin's accounts, and promptly wrote back on March 20 that he would repay 64,150 ℓ as the sum due plus interest to the cardinal, since it was borrowed "for the affairs of the dead King our honored Father of happy memory, and we recognize our duty, and permit for the above mentioned sum to be paid to our dear cousin."

As Charles's reply was unclear, Mazarin shot off another missive, demanding payment in full, to which the king responded hurriedly from Cologne that he would comply. Two months later, on May 29, 1660, King Charles II rode into the City of London in a spectacular procession with a dozen gilded coaches escorted by horsemen wearing silver doublets; a thousand soldiers; City sheriffs in gold lace; and trumpeters in cloth of gold trimmed with black velvet. Republican England was at an end.

One of Charles's first acts was to try to retrieve the dispersed collection—including the royal crown jewels—from the Continent. He naturally corresponded with Mazarin for the return of paintings, furniture, horses, and jewels, and would have particularly welcomed the return of the Sancy and the Mirror of Portugal. Mazarin declined the request.

In an odd way, we must be thankful to the cardinal for his obstinacy—of the 1,100 paintings Charles succeeded in repurchasing, all those in the Palace of Whitehall were destroyed in the Great Fire of London of 1661: 3 paintings by Leonardo, 3 Raphaels, 12 by Romain, 6 by Correggio, 18 by Titian, 27 by Holbein, 13 by Van Dyck, and 14 by William van de Velde went up in flames along with the palace itself.

There is no doubt that the cardinal was ecstatic with his acquisition of the Sancy. At last, after nearly twenty years of intrigue, he owned this exceptional and historic diamond as well as the Mirror of Portugal. For him they were the ultimate representations of his power, works of art, and far better security than the king's lands in the event of his needing to go into exile for a third time.

He had mastered the fine art of taking advantage of the indebtedness of the aristocracy and kings, and had survived the first pillaging of his phenomenal collection. When these unfortunates would pawn their valuables with the cardinal, he would allow them to inflate the value: "5 percent on 400,000 is worth far more than 5 perent on 100,000," Colbert advised.

In 1661, a year after making his demand to King Charles II, both Mazarin and Queen Henrietta Maria died. On the cardinal's death, Louis XIV accorded him a full state funeral, with a magnificent service at the Cathedral of Notre-Dame in Paris. The king himself wore mourning in honor of his godfather and mentor, and was said to have felt the loss tremendously.

An inventory was taken of Mazarin's treasures on Thursday, March 31: there were 877 paintings; 37 additional paintings excluded from the inventory; thousands of precious stones, particularly diamonds; fine furniture; sculptures; hundreds of tapestries; and more than 100,000 books and manuscripts. To help understand the vastness of this collection, today, an average museum holds only 2,500 paintings, and most municipal libraries would be hard pressed to have as many books. Mazarin had helped to make the diamond the "prince of gems." He had 50 gold enamel rings studded with diamonds, rubies, or sapphires in their settings, and several pairs of diamond earrings that he wore. He was particularly fond of the table-cut diamond, but also had several more "modern" cuts, such as the 32-facet double-sided diamond, which was baptized the "Mazarin" in homage to the cardinal.

Mazarin's heirs—his nieces for the most part—sold their inheritance to Louis XIV, who, not wishing to be accused of taking advantage of widows and orphans, paid above the inventory valuation.

The cardinal's will provided for a bequest to the crown of France: "His Eminence's intention was to gather together eighteen of the most beautiful large diamonds that exist in Europe. Having succeeded in this end, the aforementioned Seigneur gives and bequeaths them to the crown, having His Majesty's approval; they are to be called the eighteen Mazarins."

These eighteen diamonds were worth more than all of the other crown jewels of France put together. The first of the eighteen Mazarins was, of course, the Sancy. The second Mazarin was formerly the Pindar. The Mirror of Portugal was the third Mazarin. The fourth Mazarin, like the fifth and sixth diamonds, had no previous name; the fourth was a heart-shaped, rose-cut diamond weighing 24.92 carats.

The fifth Mazarin was nearly the same size and was cut as a double-rose drop, weighing 23 carats. The sixth Mazarin also was a double-rose drop diamond, weighing 20.26 carats. The seventh Mazarin, also named the Great Mazarin, and currently owned by the jewelers Boucheron, was a 21.6-carat square table-cut stone. The eighth Mazarin also was a square table-cut stone weighing 18.75 carats, and was sold to Boucheron from the crown jewel collection in 1887. The ninth Mazarin was a faceted marquise-cut stone weighing 15.67 carats. The tenth, eleventh, twelfth, and thirteenth Mazarins were all square table-cut stones and weighed 17.46 carats, 18.23 carats, 17.46 carats, and 13.36 carats, respectively. The fourteenth Mazarin was recut as a long, oval, brilliant stone by 1791 and weighed only 8.67 carats. The fifteenth Mazarin suffered the same fate, weighing a mere 8.7 carats in its new shape as a square brilliant stone. The sixteenth Mazarin, originally a 9-carat square table-cut diamond, was recut by 1791 and weighed 6.16 carats. The seventeenth Mazarin as well as the eighteenth Mazarin have been conserved at the Louvre since 1887, the first being a flat, heart-shaped 21.96-carat stone; the second, also a flat, heart-shaped stone, weighs 22.09 carats.

The cardinal also bequeathed a bouquet of fifty diamonds to Louis XIV's wife, Queen Marie-Thérèse, and the Rose of England, a 25-carat diamond also gleaned from Henrietta Maria, for Anne of Austria.

By 1661 Louis XIV was well on the way to becoming the "Sun King"—France's most brilliant monarch. His love for absolute power and extravagance had been instilled in him by his godfather and mentor Cardinal Mazarin, and Louis would, in no time at all, surpass the cardinal in both.

20

A Mere Bauble in the Sun King's Crown

1661–1710

LOUIS XIV, LIKE QUEEN ELIZABETH, is well remembered for his royal attire, and the Sancy was the most important and historic diamond owned by the French crown at the beginning of his reign. By the end of his seventy-two-year rule, the Sancy had been reduced in status to a mere bauble in the Sun King's crown. Like Queen Elizabeth, Louis was a consummate "power dresser," but unlike the English queen, his taste for ostentation and extravagance became an objective in its own right. His lust for power and greed would eventually overtake the fiscal advice and aims for a modern France given by the trustworthy and sensible finance minister Colbert. With the benefit of centuries of hindsight, we can see that the king, unwittingly, was sowing the seeds of the bloodiest civil war in Europe: the French Revolution.

Drawing from the splendor that had been written about de' Medici Florence—a splendor that his grandmother Maria de' Medici knew firsthand—Louis improved on the breathtaking parades, lavish entertainment, and sumptuous banquets. Voltaire, in describing the Sun King's progress to Dunkerque and Lille in 1670, wrote: "the ancient Asian king's pomp and grandeur [the Great Mogul of India] was surpassed by the magnificence of this journey." Eyewitness accounts portrayed the inevitable jostling that took place among the people who had come to see the king—not only to catch a glimpse of the most powerful ruler in Europe, but also to have a bit of his resplendence rub off on them.

Voltaire also wrote that the king "bestowed gold and precious stones in profusion to courtiers and ladies, who seized upon the slimmest pretext in order to speak to him." The great philosopher even devoted half a page of description to the Sancy in *La Henriade*.

Louis's court was an exceedingly grand affair. The splendid suite of seven reception rooms, called the Grand Appartement, was decorated by furniture, curtains, and hangings of embroidered velvet in winter, and white flowered silk in summer, with silver candelabra and chandeliers from which flickered a hundred thousand candles, casting a golden glow. When Louis came to the throne he owned about two hundred paintings; when he died, two thousand.

Louis's courtiers were shameless gamblers, and the palace often was referred to as a gambling den. The nobles relished playing for high stakes and were merciless cheats—howling and blaspheming, pulling out their hair and weeping when they lost, and many lost entire fortunes. The Venetian ambassador, Giustiniani, and several others gambled away everything they possessed at a single sitting without a grumble.

There were plays, concerts, and dances as the king was devoted to his *divertissements*, or entertainments. Summer evenings often were spent on gondolas on the canal, followed closely behind by his musicians, lolling back and forth with the king as they played on a floating pontoon. Naturally, the gondolas, complete with gondoliers, were presents from the Venetian Republic.

This was the age when diamonds and all other jewels took on their modern meaning—worn as a sign of beauty and wealth, to sparkle and impress. The Quai des Orfèvres in Paris had been thriving as a jewelers' guild and center of excellence (not unlike Forty-seventh Street in New York or Hatton Garden in London) since Henry IV's time, but in Louis XIV's it positively dazzled. The "jeweled leaf" or "pea pod" design had become the original signature of Parisian jewelry in his father's time, and Louis was determined to become the premier fashion icon of the world, creating the most outrageously outlandish jewels, clothes, and palaces. He succeeded in his aim.

Louis XIV in his
coronation robes.
Painting by Justus van
Egmont, date unknown.

Under Louis, Parisian goldsmiths and jewelers invented newer, lighter settings to display the brilliance of the better-cut stones. Knots, pendants, and jeweled boxes in the "French style" were all the rage. Large stones were often set in phenomenal number as clusters, dominated by diamond rosettes. These were so huge that they were commonly referred to as "rocks," and this was the first time the word was used to describe gemstones. His jewelers and goldsmiths—Jean Pittau, Louis Alvarez, Laurent and Pierre Le Tessier de Montarsy, Sylvestre Bosc, Philippe Pijart, and Pierre Bain—catered to the king's wildest excesses and were paid handsomely for their services.

An outsider looking in, Robert de Berquen, jewel merchant to the granddaughter of Queen Henrietta Maria of England, Anne Marie Louise d'Orléans, was tremendously envious not only of these men, but also of the king's merchant adventurers, the most notable of whom was the larger-than-life Jean-Baptiste Tavernier.

Tavernier (1605–1689) traveled six times to India, Turkey, and Persia (today Iran), and with each successive journey, his legend grew. Tavernier's fascinating travels were recounted in his books and described the people from these far-off lands with a detail and clarity as well as a self-effacement that was most endearing. He simply enchanted French society and brought back several fortunes in diamonds and other precious gemstones. His books were best sellers of the day and helped to popularize the diamond as the precious stone of preference.

De Berquen, in a successful attempt to claim his place in society and history, although it was unsuccessful in terms of usurping Tavernier's position, wrote his own book with the catchy title *The Marvels of Occidental and Oriental India, or New Treatise of Precious Stones and Pearls Containing their True Nature, Hardness, Colors and Virtues: Each placed according to its Order and Degree, Following the Knowledge of the Goldsmith Merchants, the Title of Gold and Silver, with an Augmentation in Many Chapters, The Reasons against the Prospectors of The Philosopher's Stone and Believers in Alchemy, And Two Other Chapters about The Price of Diamonds and Pearls*, dedicated to Anne Marie Louise, d'Orléans.

The book, published in December 1668, was well received, if not well researched when it came to history. De Berquen asserts that "The Queen of England at present owns the diamond from the deceased Mr de Sancy, which he brought back from his Embassy in the Levant and which is in the form of an almond, cut in facets on the two sides, perfectly white and clear, and weighs fifty-four carats, and valued at three gross weight in marks." According to the schedule of values in his chapter on diamonds, that would put the Sancy's value at a mere 30,600 livres ($59.4 million or £37.2 million today), far below the value indicated on the king's inventory.

De Berquen's erroneous assertions were to become one of the root causes behind the Sancy's "mysterious" past, since they were widely held to be true. Victorian lapidaries based their assumptions on his claims, and twentieth-century writers on the Victorians. Not only did de Berquen base the Sancy's provenance on one of the many lies perpetrated by Nicolas Harlay de Sancy himself—that he had acquired it during his nonexistent ambassadorship to the Levant—but he also claimed that seven years after the deaths of Henrietta Maria and

Cardinal Mazarin, the diamond still belonged to the Queen of England. But that was not the end of de Berquen's mischief.

Tavernier's books reeked of an authenticity that was difficult to match, so de Berquen created an ancestor—Louis de Berquen—who, he asserted, was the father of diamond cutting. The fairy tale claimed that Louis de Berquen returned from his studies in Paris in 1476 to Bruges, where he cut diamonds for Charles the Bold:

> He [Louis de Berquen] put two diamonds on cement, and after having rubbed them one against the other, he saw that by making a powder of diamond dust and with the aid of a mill wheel with wheels of iron, that he had found a method to polish diamonds perfectly, and even to cut them in such a manner as he wished. He executed this so fortuitously that he has had the credit for this invention since that time. At the same moment, Charles, the last Duke of Burgundy, who had heard of his skills, gave him three great diamonds into his hands to cut to advantage according to his methods. He cut these promptly, one thick, the other thin, and the third in a triangle [allegedly the Sancy] and he succeeded so well that the Duke who raved at such a surprising invention, gave him three thousand ducats in recompense. Then as the Duke found these so beautiful and rare, he gave a present of the thin one to Pope Sixtus IV, the one that was in the shape of a triangle and heart, he had put into a ring, and the reduced portion, he gave with his two hands, as a symbol of himself, to King Louis XI from whom he wished to receive intelligence. As to the third stone, that was the thick diamond, he kept it for himself and always wore it on his finger, and when he was killed at the Battle of Nancy, it was still there, one year after he had had it cut.

While there were diamond cutters in Bruges in 1476, there is no Louis de Berquen registered in the diamond guild—or even the wider merchant trade—in Bruges at the time. Diamond cutting had been documented in Europe in Nuremberg since the 1300s and in Venice a century later. The likelihood of Charles giving a valuable diamond to his mortal enemy Louis XI in the final year of Charles's life, when their bitterness was at its height, and at a time when Charles had cajoled Edward IV of England to invade France, is preposterous. The diamond owned by Pope Sixtus IV was a gift from the Burgunderbeute by Jacob Fugger, merchant banker to the pope. And finally, the Sancy was never mounted as a ring, but worn as a hat ornament by the last duke of Burgundy.

This work of fiction, based loosely on fact, is the third disaster at the root of the Sancy's mysterious past, since all lapidary texts after de Berquen refer back to him as the "fountain of knowledge." Like Saddam Hussein's minister of information, de Berquen invented a history that suited his personal purpose, but de Berquen had the supreme advantage of never becoming a laughingstock.

Tavernier, on the other hand, was the stuff of legends. A towering figure who spoke and wrote with the authority of a perspicacious eyewitness, he attributed his abilities to the education he had received as a child from his Flemish father. Tavernier wrote,

> If the effect of education may be likened to a second birth, I may truly say, that I came into the world with a desire to travel. The daily discourses upon which several learned men had with my father upon geographical subjects . . . and to which, though very young, I was with much delight attentive . . . inspired me betimes with a design to see some part of those countries which were represented to me in the Maps, from which I never keep off my eyes.

In Book I of his hefty tome, *Les Six Voyages*, Tavernier sets out a detailed table of the rates of exchange among the diverse currencies so that the reader is able to "translate" the sums mentioned throughout into the currency to which they are most accustomed. He describes the way in which diamonds are gathered; how the natives are clothed, paid, and fed; their sex and ages; and even how the governments control the various diamond mines. He is mostly concerned with diamonds, since they are the "most precious of stones" and the commodities with which he dealt the most.

Tavernier visited each of the mines and rivers where diamonds were found, and portrayed in the most picturesque detail the activities he saw there. Seven days' journey from Golconda to the east, Tavernier visited a diamond mine in the "country called Gani, meaning 'color' in Persian." It was here that the largest colored stones were found and is most likely the birthplace of the great French Blue diamond, later stolen and believed to have been cut down to make the Hope Diamond. Tavernier wrote the following about that journey:

> A league and a half from the Town is a high Mountain in the form of a half-moon; the space between the town and the mountain is a plain where they dig and find diamonds. The nearer they dig to the mountain, the larger stones they find; but at the top they find nothing at all. . . . For they found a great number of stones from ten to forty carats, and sometimes bigger; among the rest that large stone that weighed nine hundred carats [the Great Mogul diamond], which Mirgimola presented to Aureg-zeb.

Tavernier traded with the locals, rapidly picking up their language, observing their habits, and then adopting them. He was well regarded, though a stranger, and made a fortune with each successive journey by selling his gems to Louis XIV and royal jewelers and merchants across Europe. After his sixth voyage he remarked on the differences in appreciation of the clarity, or water, of diamonds:

> As for the water of the stones, it is remarkable that whereas in Europe we make use of daylight to examine the rough stones, and to judge their water, and the specks [impurities] that are found therein, the Indians do all that in the nighttime, setting up a lamp with a large wick in a hole which they make in the wall, about a foot square; by the light whereof they judge the water and clearness of the stone, which they hold between their fingers. The water which they call celestial is the worst of all, and it is impossible to discern it so long as the stone is rough. The most infallible way to find out the water, is to carry the stone under a tree thick of boughs, for by the greenery of that shade you may easily discern whether the water is bluish or no.

Tavernier makes it clear that the pure white flawless diamond was still the most highly regarded, and the most valuable, and like de Berquen, devised a simple way of valuing stones. If the diamond was thick, well proportioned, with a clear and lively water and flawless, be it cut as a tablecut or rose cut, like the Sancy, it would be valued at 150 livres for the first carat. Since these stones were many-faceted, or

many-sided, Tavernier believed that the true value could be determined by "squaring" the weight of the diamond, then multiplying
that result by 150 livres. In the case of the Sancy, where its weight in
old carats was 54 carats, the mathematical equation was: 54 carats $\times$
54 = 2,916 $\times$ 150 livres = 437,400 livres.

In the inventory of 1691 the Sancy diamond was described as
being "without equal" and "priceless," yet according to that inventory
was estimated at 600,000 ecus, or 200,000 livres ($24.2 million or
£15.2 million today). It would seem that neither de Berquen's nor
Tavernier's form of valuation was adopted by the crown.

Notwithstanding this, Louis XIV proved to be Tavernier's best
customer, and by the time the merchant adventurer had published his
book in 1669, the king's diamond collection comprised 1,302 rough
diamonds and 609 cut diamonds, with colors ranging from violet to
peach blossom, and shapes from helmets to hearts.

In his infinite wisdom, Colbert had devised the "King's Gem
Ledgers" in that same year, foreseeing the need to keep track of his
monarch's passion for diamonds and other precious stones. He also
supervised the daily update of the inventory by personally writing
"correct" beside the entries of purchases from merchants, as well as
"exits" in the form of gifts made by Louis. Colbert's methodical super-
vision was required for these various changes to the inventory, since
the personal collection of the king (as separate from those of the
crown jewels) had political ends.

The first of these political ends was the obvious impressive opulence they created for visiting dignitaries and Louis's own aristocracy.
When Louis was preparing for the state visit from the king of Siam
(now Thailand) in September 1686, the order went out to ensure
that His Most Christian Majesty should be "bedecked with diamonds
of extraordinary size which are worth more than the whole Kingdom
of Siam." Louis was often bowled over by an exceptionally fine
jewel—or repulsed by an ugly one.

Like for all his predecessors, the king's gems were more than a
tremendous source of transportable wealth. They also constituted a
ritual "presentation" to those deserving his benevolence and friendship, and were important tools of government. Even the duke of Marlborough, who had so decisively defeated Louis's armies in the War of

Spanish Succession (1701–1713), received a "presentation" box with a jeweled miniature portrait of the Sun King. The box was Louis's signature piece: it comprised an enameled portrait miniature of the king, mounted on a gold plaque set with twenty to sixty diamonds and enclosed with another gold plaque with the king's cipher on the reverse. To receive a presentation box from Louis XIV was tantamount to a knighthood, or receipt of a Congressional Medal of Honor. Only 3 of these boxes are known to have survived from the original 338 made between 1669 and 1684.

Louis XIV understood the value of diamonds and their place within his court. They were essential to his persona, and from the beginning, he set out on a comprehensive program to make the French crown jewels the largest in Europe. He commissioned the first diamond buttons, which today are represented in the fashion history as rhinestone buttons. In 1665 he bought the 34-carat, rectangularly shaped de Guise diamond, which he gave to Marie de Lorraine de Guise. Four years later he purchased in one transaction with Tavernier 46 large diamonds and 1,102 smaller ones.

The Tavernier engravings of the 20 largest diamonds at that time survive today. Three were in the rough, with the remaining 17 stones having been cut in India in the characteristic mogul cuts. The king had all of the stones recut in the European style by his diamond cutter, Pittau, to bring out the water of the stones. The largest and most beautiful of these was the absolutely pure French Blue, weighing 115.28 carats—more than twice the size of the Sancy prior to cutting. Later, in 1673, Pitau recut this stone into a splendid heart-shaped seven-sided brilliant cut with a star pattern on the pavilion weighing 69 carats.

Shortly after Louis's reign, the Pitt diamond, owned by Thomas Pitt (1653–1726), a great-grandfather of Prime Minister William Pitt during George III's reign, also would become part of the French crown jewels, supplanting the Sancy as the largest white diamond in Europe. Pitt had acquired the diamond some years earlier in India under mysterious circumstances. Thomas, who became known as "Diamond Pitt," had developed an Oriental trade that frequently brought him into conflict with the immensely powerful East India Company. Despite this, while in India, Pitt continued to trade on behalf of the East India Company, as well as for his personal account, and had a particular fondness for diamonds. The diamond, weighing 410 old carats in the rough, was reputed to have been stolen from the Golconda mines by a slave, who in turn was murdered by the ship's captain, with whom he had negotiated his escape to freedom in exchange for half of the sale value of the stone. The legend claims that the ship's captain sold the diamond to Pitt for £1,000 ($100,000 or £63,000 today) but was so overwhelmed by remorse and grief that he squandered the money and hanged himself.

Pitt arranged for this fabulous stone to be cut in London by the most admired diamond cutter of his day, Joseph Cope, who took two years and charged £5,000 to complete his task. The result was a cushion-shaped brilliant weighing 140.64 metric carats, measuring 25.4 mm in breadth, 25.4 mm in length, and 19 mm in thickness. It is considered to be the most perfectly cut of all the celebrated historic diamonds today. The Sancy was no longer the largest white diamond in Christendom, its position now held by the Pitt.

But, as with most of the Sancy's owners, the Pitt brought more hardship than benefit with its ownership. Pitt, now reputed to be a man of naked ambition, counting his enemies simultaneously with his cash, was in constant fear of being robbed and possibly of losing his life. He never slept two nights in the same place, and never let anyone know his plans or his intended whereabouts. Peace of mind comes at a cost, so not surprisingly, he first tried to dispose of the diamond in 1712 to various crowned heads of Europe, but without success. It was only when John Law, a fast-talking, persuasive charlatan, entered the scene that the priceless goods were entrusted to him for sale to the French crown. The Pitt diamond soon became known as the Regent diamond.

While Tavernier was undoubtedly the most well known of the king's merchant adventurers, Louis also bought diamonds and gemstones from others. In 1669 a Dutch merchant sold the king a tremendous number of pearls and precious stones, including 14 large diamonds and 131 smaller ones. The largest, a bluish-color table-cut diamond called the Bazu, weighed 43.67 carats after recutting, making it the fourth-largest diamond in the crown jewels collection.

Another merchant of Portuguese Jewish origin, Master Alvarez, was commissioned to cut 12 large and 653 smaller diamonds for the

French king. Like Tavernier, he traveled to India and bought stones at the court of the Great Moguls, and it is thought that he may have cut the Five-Sided Pink diamond weighing 21.32 carats, which Napoleon later called the Hortensia, after Josephine's daughter. This is the earliest surviving example of this type of Parisian cut stone, and is esteemed not only for its beauty but also for its historic value. Alvarez was so highly regarded that he became one of the writers of the 1691 inventory for the king.

Louis's profligacy and belief in himself as an absolute monarch prevented France from becoming a modern state. The country had been overshadowed by years of military conflict and extravagance promoted by the king in his attempt to outshine and conquer the Habsburgs. Through Louis's marriage to Philip IV's daughter Marie-Thérèse, infanta of Spain, he believed he had a claim to the Habsburg Spanish throne and plunged France into a series of long, bloody, and bitter battles with not only the Spanish Habsburg family, but also the Austrian Habsburgs.

It was this first war against the Habsburgs that was the motivating factor behind the 1691 inventory, since Louis had had to melt down 27 tons of the silver furniture from the Palace of Versailles to pay the troops earlier that year. The inventory revealed that there were 5,885 diamonds in excess of 0.5 carat. Fortunately, he would never need to use the crown jewels despite losing most of his international battles, which lasted for more than thirty years.

At the time, Europe feared absolute domination by the French, and at the end of the day it fell to the English commander, John Churchill, duke of Marlborough, leading a vast European army, to utterly defeat Louis's expansionist plans. The duke's military prowess and organizational skills led to decisive victories over the French in only a four-year period—at Donauwörth and Blenheim (1704), then Oudenaarde and Lille (1708)—for which he received the 1,800-acre magnificent estate Blenheim Palace—now a World Heritage Site—in the Oxfordshire countryside.

Louis and his armies were utterly defeated, and his plots against the Habsburgs thwarted. The French victory in 1712 at the Battle of Denain gave one last breath to Louis's dying cause, before the Peace of Utrecht was signed between France on one side and Britain and

Spain on the other in a series of treaties dated from April to July 1714. The defeat was the worst suffered by the French since Agincourt in the Hundred Years' War in 1415. France was forced to forfeit her North American colonies (Hudson's Bay; Newfoundland; and Arcadia, or Nova Scotia) to Britain. France's lucrative *asiento* trading contracts to supply slaves to the Spanish colonies were made over to the South Sea Company, which had received a royal charter in England three years earlier. Britain also received St. Kitts in the Caribbean, and Minorca and Gibraltar from Spain. This also was the first international treaty in the French language, rather than Latin, and enshrined the concept of balance of power in Europe for the first time.

Yet Louis remained determined to maintain his absolute power and authority within France and strove to preserve the unity of the state and the French church, where he, like Henry VIII in England, was its spiritual head. This often led Louis into conflict with the Huguenots and the pope, with damaging repercussions. Louis often held the opposing view from the pope with regard to vacant sees and abbacies and openly persecuted Huguenots and Jansenists. Eventually Louis revoked the Edict of Nantes, signed by Henry IV in 1598, leading to a mass exodus of adherents of the "Reformed Religions" to the New World.

On a personal level, the king is probably best remembered for his voracious sexual appetite and his mistresses—the most notable of whom were Louise de la Valliere and Madame de Montespan. One of his first paramours was the youngest daughter of Queen Henrietta Maria, Princess Henriette, who had married Louis's younger homosexual brother and allegedly died of poisoning. After Queen Marie-Thérèse's death in 1683, Louis secretly married another of his courtesans, Madame de Maintenon. Some French bishops prayed for the king's moderation, telling him to his face that he was becoming another Henry VIII—for his women as well as for taking over as head of the French church. Louis enigmatically replied "What I have just heard is *considérable*."

By the time of his death at age seventy-seven in 1715, France had lost its international colonies, its European war, and much of its treasury pursuing the Sun King's impossible dreams. Louis had outlived his children, all of his grandchildren, and three of his great-grandsons during his seventy-two-year rule. While he was the greatest of France's monarchs, his rule in old age was marred by court intrigue and bigotry—the one thing he had hoped to extinguish by moving the court to the Palace of Versailles in 1682. But the court was rife with incessant rumors of poisonings; jockeying for position close to the king; and, of course, more than a smattering of infidelity and using sex as a weapon.

The king's physician, Dr. Fagon—nicknamed "the killer of princes"—oversaw the deaths of many of the king's children, and prescribed asses' milk for the dying king as the remedy for "sciatica." Louis did not have sciatica, but rather gangrene, and Fagon soon would be elevated to the status of a killer of kings.

Louis sent for his great-grandson and heir to the throne, five-year-old Louis. The two looked gravely at each other for the last time. Then the king said, "*Mignon*, you are going to be a great king. Do not copy me in my love of building or my love of warfare; on the contrary, try to live peacefully with your neighbors. Remember your duty and your obligations to God; see that your subjects honor Him. Take good advice and follow it, try and improve the lot of your people, as I, unfortunately, have never been able to do." Then he asked for the little boy to be brought closer so that he could kiss him good-bye.

Louis's bedroom glowed with its candlelit vigil, filled with religious music and the murmuring of prayers, and after three weeks of intense suffering, he quietly expired. The duc de Bouillon stepped out onto the balcony of the king's bedchamber wearing a black feather in his hat to announce to the doleful crowd "*Le roi est mort*" and returned indoors wearing a white feather proclaiming "*Vive le roi*."

21

Just Another Symbol at the Heart of Power

1715–1773

UNDER LOUIS XV, the Sancy became far less important as a symbol of power. No longer the largest white diamond in Europe—or, for that matter, in the French crown jewels—it was the Sancy's history rather than its size that made it exceptional. Furthermore, since the king himself was a mere child, it would be some fifteen years before any of the crown jewels would once again be worn by an adult monarch. This, in many ways, placed the onus of the pomp and circumstance of kingship squarely on the shoulders of Louis's regent Philippe II, duke of Orléans.

Philippe was a nephew of Louis XIV and became regent to the child king Louis XV in 1715. The situation in France was precarious to say the least. The country had been ravaged by the Sun King's disastrous international wars, there was no money from the colonies since they had been forfeited to the British, and the state treasury was dangerously low. The gap between the aristocracy and the middle classes had narrowed, but the gulf between farmers and peasants and the middle and upper classes had become an ocean. Agriculture was fearfully neglected, since noble landlords were either too busy enjoying the social life and vices of the capital or held virtual prisoners at court in Versailles.

Versailles lay empty for the first seven years of the young Louis's reign, its golden rooms, priceless paintings, and furniture and meticulous gardens maintained and enjoyed by servants alone. The *noblesse de court* (court nobility), who had sprung up as virtual prisoners in one perpetual, provincial house party at Versailles, escaped back to Paris, relieved from their duties and political exile. Life at Versailles would spring back to life only after the king's coronation in 1722.

Louis had no brothers or sisters, since all of them had been killed through the ineptitude of Dr. Fagon. His reputation for human devastation was such that French historians have long wondered whether, if Dr. Fagon had not existed, the French Revolution would have been avoided. Louis XV himself had escaped the same fate due to the wisdom of his nursemaid, the duchess of Ventadour, who hid him away from the rest of the family, who alternatively died of measles or the "dear" doctor's prescriptions. Even Louis XIV recognized her importance when he told the little boy on his deathbed to "remember all that you owe to Madame de Ventadour." Fortunately, the duke of Orléans also had survived, and installed Louis at the Tuileries Palace, across from his own Palais-Royal. The duke served the child king faithfully as long as he lived.

Philippe of Orléans had never been allowed to participate in public life under Louis XIV, not because the king had any personal misgivings about the duke but rather because Louis mistrusted all of his nobility. Deprived of any real role, Philippe was the perfect rake. When, at age forty-one, he effectively became France's ruler, the years of dissipation had taken their toll, but he was determined to rule well. He governed much as Louis XIV had done and rapidly commanded the same deep respect, but he ruled with good humor rather than hatred and fear.

Despite ordering the bawling Louis wrested away at age seven from Madame de Ventadour and handed over to a governor for the good of France, Philippe loved Louis more than his own lackluster son. Philippe told Louis, "You are the master, I am only here to tell you what is happening, to make suggestions, to carry out your orders." Louis, like so many others, became enchanted by his distant cousin and soon joined in council meetings, clasping his pet cat in his arms, too shy to speak a word.

The duke knew that the wheels of power that kept France glued together politically and socially—the complex relationships among king, nobles, and church—made progress as impossible as dancing in molasses. Investment in France's future had to take place. But how? There had been financial speculation in France's American colonies fueled by the Scottish scoundrel John Philip Law, who had set up the Mississippi Company as a great financial experiment in France. This company was to raise credit for entrepreneurial enterprises, but like the South Sea Company, of which Law was a mover and shaker as well, foundered on a tide of greed. Investors in the Mississippi Company were often investors in the South Sea Company and vice versa. Law bribed politicians and King George I's mistresses with stock so they would influence the king to invest. Deplorable methods were used to inflate stock prices for rapid capital gains in much the same way they were employed to create the Internet bubble almost three hundred years later.

All the investment capital in France and England that had been placed in the financial markets since the outbreak of peace in 1714 had been to a greater or lesser extent in one of Law's companies. Speculation fever gripped London and Paris, and new companies funded by the South Sea or Mississippi companies—legitimate and bogus—sprouted like fungi. In September 1720 the South Sea bubble burst, and Law exiled himself back to France and security. Like the Internet bubble, the collapse shook the very foundations of government. Ministers were in abject terror for their lives. Investors had been bamboozled into making investments in companies that had no assets, and the enraged victims—some of whom were bankrupt, others destitute—screamed for justice and revenge.

France was in a shakier state than Britain when the bubble burst, but unlike England, its underlying economy was not sound. A bold act to inspire confidence in the crown and France's finances was required, in the duke's opinion, to maintain business confidence. Diamonds had long been used as a means for inspiring such confidence, and it so happened that the most amazing diamond ever to be seen in Europe was put up for sale.

Since Law was "exiled" in France—and claiming to help France to extricate itself from its financial difficulties—he went to the regent, the duke of Orléans, showing him a glass model of the Pitt. At first the regent was reticent—it was an awful lot of money to spend when matters were so tenuous for the crown. Law and his French cohort the duke of St. Simon pandered to the duke's ego—suggesting that such a stone should after all be called "the Regent." Law's blandishments at last succeeded.

On June 6, 1717, after a meeting of the council, the duke agreed to purchase Pitt's 140.64-metric-carat diamond for 2 million livres, the equivalent of 745 kilograms of pure gold ($2.8 billion or £1.8 billion today). Law was paid £5,000 in fees for the transaction. The regent rebaptized the diamond "the Regent," and it was added to the state crown jewels collection in 1719. The official description read:

> Today, on the fourteenth day of June, one thousand seven hundred and nineteen, a diamond has been added to this inventory; purchased in England, of the first water, weighing 546 grains, brilliant-cut of slightly elongated square shape, with rounded corners and all its steps. There is a small crystal in its cleavage plane and a notch in its lower part. It is of inestimable value, but for the inventory, Messrs. Rondé, father and son, have estimated its worth at six millions. The aforementioned diamond has been given the name of the Regent.

The diamond was intended to give confidence to the people that their monarch was invincible and almighty—with the more modern twist being added that he was not insolvent.

The Regent was mounted in the front fleur-de-lys of the coronation crown of Louis XV in 1722 and in that of Louis XVI in 1775, with the Sancy set at its summit. After the coronation ceremonies, both diamonds were replaced by paste replicas and were worn separately. The Regent was often kept as a single diamond in its own mounting, or as part of a setting in a knot of pearls with diamonds as a shoulder ornament, and would remain so until the French Revolution. The Sancy was worn as a large agraffe in Louis's hat, or as a pendant in a necklace worn by his queen.

But the choice of a queen for the young monarch was to prove yet another delicate matter. Louis spurned his first intended fiancée, the infanta of Spain, for being too young (she was only five and he fifteen when they were betrothed). If they were to marry, he would have to wait another ten years before he could consummate their relationship. So the infanta was packed back off to Spain and the hunt for a suitable replacement was on.

The king's favor fell on the most unlikely of candidates: the daughter of the penniless and exiled King Stanislaus of Poland, Marie Leczinska. It was a poor choice for a monarch wishing to instill confidence in his power and authority, according to Nancy Mitford in her biography of Madame de Pompadour, since his bride had "neither worldly goods, nor powerful family connections, nor beauty, nor even youth, since she was seven years older than the king." What Louis's detractors omitted to note was that he could quickly get on with the business of creating heirs with an older woman, particularly with an older woman of excellent health with broad childbearing hips. By the time Louis was twenty-seven he and Marie had had ten children. Unfortunately for their marriage, Marie only took an interest in the children and had a reputation for being a bit of a bore. She did nothing to make herself attractive or interesting to her young husband, and seemed to have wandered quite happily into middle age. He naturally sought love elsewhere.

With the marriage, Louis set up house once again at Versailles. The palace throbbed with activity, housing over a thousand nobles and their families. It was the heart of power, and a public exhibition hall for the king. The entire palace and gardens were thrown open to the public with the formal *lever* (rising-from-bed ceremony) and *coucher* (retiring-to-bed ceremony) of his great-grandfather restored for the court.

Yet Louis remained shy and aloof, delighting in little things and small details. At first he created the *petits appartements* (private rooms) for himself in the north wing—some fifty rooms with seven bathrooms for his own private pleasure—where only those who had been invited for the *grandes entrées* (official presentations) could go. Eventually the king would arrange a series of other truly "private" apartments that were accessed by a series of hidden staircases and secret passages overlooking internal courtyards. These rooms—referred to at the time as "rats' nests" by Robert de Cotte, son of one of the architects of Versailles—are some of the most exquisite at Versailles, and show off the king's taste for fine detail. Despite his preference for solitude and the smaller, finer things in life, Louis never shirked his duties as king, and made all the public appearances that were his duty.

The king had matured into a kind, loving, and caring ruler despite his shyness, but the fundamentals underlying the French social, political, and economic structure were rotting—and neither the king nor his ministers had the slightest clue as to how to change the situation. Isolated from Parisian society at Versailles and remote from any form of public opinion, Louis lived in a glass house looking inward. He was unable to see that by falling back into the miserable etiquette and mannerisms of his great-grandfather's court he had sealed the fate of the nation.

His queen utterly bored him, and Louis, above all else, needed love. He let it be known that he required a mistress, and since the king was considered a god, there were plenty of young and intelligent women wishing to fill the position. There was no shame attached to such a venerable and materially beneficial position. In February 1745, when Louis's and Marie's eldest son, the dauphin, married the younger sister of the infanta of Spain, Queen Marie arrived at the ball in a shimmering dress covered in clusters of pearls, with the Sancy and the Regent sparkling in her hair. Louis, disguised at the masked ball and first spied taking cover amid clipped yew trees, was bedecked in his "White Suite" of the Order of the Golden Fleece, which held, among other diamonds, the second (the Pindar) and twelfth Mazarins, as well as the great French Blue. Later that night, Jeanne-Antoinette d'Étoiles, better known as Madame de Pompadour, dazzled Louis for the first time and became his beloved mistress.

Although Madame de Pompadour is not remembered kindly by historians—perhaps undeservedly—she can hardly be blamed for the crumbling French political and social infrastructure for which some of her more unkind detractors accuse her indirectly. True, the feud between Louis and the church had become inflamed with her arrival on the scene, but she was not the underlying cause of the bitterness between the two. By 1749 the state's finances were in appalling disarray due to the political and economic structure of French society. Rather than address the underlying causes of the malaise, Louis ordered la vingtième, a 5 percent tax on total income, to be levied on all classes to keep the status quo and avoid drastic slashing of court expenditures. For the king, *la vingtième* had the added benefit of particularly targeting the clergy, who had hitherto been exempt. Louis, knowing the level of resistance to his new tax, also demanded a complete declaration of church property. Until then, the church paid its taxes by gifting sums to the state for amounts of its choosing and at intervals to suit its religious needs. Paying taxes was bad enough—but declaring income and assets was considered to be impossible. The church stirred up as much turmoil as it could for the sovereign by denouncing ministers, Parlement, Protestants, and Jansenists—the evangelicals noted for their self-flagellation and loathed by all non-Jesuits.

It was a clever ploy, since the Jesuits and neo-Jansenists (the real Jansenists having been destroyed under Louis XIV) were the staunchest supporters of Parlement. The quarrel that had begun between king and church now embroiled the French legislature. The senior president of Parlement wrote to the king, "Your Parlement has never been brought to the steps of your throne by a matter of such gravity." The king had begun to think of his own Parlement as being rather too Cromwellian for his own good, and feared a turn to republicanism, so he obligingly sided with the church. The high court of Parlement, or Grande Chambre, was exiled to Pantoise in May 1753, and Louis proclaimed that only he could be the arbiter on matters regarding the sacraments and matters of state.

This was a tremendous error. At Pantoise the presidents lived lavishly and ignored the court, spreading propaganda that only *they* were the defenders of justice and liberty. When the harsh winter led to starvation and unemployment, the first banners with *"Burn Versailles"* written in red were held aloft in the streets. Bloodshed was averted for the time being when Louis finally reinstated Parlement in September 1754 amid scenes of jubilation. Naturally, the clergy never paid the hated taxes. Ironically, the same week that the crisis was diffused, the future Louis XVI was born.

Politics abroad also posed serious problems for Louis. The British and French had been skirmishing on the high seas in India and Canada, as France tried valiantly to reestablish a colonial presence after the debacle in Europe and the Peace of Utrecht in 1714. George II, the second Hanoverian king of Britain, was on the throne, and Louis feared that another disastrous Continental war was about to break out. In the end, the sea battles in the colonies rose to fever pitch, and despite the king's best endeavors, war could not be avoided. In May 1756, a simple declaration of war from London read, "We declare war on France who has so unrighteously begun it."

Initially the French had an important military success, recapturing Minorca from the English, but when the English king's cousin Frederick the Great of Prussia invaded Saxony, igniting the Seven Years' War, matters went from dangerous to downright abysmal. The British, ever able at playing one Continental power off against another, had the distinct advantage of family ties between Frederick the Great and their own Hanoverian king. They provided funds to subsidize Frederick's armies and allied themselves to their German cousins. Louis's armies were driven back across the Rhine and were defeated at the Battle of Krefeld in 1758. When Britain entered the war in 1756 it had some colonial possessions. When the war was over in 1763 it had the greatest empire the world had seen since ancient Rome. Louis had been thrashed, Montreal was taken in 1760, and French Canada was at last in British hands.

Yet perhaps the most important development of all was not in the battlefield but in the field of thought. The philosophical principles of the Age of Enlightenment had taken hold. In France, Voltaire, Montesquieu, and Diderot were contributing to the great body of scientific and philosophical work throughout Europe. Newton's *Principia* (1687) and *Optics* (1704) had laid the foundations for scientific research, taking thought forward from sorcery and magic into a deeper understanding of the natural world. However, Louis, now an old man, did not grasp the fact that the absolutism inherited from his great-grandfather no longer had a role in a rapidly changing modern world.

He was still stuck in the feud with the church that had by now become a vendetta, with continued thrusts and parries hitting the chest of the other with alarming regularity. Yet as much as the church was hated by king and country, public feeling against the aristocracy was even more intense. At first Louis had almost imperceptibly lost control of the warring factions, amusing himself with his latest mistress, the former prostitute Madame du Barry. Finally, in 1771, an exhausted Louis supported the judicial reform that would see the rise of the powers of Parlement. It was the beginning of the endgame.

But Louis would broker nothing but his "absolute" rule and continued to veto any notion of power passing into the hands of his loathed aristocracy or untrustworthy church. The king had outlived his sons and was grooming his grandson to take the reigns of power on his death. Louis, now sixty, ordered that the matter be settled without delay. A suitable bride was selected—the youngest of the Austrian Habsburg queen Maria Teresa's daughters, Marie Antoinette. On April 17, the fifteen-year-old Marie swore to renounce her right to the Austrian hereditary lands as well as to Lorraine. Two days later, a proxy wedding to Louis Auguste, dauphin of France, took place in Vienna.

Two and a half weeks later, the young dauphine arrived at the French border in her velvet and gold carriage. She was stripped of her Austrian wedding attire (down to her undergarments), made to wear French-made clothes, and taken to meet her husband and the French king in a forest near Compiègne. Whereas the monarch was still reputed to be the handsomest man at court, his grandson had heavy-lidded eyes; thick, dark eyebrows; was overweight; and had an overtly awkward manner. He, too, was only fifteen. Not surprisingly, when the party returned to Versailles, it was widely rumored that nothing had happened on the teenagers' wedding night to assure the succession of France. The young dauphine's reputed inability to inspire her husband with sexual passion would soon become a matter of considerable worry and relentless court gossip.

The dauphin's sexuality, or rather lack of it, remained in sharp contrast to the king's nocturnal escapades with his latest mistress, Madame du Barry. Years of the king's personal decadence had led to morals generally being loosely worn at Versailles. Nobles married young, had children, then lapsed gracefully into finding their pleasures of the flesh elsewhere. The dauphine expressed an intense dislike for the morals at Versailles, and in particular for Madame du Barry, when in a surviving letter dated July 9, 1770, to her mother in Vienna, she wrote that du Barry was "the most stupid and impertinent creature you can imagine." Marie even ventured that she pitied the king for his "weakness" for the "harlot." Within two months of her arrival at court, the dauphine decided to offer no formal acknowledgment of the king's mistress. It was not an unusual reaction from a straitlaced teenager who took five years to consummate her marriage, but a rather unwise decision for a foreign princess.

The relationship between the quiet and studious Louis, who would have made an ideal librarian or scientific researcher, and the imperious yet fun-loving Marie was difficult from the outset. Soon she would come to love and outdo the French at their own game, becoming the ultimate symbol of frivolity and conspicuous consumption. Thomas Jefferson wrote in his autobiography that he "had ever believed that had there been no queen, there would have been no revolution." Harsh words for a country that was held together only by an aging absolute monarch.

22

The Hated Diamond

1774–1789

❖

ON THE EVENING OF APRIL 27, 1774, as Louis XV bent over a candle in the Petit Trianon, the pleasure palace built for Madame de Pompadour on the grounds of Versailles, blotches were visible on his face. Twelve days later he was dead of smallpox. The dauphin, Louis Auguste, and his wife recalled hearing a "terrible noise, exactly like thunder" as they awaited news of the king's demise. The noise was the sound of the courtiers stampeding from the dead king's bedchamber to the dauphin's to be the first to cry out to the new king, "*Vive le roi!*" Louis Auguste and Marie Antoinette fell to their knees and prayed, "God protect us. We are too young to reign."

It was true. But the greater truth was that to avoid bloodshed France needed a strong, reforming monarch sensitive to the public's needs and able to keep a firm hand on the different factions. Louis was not that man, and life at Versailles was so far removed from reality that it would have been difficult for him to understand just where to begin to make changes—other than to exile Madame du Barry to a convent. The royal system was essentially corrupt, and well entrenched. There were myriad special interest groups lounging around court, more than a thousand nobles, ambassadors, and servants. The Spanish ambassador alone had seventy servants. It was not uncommon for a dinner party of eight or so to have twenty-five servants waiting on them. Thomas Jefferson was so disgusted by the French and their lifestyle that he wrote, "the roughness of the human mind are so

231

thoroughly rubbed off with them that it seems as if one might glide through a whole life among them without a jostle."

This did not mean that they were clean. The palace was infamous for its dirt, and its odd menagerie of animals. Pets were treated fabulously—decked out in diamond necklaces, and eating from tables. Exotic white monkeys and innumerable Persian and gray Angora cats were often seen roaming the palace.

In the new court, ruled by Queen Marie Antoinette, excesses were taken extremely seriously. One of the first signs of these was the creation of jeweled snuffboxes, with a cameo portrait of the young and beautiful queen surrounded by black, bearing the inscription "Consolation of Grief." Considering that the queen disapproved of Louis XV and his sexual escapades, the hypocrisy of the token was not lost on either the court or the people.

Excesses also took the form of increasing the queen's household. Marie Antoinette had a phenomenal number of personal servants. There was the grand almoner, a first almoner, and an ordinary almoner, with four other almoners who rotated quarterly, four chaplains on a rotation as well, four chapel boys, and two chapel summoners. There was an official trainbearer, who naturally had to be of noble birth, a first gentleman usher, pages, cloak bearer, any number of ordinary ushers, and equerries—and these servants were employed only for when the queen went out.

The teenage queen did not understand that court intrigue needed to be controlled and avoided. Her own household was plagued from the outset by her own incompetence in naming the ineffectual and easily led princesse de Lamballe superintendent of the household— superior to all other princesses of the blood. It was a position that was meant to be retained for the princesse's natural life. When the princesse de Lamballe, with whom it was rumored that Marie had had a lesbian affair, fell from grace and was replaced by the sweet and docile Yolande de Polignac in her affections, Marie Antoinette could not withdraw the supreme honor that she had bestowed on the princesse.

By the following year, the queen's inability to bear an heir to the French throne became a real problem, and plans for her to be crowned in the coronation ceremony with her husband were rebuffed. The compliant king followed his first minister's advice and agreed that the

Marie Antoinette—
arch-manipulator or
much abused? Painting by
Jean-Baptiste Gautier-d'Agoty,
1775.

expense of a double ceremony would be unwise. The queen had no alternative but to express herself as being indifferent to the entire affair. Instead, she would concentrate on the important matter of her dress for the coronation, and her jewels. She commissioned a jeweled gown from a new fashion couturière, Rose Bertin, that was so heavy that the dressmaker proposed that the mistress of the robes should convey it to Rheims on a specially constructed stretcher. Despite the cost of the queen's gown, it paled into insignificance when compared to the attire ordered by her husband. Louis XV's crown was too small for his grandson's head, so the royal goldsmith, Auguste, had to make it bigger. The price tag attached to this exercise was 6,000 livres, with most of that sum spent on additional rubies, emeralds, sapphires, and the resetting of the Sancy and Regent diamonds in their original places.

To have engaged in such an extravaganza for the coronation was folly. Turgot, the king's new controller-general of finance since August

1774, had been battling to remedy the finances of the state that had never recovered from the ravages of the Seven Years' War. The state deficit stood at 22 million livres, with another 78 million livres projected by the close of 1775. Turgot had a plan to reform the tax system that included reduction of financial privileges accorded to the nobility, as well as creating a free market for grain. Instead of implementing the plan successfully, the harvest in 1774 had been disastrous, people were dying of starvation, and prices had skyrocketed. The nobility ignored the financial restraints put on them, and quite naturally, the populace protested violently. By May the grain riots known as the Flour War had reached Versailles, and these were put down just as violently by the king's men.

While Turgot counseled the king to hold his coronation ceremony in Paris, where it would be less expensive, Louis feared that the rebellion of the grain riots would mar the occasion. So the king and queen traveled to Rheims for the coronation on June 11, 1775, going across country, with much of the nobility accompanying them trampling the newly planted fields along the way. It was an act of callousness that the people would not forget. The peasants, who stood powerless at the roadside, were said to be no better than scarecrows by the aristocrats who passed them in their gilt carriages or on horseback.

It was most likely during the Flour Wars era when the famous phrase "let them eat cake" (*qu'ils managent du brioche*) was allegedly uttered by the queen. History has shown us, however, that the bride of Louis XIV Maria Thérèse said in 1737, "if there was no bread let the people eat the crust (*la croute*) of the pâté." Queen Marie Antoinette was insensitive to her own extravagant ways but was genuinely kindly in her feelings—at least at this stage—toward her people. In fact, when a little boy age four or five fell under her horse and was fortunately unhurt, the queen made an offer to his mother to raise him at Versailles and supervise his education. The mother, given the opportunity to have one less mouth to feed, gratefully accepted.

Yet, by autumn, the pamphleteers of Paris were having a field day, satirizing the queen and king and speculating mostly about both of their sexualities. Marie Antoinette wrote to her mother, Queen Maria Theresa of Austria, shortly before Christmas that she "needed the quality of a mother to be regarded as French by this petulant and frivolous nation," which also resented any influence she might have over king or country.

In fact, the queen's attitude to her husband was not as it should have been. She frequently referred to him as the "poor man," and did as her heart desired without any regard whatsoever for her station as queen or how her actions might be interpreted. When she was admonished by her mother, Marie Antoinette wrote back to one of her "approved" Austrian correspondents, "You know Paris and Versailles, you have been there, you can judge . . . my tastes are not the same as the King's, who is only interested in hunting and his metalworking. You will agree that I would cut an odd figure at a forge. . . . If I played the role of Venus that would displease him a great deal more than my actual tastes of which he does not disapprove."

Her allusion to Venus meant that she would not have love affairs—though her flirtations were scandalous enough. Louis, for his part, had by now fallen madly in love with his willful queen. He did disapprove of many things she did, but as a kind, generous, and weak man in love, could not bring himself to be harsh with her. She, in return, appeared most submissive to her husband in public. But her spirit for dissipation was growing daily. Her twenty-first birthday, in 1776, was an orgy of gambling lasting nearly three days, and when the king took her to task on the third day, she replied, "You said we could play, but you never specified for how long."

The obligatory flirtations between the queen and courtiers were generally seen by the king as being of no consequence—but it was her unquestionable enjoyment of the company of her brother-in-law, Comte d'Artois (the future Charles X), that gave the pamphleteers the best run for their money. Artois was manly; Louis, reputedly impotent. The pamphleteers' publications infuriated the king, but he was powerless to stop them—their seditious works were licensed and published in Holland or England and clandestinely imported to France.

In truth, the queen was accountable to no one except the king, and he indulged her every whim. When she wanted to watch the dawn break, the entire household followed, save the king, who valued his sleep more. When she began to wear her hair and wigs piled on top of her head three feet high decorated with gems, feathers, and ribbons, the king not only acquiesced, but also gave her a jeweled feather, or *aigrette*, ornamented with some royal diamonds. These hairstyles, called *poufs*, became the rage throughout Europe, and France assured its place as the heart of fashion for luxury and semiluxury goods. Even the American ambassador to Paris, Thomas Jefferson, sent back fashion plates to ladies of his acquaintance in America from the magazine *Cabinet des Modes*, the *Vogue* of its day.

It was the queen's extravagance that would be her undoing, though she could hardly be single-handedly to blame for the French Revolution, as Jefferson had so unkindly written. The queen's wardrobe, created by the imaginative and talented Rose Bertin, was filled with expensive works of art—with real diamonds, sapphires, and rubies often sewn onto the silk—and the queen's dress allowance was consequently never large enough. Bertin, also a clever businesswoman, would tell all of her customers who came to visit her shop on the rue de Saint-Honoré, "Show Madame my latest creation for Her Majesty," and was quickly nicknamed the "minister of fashion" by the pamphleteers. By the end of 1776 the queen, who had been given a generous dress allowance of 150,000 livres ($153.3 million or £95.8 million today), had debts to her couturière for practically 500,000 livres. In the summer of 1776, Marie Antoinette had bought a pair of chandelier diamond earrings—partly with diamonds and gems she already owned, partly on credit—from a celebrated jeweler of the day, Charles-Auguste Boehmer. Shortly afterward she bought a pair of diamond bracelets for 400,000 livres, and when the reckoning day came for payment, she simply borrowed the money from the king.

Four new pairs of shoes weekly, three yards of brand-new ribbon to tie the royal peignoir, and two spanking-new yards of green taffeta daily to cover the basket in which the royal fan and gloves were carried were minor extravagances. Candles, often replaced even if they had not been used, cost 50,000 livres annually. The queen's wardrobe was worn once, then distributed among her household. Her wardrobe book was presented to her daily, with swatches of her court dresses next to each item, and Marie Antoinette would dreamily select what she wanted to wear that day by pricking the book with a pin to indicate her choices. Her porters would then go into the three large rooms filled with closets, drawers, and dressing tables to fetch the queen's clothes.

Then there were the diamonds. While fashions changed, and the muslin dress—to the disgust of the French silk industry—became the "in" thing to own, the queen truly loved her diamonds. She had had virtually all of the crown jewels reset on several occasions since becoming queen of France, and had Louis foot the bill. When Louis inherited the crown and thereby the crown jewels in 1774, there were 7,482 diamonds. By 1784 there were 3,536 additional diamonds purchased for the royal couple. In addition, the queen had her own personal jewels, some of which had come to France with her from the Habsburg court in Vienna.

Interestingly, Marie Antoinette was extremely supportive of the American cause, and where Louis "hated" republicans, he allowed his aversion for them generally, and Benjamin Franklin in particular, to be overcome for political reasons. In 1776 Louis sold diamonds worth 75,050 livres ($76.7 million or £49.9 million today) to help finance the American Revolutionary War. Fortunately, neither the Sancy nor the Regent was among the lot. The French support for the Americans at this time was not driven by idealism or political, philosophical, or social enlightenment. It was the product of revenge against the British, who had "stolen" French colonies in Hudson Bay and French Canada by the Peace of Utrecht.

It was diamonds that would finally seal the queen's fate as a figure of hatred in the Affair of the Diamond Necklace. Cardinal de Rohan, who had been at the Austrian court and who was loathed by Marie Antoinette's mother, had been trying since his return to France to be admitted to court. The queen, driven by her mother's poisonous correspondence against the cardinal, refused to have anything to do with him and froze him out. Her actions were so successful that the cardinal became obsessed with winning over France's queen.

On July 12, 1785, Marie Antoinette received a letter from the crown jeweler, Charles-Auguste Boehmer, which read:

> Madame,
> We are at the summit of happiness to dare to think that the latest arrangements which have been proposed to us and to which we have submitted with zeal and respect, are a new proof of our submission and devotion to the orders of Your Majesty. We have real

satisfaction in the thought that the most beautiful set of diamonds in the world will be at the service of the greatest and best of Queens.

The queen was frankly bemused. Boehmer had, of course, reset all the crown jewels for her and Louis, including the Sancy, which she had worn as a necklace and a diadem, or tiara. Boehmer had approached her as well for the purchase of a diamond necklace more than a year earlier; she had refused on the grounds that her "jewel cases were rich enough." When he persisted, Marie Antoinette bluntly replied, "We have more need of ships than diamonds."

When queried, Boehmer answered truthfully that he was not trying to *sell* the queen his necklace, since Her Majesty had already bought it with 30,000 livres advanced by Cardinal de Rohan. The cardinal had advanced the princely sum in the hope that this would, at last, buy him the queen's favor. Further, Boehmer claimed to have letters of authority from the queen for the purchase of the diamond necklace for 1.5 million livres that included an instruction that Boehmer was to say that he had sold the infamous necklace in Constantinople, should he be asked. The queen was flummoxed and could not conceive that de Rohan would have involved himself in such an affair. She said that it was "a labyrinth to me and that my mind was lost in it."

De Rohan was scandalized that the queen claimed to know nothing of the transaction. As the truth of the matter unfolded, the queen and her advisers saw this as an opportunity to destroy the ambitious cardinal, rather than the true necessity of fighting a rear guard action to protect Marie Antoinette's reputation, which had been persistently attacked by the pamphleteers in their *libelles*. This was a catastrophic misreading of the national feeling against the queen, especially as she was about to go on the attack against one of the most respected families of France—the de Rohans.

When Louis cross-examined the cardinal in front of the queen the following August, he gleaned from that interview that the cardinal had been given the letter instructing him to purchase the necklace from a lady called Comtesse de Lamotte. Jeanne de Lamotte was brought up as a virtual beggar by her peasant mother, but had been told that she was a direct descendant of the Valois king Henry II.

She, like so many other hangers-on, staked out her position at court, and eventually had an affair with the cardinal on his return from Vienna. At the time she was already married and living in a ménage à trois with her husband and her lover Rétaux de Villette, a known and accomplished forger. The truth slowly dawned on the cardinal that he had been duped by the trio and that it had been Madame Lamotte's intention all along to swindle him and Boehmer out of a fortune in cash—not to mention the diamonds themselves.

The queen asked how the cardinal could have possibly imagined that she would have first confided such an important acquisition to a woman of that nature. How could he think that she wished to use a man to whom she had not spoken since the day of her arrival in France? De Rohan replied truthfully that he had been blinded by ambition and the need to be of service to Her Majesty.

Rather than let matters lie there and pursue the true culprits, since Comte de Lamotte had escaped to London with the diamonds, which had been brutally pried from their settings and damaged, the king and queen ordered Cardinal de Rohan to be arrested along with Jeanne de Lamotte, who had remained in Paris. Rétaux de Villette was also sought from his hideout in Geneva. The comte de Lamotte remained at liberty in England. Jeanne de Lamotte was not prepared to go down without a fight, and in December 1785 her trial brief was published, recounting details of an alleged sexual intrigue between the queen and the cardinal. Naturally, the public believed every word, and more than twenty thousand copies were sold. As Marie Antoinette was now pregnant again, it was widely supposed that the cardinal could well be the father—an anathema beyond comprehension to the queen.

When the cardinal came to trial in Parlement in May 1786, it was sensational. One of the defendants, a young prostitute named Nicole d'Oliva, described how she had been hired by the comte de Lamotte to portray the queen in a dark nighttime tryst with the cardinal in the Grove of Venus in the gardens of Versailles, where she gave the cardinal further verbal instructions for the purchase of the necklace. Nicole was acquitted of all crime except that of impersonating the queen, and received only a verbal rebuke for that. De Villette, for his role as master forger, was banished from France with the clothes on his back as his only possession. The de Lamottes—the husband in abstentia—were handed out fierce sentences that included public flogging, branding, and life imprisonment. Yet the cardinal was acquitted, providing he apologize publicly for his "criminal temerity" in believing that he had met with the queen in the Grove of Venus. He was forced to divest himself of his offices and make a donation to the poor. The last condition was that he be banished from court forever. The verdict reinforced the image of the queen's loose morals—after all, how could an educated man like the cardinal believe he had met with the queen in such a manner if it was not her habit to do so?

Although all the ministers had begged the queen to spend less on diamonds and jewels and had failed, the Cardinal de Rohan had succeeded. Diamonds, and most notably that "cursed Sancy diamond," became objects of disdain to Marie Antoinette. After all, Charles the Bold had died owning it, Antonio de Crato had lived a tragic and nomadic life, Henrietta Maria had died penniless and without a crown. Surely, Marie Antoinette reasoned, there was something to the theory of a malediction on the stone. Even the Regent diamond was spurned by the queen, since Pitt had been made miserable by its ownership. These cursed diamonds had become her source of unhappiness.

The queen's baby girl was born prematurely, and Marie Antoinette would take many months to get over complications of the last pregnancy. Despite all the rumors about the royal sexuality and her "affairs," Louis never questioned the paternity of any of his four children by Marie Antoinette, despite the heyday enjoyed about this subject by French pamphleteers. But the royal family's life was threatened by more than scurrilous pamphlets. The new baby was not flourishing. Their eldest son, the dauphin, was feverish, and it was evident to all that a cloud hung over Versailles. But most pressing of all their problems in 1786 was the incontrovertible fact that the monarchy was essentially bankrupt, and Louis could no longer avoid the inevitable; financial reform was essential.

The tax system was based on inequality and feudal rights. There were the three divisive factions among the aristocracy: the *noblesse de court*, *noblesse d'épée*, and *noblesse de robe* (nobles of the court, sword, and wardrobe, respectively); each had its own system of garnering power and favor. While many of them should have been paying taxes, the burden more frequently fell on their tenants or peasants. These four hundred thousand privileged individuals of the aristocracy owned a fifth of all the land in France. The church had managed to avoid the *vingtième* that Louis XV had tried to institute against it, and although it owned a tenth of the land in France, as an institution it was phenomenally wealthy and powerful, even if the average priest could barely scrape enough together for a decent meal. The myriad taxes levied—*la gabelle* (salt tax), *la taille* (tax on total income in the north, on property in the south, and successfully levied only on commoners), *les aides* (tax on wine, playing cards, and soap), *la capitation* (tax on commonors determined by profession), and the dreaded *vingtième* (5 percent income tax)—remained uncollected or subject to thousands of exemptions. The limitations placed on the bourgeoisie by the system were a serious bone of contention, and talented professionals became mouthpieces for the downtrodden. All of these classes of society loathed one another, and did not trust the future of France to any of the other groups.

In November 1788 the Committee of Thirty, of which very little is known other than the fact that three of its members—the marquis de Lafayette, who had distinguished himself in the Revolutionary War in America; Abbé Sieyes; and Abbé de Talleyrand-Périgord, better known as Prince Talleyrand—became the self-appointed conscience and leaders of the revolt against the crown. As in the Revolutionary War in America, the inequity of the social and economic system was at the heart of the bloodshed to follow.

Despite having recalled Parlement in 1774, the present king found that nothing could quell the unrest. After years of fiscal abuse and failed harvests, most of France's twenty-one million people were ragged and starving. Most of them were made to endure outrageous social indignities and had virtually no education. With clergy and nobility refusing to pay more in taxes, and the masses unable to do any more than they had done, Louis found himself in the invidious position of needing to recall the Estates General for the first time since Louis XIV's reign. With the First and Second Estates representing the clergy and nobility, respectively, the Third Estate became the voice of the people in 1789, joined by the powerful and persuasive bourgeoisie. When the elections were held, 291 nobles, 300 clergy, and 610 members of the Third Estate took office and presented their *cahiers de doléances* (books of grievances). No matter which faction authored these grievances, they were universal in their condemnation of the absolute monarchy, but none went so far as to suggest government without a king. It looked as if, at last, the three factions had agreed on something.

On June 29, 1789, sixteen days before the storming of the Bastille, Thomas Jefferson wrote to John Jay from Paris with an uncharacteristic lack of foresight: "A perfect cooperation with the Tiers [Third Estate] will be his wisest game: This great crisis being now over, I shall not have matter interesting enough to trouble you with, as often as I have done lately."

In the words of the philosopher-writer Alexis de Tocqueville, "Never was any such event so inevitable, yet so completely unforeseen."

23

Slipping through the
Deft Hands of Thieves

1789–1799

❖

By the time thomas jefferson's letter reached John Jay in America at the end of June 1789, the young dauphin had died, the Third Estate had rebranded itself the National Assembly, with the king ordering the clergy and nobility to join it, and a constitution was to be drafted to reflect the revolutionary change in French society. Two weeks after Jefferson's letter, when most of the clergy but only forty-seven nobles had obeyed the king's orders, the king tried to disband the National Assembly, and the people took to the streets. Private and public property were attacked by the marauding mobs—many of whom were looking for arms at the gunsmiths' and sword cutlers' shops of Paris—and they organized themselves into vigilante militias. The hated Bastille, though slated for demolition with few inmates left inside, had become an intolerable symbol of the absolute monarchy and ancien régime. It was stormed and taken by the mob, and the French Revolution had begun.

Within a month, the National Assembly had outlawed all feudal rights and made its Declaration of the Rights of Man and the Citizen, largely modeled on the American Bill of Rights. In October, Louis was legitimized as king of the French by the National Assembly. The following month, all church property was nationalized. By June 1790, all hereditary titles were abolished, and eight months later, the first

243

bishops of the new constitutional church were elected. In March 1791 the pope finally spoke out against the ravages perpetrated against the church, and the royal family could visualize the writing on the wall in their own blood. On May 28, 1791, the National Assembly ordered a new inventory of the crown jewels and confiscated the personal jewels of the king and queen. By spring 1792 the nobility had fled France by the thousands, mostly to England and America—but not before they were despoiled of their riches, and especially their gems, furniture, and paintings. All of the booty was stored in the *garde-meuble* at the Louvre and would become the basis for the national collection to be housed at the former royal palace. It was time for Louis and his family to escape. The date was set for June 20, 1792.

The debonair Swedish diplomat Count Fersen, who also was Marie Antoinette's lover, offered the king and queen all the money he had—some 60,000 livres. Count Fersen also arranged for a carriage for the royal family and masterminded the escape route, including soldiers to protect them. The carriage was a sumptuous coach with dark green and yellow bodywork, pale yellow wheels, and white velvet upholstery. It was ordered in the name of a friend of the count's, the baroness von Korff, and made conspicuous around Paris, so that it would not arouse suspicion when the royal family took flight. The king disguised himself as the comte de Choiseul, whom he resembled, and the queen dressed as if she were the children's governess.

Through clever subterfuge arranged by Count Fersen, Louis, Marie Antoinette, their children, and their governess were able to walk out of the Tuileries in Paris into their waiting carriage, with the count as its driver. Once safely past the outer Parisian checkpoint at Porte Saint-Martin, the king took the reins, and Fersen escaped across the border into Belgium. The royal family was heading toward Germany and on, they hoped, to the Habsburg royal court in Vienna.

As they passed Châlons-sur-Marne, the king looked at his watch and remarked with considerable relief, "Lafayette must be feeling most embarrassed by now."

But Lafayette was not embarrassed at all. He was apoplectic. Surpassing any authority granted to him, he immediately dictated an order to his aide-de-camp:

The King having been removed by the enemies of the Revolution, the bearer is instructed to impart the fact to all good citizens, who are commanded in the name of their endangered country to take him out of their hands and bring him back to the keeping of the National Assembly. The latter is about to assemble, but in the meantime I take upon myself all responsibility of this order. Paris, 21st June 1791. Lafayette.

He need hardly have bothered. The royal carriage had missed its appointed rendezvous with the soldiers loyal to the king by more than three hours. The soldiers, who had been loitering in the village near the meeting point, immediately aroused suspicion among the townspeople, who suspected that they were in the village to collect unpaid taxes, rather than the cover story, which was that they were the escort for a carriage that carried payment for the armies in the east. With pitchforks brandished and muskets pointed at their faces, they beat a tactical retreat.

When the king arrived at last in the village of Sainte-Ménéhould, the villagers knew that something extremely odd was going on. He understood right away that he had caused a stir, and rode on ten miles to the little town of Clermont en Argonne, where he changed horses. The attendant heard a shout from the carriage, "Take the road to Varennes." The pursuing villagers were told what he had heard, took a shortcut known to locals, and arrived at Varennes at the same time as the carriage.

A local official—a grocer, one Jean Baptiste Sauce—stood in the middle of the road with the National Guardsmen behind him, bayonets fixed to their muskets, and cried out, "Halt! One step more and we fire!" The horses were reined in and clattered to a halt. Sauce approached and asked for the passports of the occupants, and was satisfied that they were who they claimed to be—the baroness von Korff and her party. Drouet, a young postmaster, who had been pursuing the carriage for miles, knew better, and demanded that they be detained, or Sauce would be charged with treason.

The royal party was taken to Sauce's bedroom above his shop and awaited the arrival of a local judge, who had spent much time at Versailles and had met the king on several occasions. When he took one look at the huge figure in a green overcoat, the judge immediately knelt before him and cried out, "Oh, sire!"

Louis answered him without faltering, "Yes, I am indeed your king." The king explained why they had left Paris and that they had no wish to harm anyone, and was promised that in the morning they would be provided with an escort to complete their journey.

But before dawn, one of Lafayette's aides-de-camp, Jean Louis Romeuf, arrived at Varennes with Lafayette's order to return the royal family to the Tuileries. The king asked to read it, and on doing so, placed the order on the bed where the royal children were lying. The queen scooped it off the bed and threw it on the wooden floor, shouting, "I will not have my children contaminated." This one comment set the hitherto sympathetic people of Varennes against her.

By the time the king and his family had been brought back to the Tuileries in Paris, the people had been whipped up into a frenzy. A month later, in August 1792, all over the city pamphlets titled *The Great Treason of Louis Capet [the King]* were scattered, revealing the "discovery of a plot for assassinating all good citizens during the night of second and third of this month." By the beginning of September, Paris descended into mob violence. Priests who had been held prisoner were brutally murdered and, once dead, dismembered. Other prisoners received "justice" in kangaroo courts that were no more than back rooms lit by candles and facing judges who knew nothing of the law. Then they were tortured to death with the most appalling animalistic ferocity. At the Conciergerie, where prisoners awaited trial at the Palais de Justice, gangs of assassins hacked to death 378 of the 488 prisoners in their cells, and their disemboweled remains were thrown into heaps in the courtyard.

The authorities did little to curb the massacres. Indeed, they were given tacit approval by the bloodthirsty Jean Paul Marat—a vituperative physician turned pamphleteer—who reasoned that they were only killing the enemies of the Revolution. But as is so often the case with mob violence, the unexpected happened.

From September 8 to 15, 1792, thieves broke into the *garde-meuble* on the first floor of the Louvre and helped themselves to the crown jewels. The Sancy, the Regent, all the other Mazarins, the crowns and coronation regalia, and all other gems, ornaments, and valuables were stolen. This treasure, while no longer of any use to the king, was the intended means of extricating the French treasury from its hole and had been intended for sale at the right time.

The police and revolutionary militias of Paris combed the city and apprehended some of the thieves, and Commissioner Alizard had them thrown into the Conciergerie. Wild stories—believed by most—that the queen had hired these men to recover her precious jewels so she could sell them for her own account, circulated by word of mouth and again in the dreaded pamphlets.

One of the thieves, a man named Badarel, claimed to have buried his loot with an accomplice called Gallois on the night of September 15, shortly before he returned to the scene of the crime to see what the ruckus was about. When he was incarcerated at the Conciergerie, he had three diamond chains in his pockets. On September 20, other jewels, which had never been documented—not even in the inventory of 1791—were recovered with the help of a Jew named Anselme Lion, who reported an attempted sale to him by a shady character. He arranged for the sale to take place later in the day when the police were present, and the thief was arrested.

From the National Assembly's viewpoint, it was exceptionally important to dispatch justice, and to do so rapidly. The charge against the thieves, aside from the obvious charge of theft, was "an armed plot with the intent of overthrowing the newly constituted government of France." The men charged were named Douligny and de Chambon. Badarel and another man, Picard, who also were in custody, were brought along to testify at the trial on September 24. After forty-five hours of questioning and cross-examination, Douligny cracked. He named all his other accomplices, including a fellow cellmate from a previous stint in jail, a man named Roudany. When the two men were condemned to death by the tribunal, they cried out other names—other accomplices—to save their skins. Douligny said that a man called Francisque, and another called Depeyron, as well as Badarel, were the masterminds.

Badarel was hauled back in front of the tribunal and confessed that he had hidden jewels in an alley, now avenue Montaigne. A court official was sent to verify Badarel's claim and, according to the court records, returned with:

> A package containing an enamel piece with nine large pearls, four small pearls, nine emeralds and rubies of different sizes, two pearls that had no mounting, an onyx religious piece representing a saint mounted in gold, a medal of a person made of gold with the top made of white enamel, fifteen large brilliant-cut diamonds in their boxes that were covered in silk casings, ninety other diamonds also in their boxes with silk casings and nine roses and four brilliant-cut diamonds.

The find was compared with the inventory of May 28, 1791, which had been compiled by Boehmer, the unlucky jeweler in the Affair of the Diamond Necklace. The onyx piece had been offered by Holy Roman emperor Charles V to the treasure of the Sainte-Chapelle. The golden medal had once belonged to the chapel of Richelieu, and had been worn as part of the court attire of Louis XVI.

Naturally, this recovery gave the authorities cause to hope that the two condemned men might make further confessions, and decided on September 24 to grant stays of execution. Badarel and Depeyron also were condemned to death, but Badarel, too, received a stay of execution "in consideration for the important services rendered to the Republic by his multiple avowals and specific information that the accused had given about his movements."

Depeyron, however, was taken to the scaffold at the appointed time and on the appointed day. As he mounted the scaffold, just as in the movies, he cried out "Wait!" and demanded to see the president of the tribunal, with the promise of revealing all. His cache of diamonds, he swore, was of tremendous value to the Republic. The president, duly summoned, promised him mercy only if what he was about to reveal was truly as important as he claimed. Depeyron, still manacled, took the president to his home in the dead-end street picturesquely named Sainte-Opportune, went into his close closet, or toilet, and pulled out of the space between the roof tiles two packets of diamonds that represented a total value of 1.2 million livres. The gems were the *fleur-de-pêcher*, the five-pointed Rose diamond (soon to be renamed the Hortensia), the Great Mazarin, and diverse diamonds between ten and fifteen carats. Depeyron's cache was exceptionally valuable, especially when up to this point only 300,000 livres in gems had been recovered.

Throughout the month of October other thieves were tried, with the same pattern of condemnations of executions being reversed at the last minute when the hidden gems were given up in return for their lives. It was only on November 20 that the so-called leader of the robbery, Paul Miette, was put on trial. He had been fingered by Douligny and de Chambon during their trial, and he, in turn, squealed on others. Like the others, he was spared, despite being the mastermind. Only one thief, François Mauger, was executed; unfortunately, he had no jewels left with which to bargain for his life.

Despite numerous recoveries and a more complete picture emerging about the theft, the Sancy, the Regent, and the French Blue—the three most valuable diamonds in the crown jewel collection—were still missing six months after the initial theft. The trail seemed to have gone cold.

Then, as so often in these cases, a lucky break came. A Madame Lelievre and her sister, Madame Morée, were released from prison. Madame Lelievre was the mistress of a man named Bernard Salles, who had participated in the theft on the first night from the *garde-meuble*. Salles had been executed—not for the theft, but for forging documents shortly after the theft. The Regent was recovered when after her release, she tried to fence the gem, which had either been stolen by Salles or hidden in their garret. On December 10, 1793, it was announced in the *journaux judiciaries* that:

> Your Committee of General Surety never ceases to make progress in the search for the accomplices in the theft at the *garde-meuble*. Yesterday, another accomplice was apprehended, and another precious stone recovered. It is the diamond known as the Pitt or the Regent, which was valued in the 1791 inventory for 12 millions. To hide it, the thief had hidden it in the floorboards of her attic in a hole an inch and a half in diameter. The thief and the fence have been arrested. The diamond has been taken into evidence for their conviction. I propose to you, in the name of the committee, to decree that the diamond shall be transported to the national treasury and that the commissioners of this establishment hold this gem for the good of the nation.

Three months later, in March 1794, the Sancy was recovered in the home of a Monsieur Tavenel and his sister, the widow Leblanc, along with a huge number of other stones worth several million livres. With the Sancy was the de Guise diamond and most of the Mazarins. The thief had been unable to move or sell the Sancy and his other booty in France, since it had become a treasonous offense to possess it. Nor did he have the means to take it outside of the country. He had "owned" the greatest treasure of the French crown for nearly eighteen months but had been unable to turn that ownership into a profit. Tavenel and his sister were condemned to eighteen years' hard labor in irons, but Tavenel managed somehow to escape by means unknown to this day, leaving his sister in the custody of her jailers.

While in the process of overseeing the recovery of the stolen crown jewels, the National Assembly had made it "law," from 1792, to confiscate all the possessions of its emigrant nobility. Religious artifacts of value also had been confiscated from abbeys and churches, and these were taken to the Louvre, along with all the other treasures. By mid-1794, 17 million livres' worth of jewels recovered in this manner were housed in the former royal palace.

With the royal family virtual prisoners at Tuileries since their return to Paris, it most likely came as little surprise when the palace was stormed by a mob on August 17, 1792. The only reason why this had not happened earlier was certainly because in August 1791 the Declaration of Pillnitz between Emperor Leopold, Marie Antoinette's brother, and the king of Prussia considered the situation of the French royal family "an object of interest to all the sovereigns of Europe" and wished to restore a monarchical system in France. The mistake made by Prussia and Austria was that neither could act without the cooperation of other European powers.

With the Declaration of Pillnitz, cries for war against foreign powers from the sanguine revolutionaries in charge of France had grown louder and louder. The queen's sentiments that these "foreign powers" might present themselves as the king's only salvation were well known. Louis had been reduced to a mere figurehead for the revolutionary government, and was made to endure the final humiliation when, on the death of Emperor Leopold, he was compelled to declare war in a preemptive strike against both Prussia and Austria. The fact that the French army—a ragtag force of fewer than 140,000 insubordinate and ill-trained volunteers—was no match for the fine armies of Prussia and Austria was not known to those with the real power in France.

As the war got under way, with the invasion from France through Belgium toward Prussia in April 1792, the reality of France's disastrous policy became plain. Generals were murdered by their own troops, battle after battle was lost, and the marquis de Lafayette returned to Paris from Belgium in June in the hope of restoring order to the capital by mounting a coup d'état.

Lafayette ordered the king to disband his six thousand men who were household guards—probably the best-trained French soldiers—which Louis did without objection. But Louis rejected utterly the treatment of obstinate priests as being counterrevolutionary—a policy that could result in their being deported to French Guiana on the denunciation of a single citizen—as well as the establishment of twenty thousand National Guardsmen on the outskirts of Paris. This, combined with the inauspicious beginning of the war, meant that the squabbles among the myriad revolutionary factions—Feuillants, Fédérés, Girondins, Jacobins, and Sans-culottes—exploded into a full-blown civil war. The Tuileries was stormed by the Girondins initially, but when Louis persuaded them that he supported their cause, he was left in peace.

A month later, the Sans-culottes stormed the palace—this time under fire from the king's Swiss guards. Wave after wave of Sans-culottes ascended the steps of the Tuileries, shouting "Treason! Death to the traitors!" When the Swiss guards, having exhausted their ammunition, surrendered, they were hacked to death along with all the ushers, pages, doorkeepers, cooks, maidservants, and the dauphin's subgovernor. Their bodies were tossed out the windows of the palace, their heads impaled on pikes. All the rooms were looted, furniture that was not taken away smashed, jewelry and ornaments pocketed, and official papers strewn over the floor. A witness to the carnage saw two very young boys playing ball with human heads, while another uttered, his hands stained dark red with blood, "Providence has been very good to me. I killed three of the Swiss with my own hands." Five hundred Swiss guards had been slaughtered in the palace or its gardens, and sixty others were escorted to the Hôtel de Ville, where they were immediately massacred. Three hundred "citizens" and ninety National Guardsmen also were killed.

At nightfall, the royal family was escorted to a convent, where they were given makeshift beds. In the morning they were taken before the National Assembly, where the king was ousted from his functions, and the National Convention—as the National Assembly decided to rebrand itself—was to be elected based on universal manhood suffrage. The king and his family were confined in a secure building called the Temple, which had formerly been occupied by the king's brother the comte d'Artois, who was now in exile. The National Convention had imprisoned the king without deciding with what to replace the monarchy. The Reign of Terror had begun.

Four months passed with the royal family incarcerated in the Temple. During the day, the king helped instruct the dauphin and read works by Montesquieu and Racine to the young boy. He also gave the dauphin maps to color as a way of teaching him geography. In the evenings, after the children played, then said their prayers before going to bed, the king studied in his room until midnight—often rereading the life of Charles I of England, perhaps in an attempt to understand where he had gone wrong, and if there might be any escape. The queen passed her days making tapestries, embroidering, or knitting, then played with her daughter or her Scottish terrier. While Louis had slimmed from worry and a poor diet, Marie Antoinette had become skin and bones. Her hair was gray, streaked with white, and she was only thirty-seven years old. Their jailers were cruel—rattling keys in their faces, scrawling obscenities on the walls, or singing revolutionary songs at them in the garden when they were allowed out for a walk in the afternoon. Their jailers tore apart their food with their grimy fingers to ensure that nothing had been smuggled in to them, then shoved the crumbled bread and dissected meal under their noses. They all knew that the end would come, even if they did not know when or how.

When the King was summoned before the National Convention, the queen tenderly kissed him good-bye. Louis knew that the verdict was never in doubt, only the punishment that would await them all. A former lawyer of the king, Chrétien de Lamoignon de Malesherbes, returned from Switzerland as the king's counsel, stating, "I owe him a duty now that many people deem dangerous."

The king was found guilty unanimously, as he had always supposed. Where the wrangling occurred was on his sentence. Some Girondins felt his life should be spared as a matter of "expediency." One of their leaders, Jacques Pierre Brissot de Warville, declared that "no Republican will ever be brought to believe that, in order to set twenty-five million people free, one man must die." One of the secretaries of the convention, Rabaut Saint-Étienne, added, "Louis dead would be more dangerous to people's freedom than Louis living in prison." These pleas for mercy were derided in the streets by the Sans-culottes and by more hawkish Girondins. The king was sentenced to die by a majority of fifty votes, and the Girondins were now suspected as royalists by the violent Sans-culottes. The vote lasted seventy-two hours. A deputy recorded, "The uppermost galleries, kept open for the common people, were filled with foreigners and people from all walks of life. They drank wine and brandy as if they were in some low, smoke-filled tavern. At all the cafés in the neighborhood bets were being laid on the outcome."

The king accepted his verdict of death calmly, and returned to the Temple. There he was aroused from his sleep shortly before dawn on January 20, 1793, to be told that he would be executed the following morning. According to historian Christopher Hibbert, the king said good-bye to his family that night amid "lamentations that could be heard outside the tower." When he was fetched the next day at dawn by Jacques Roux and other commissioners of the National Convention, Louis kept them waiting a few moments while he said his last prayers. When he stood up, he handed a small parcel containing what remained of his few personal belongings and his will to Roux, and with a broken voice whispered, "For the queen . . . for my wife." Roux coarsely replied, "I am not here to run your errands, I am here to take you to the scaffold." Louis graciously replied, "That is so," then offered the parcel to another man, who quietly took it from the king.

The king's death carriage arrived at the Place de la Révolution at above nine-thirty, and Louis XVI mounted the scaffold amid a roar of drum rolls and shouts from the bloodthirsty throng. Despite his protestations, his hands were bound behind his back, and his hair cut short. He asked to be allowed to address the crowd, and when the drummers stopped said in a loud, authoritative voice, "I forgive those who are guilty of my death, and I pray to God that the blood which you are about to shed may never be required of France. I only sanctioned upon compulsion the Civil Constitution of the Clergy—" The rest of his words were drowned out by the drummers recommencing their beating. When it fell, the guillotine blade failed to sever the king's head, and was raised a second time, then lowered again. The king's head fell into the awaiting basket, and an eighteen-year-old guard held it aloft to the jeering public, who cried, "*Vive la République! Vive la nation!*"

The monarchies of Europe, which had been reeling from events in France, were in utter shock. Georges Jacques Danton, the new head of the National Convention, had claimed France's right to natural borders—and therefore that the country intended to extend its borders to the sea, the Alps, the Rhine, and the Pyrenees. It was tantamount to a declaration of war on Switzerland, the German states, Spain, and Great Britain.

The queen was separated from her children in July 1793 and incarcerated in the Conciergerie. When it came time for her trial, she was accused of crimes ranging from conspiracy with her brother to incest with her son. When she gave no answer to the kangaroo court's obscene accusations and was pressed on the point, she replied with great dignity, "If I give no answer, it is because nature itself refuses to accept such an accusation brought against a mother. I appeal to all the mothers here present." For a moment there was hope—her spirit had aroused sympathy in the court. When the president saw the unexpected turn of events, he angrily threatened to clear the court, and sped up the proceedings, hardly giving others the opportunity to pronounce their guilty verdict and death sentence.

The queen was taken the next morning to the scaffold, her hands bound behind her back and her hair roughly shorn, wearing a white piqué dress, white bonnet, black stockings, and red high-heeled shoes. She trembled at the sight of her death cart, and had to have her hands untied so she could relieve herself on the courtyard wall. The streets were lined with the ferocious citizens of Paris as she slowly made her way to the guillotine, and when she alighted from the cart, her eyes vacant and sunken, cheeks pale and drawn, she stumbled and stepped on her executioner's toe. As he cried out in pain, she apologized, "Monsieur, I beg your pardon, I did not do it on purpose." These were her last words.

During the next years, the guillotine blade rose and fell more times in a day than there were days in the year. Even Danton fell under the executioner's blade. His replacement by Maximilien Robespierre made no difference to France's neighbors—the country had had the taste for blood, and under Robespierre the French threat grew abroad. Any vestige of the France prior to the Revolution was systematically wiped out—the currency was changed, and even the months and years were given new names.

Even with the execution of Robespierre and his followers in July 1794 the bloodshed continued, and only with the brilliance of France's few good generals, such as Louis Lazare Hoche, was the country able to make any advances in its foreign wars. By the beginning of 1795 the French had occupied Amsterdam, and in April France signed its peace with Holland and Prussia. The National Convention was dissolved and replaced by yet another rabid constitutional committee, called the Directory, in October of that year. The government of France—no matter what it called itself—was, as it had been in the king's time, essentially bankrupt, and had dispatched two agents named Perrin and Cablat to Constantinople with a huge number of valuable diamonds. The Mirror of Portugal and most of the Mazarins were sold to the sultan at the Porte for an undisclosed sum and were lost forever to the public eye.

The larger remaining crown jewels, including the Sancy, were put on exhibit at the Museum of Natural History, where they were deemed "necessary for the instruction of the public, and which were separate from objects of luxury." But this exhibition was exceedingly short-lived. With fourteen armies in the field in 1796, money, arms, food, and men were the primary concerns of the Directory. Even these "historic" and "educational" crown jewels would need to be forfeited for the "glory" of France.

The moneymen who had been financing the French with arms and horses now demanded payment or they would cease their deliveries.

Baron von Treskow, who had provided both arms and horses, was owed millions of francs. After some negotiations, the Regent was sent to him in pawn for a bargain of 3 million francs, reimbursable at a time to be determined. Another banker, Vanlenberghem, in association with others in Belgium and Holland, paid off the debt to von Treskow and took possession of the gem, which Vanlenberghem's wife wore under her clothes at all times.

The alleged provider of exceptional horses from Spain, the marquis of Iranda, was cajoled into providing hundreds more horses for an advance of 1 million francs, secured against the Sancy and other gemstones. Iranda estimated that the jewels he now possessed in pawn to be worth a mere 300,000 francs instead of the 1 million francs valuation that the Sancy alone had provided in the inventory of 1791.

Iranda's horses, whose payment was secured against the Sancy, were sent into battle under a little-known and newly appointed general, Napoleon Bonaparte, for his first great victory in charge of the Army of Italy at the Battle of Marengo. Three years later, on the 18th of Brumaire of Year VIII—November 9, 1799—Bonaparte ended the French Revolution by a coup d'état.

24

The Bonaparte Legacy

1799–1828

❧

NAPOLEON'S METEORIC RISE TO POWER was assured at Marengo—by the splendid Spanish horses acquired on a deferred payment plan using the Sancy as security. Napoleon's ascent could not have been predicted at the time, but it was inextricably linked to the loss of the Sancy to France.

In 1799 the mood of the French army was very different from what it had been at the outset of the Revolution. Antagonism toward church, king, and aristocracy was as strong as ever. Hatred and bloodshed had become a way of life, ingrained by the events of the preceding ten years. The Revolution no longer represented a rallying call for France's "freedom fighters," nor was it any longer an emotionally or psychologically uplifting cry. In fact, in 1799 the army felt detached from government and took pride only in their regiments and their victories. Their commanders were their gods, and Napoleon had promised and delivered "rich provinces, great cities . . . honor, glory, and wealth."

What the army—and the people—wanted was leadership after ten long years of bloodshed, committees, and mob rule. Paul-François Barras, who had come to power during the Directory at the head of the police after the fall of Robespierre and the Reign of Terror, had spotted Napoleon's talent during the *journées de Vendémiaire*, when royalists had threatened to overrun Paris, and put Napoleon's name forward in March 1796 to head the Army of Italy. His appointment was unanimously endorsed by the entire Directory, as they knew that Napoleon would have no scruples about replenishing the country's empty coffers with treasure looted from defeated countries.

The economic situation in France was nothing short of abysmal. The value of interest-bearing bonds, called assignats, had fallen so much that one hundred livres was worth only 15 sous. Paper currency retained only 1 percent of the value it had held between 1795 and 1796. Beggars and peasants alike would accept only gold or silver coins, claiming that the paper money was only fit for their horses to eat. The harvest was again poor, and fuel prices skyrocketed. The impoverished could not afford to cook, let alone heat their homes. This situation was made worse by the flamboyance and excesses of the rich, their thirst for pleasures of all sorts—like gambling, where, according to Napoleon's biographer Vincent Cronin, it was not uncommon to lose 1 million livres on a single card—or the outrageous fashion of dressing *à la sauvage* with bare breasts and flesh-colored tights covered only by "circles of diamonds set around the ankles, wrists, and thighs."

France undoubtedly needed a leader to drag it out of the quagmire of political, social, and economic decadence, and Napoleon saw himself unequivocally as that man of destiny. He was only twenty-six at the time, the son of a Corsican lawyer of noble Florentine origin and a native Italian-speaker—in fact, the name was spelled Buonaparte, meaning "the good party," until he became first counsel. Although both his parents were noble by birth, they had none of the inbreeding, wealth, or privileges common among the nobility. Napoleon spoke French with a marked Italian accent, misspelling and mispronouncing words, until his death.

A week after Napoleon's appointment as commander in chief of the Army of Italy, he married the alluring Rose de Beauharnais, whom he had nicknamed Josephine. She was from the island of Martinique, the widow of the guillotined Vicomte de Beauharnais, and former mistress of Paul-François Barras. Josephine was six years older than Napoleon, and certainly not in love with him when they married, complaining to her friends at the time that it was her "tepidness toward him—and his belief that she should be his alone—that annoyed her." Nonetheless, she seemed happy to do so, since Barras had wished it and promised her his continuing protection if she accepted Napoleon's proposal. At thirty-two, with no money or prospects and two young children, she needed to look to her own future, which would become bleaker the older she became. Barras had promised her, as a wedding present, to secure for Napoleon the Army of Italy so she could live well. Compliant, she agreed.

The marriage contract was favorable to Napoleon. He agreed to pay his wife 1,500 livres for life, which in view of the civil marriages in revolutionary France, and the likelihood of divorce, was exceedingly stingy. The wedding itself was a sad affair. In a dingy room of the town hall, the bride and groom were accompanied by their three witnesses, as required by law—Josephine's two former lovers Barras and Tallien, with whom she had been incarcerated at the time of her husband's demise, and her lawyer. Josephine had borrowed her younger sister Catherine's birth certificate—since hers was in English-occupied Martinique—for the ceremony. The wedding vows were equally devoid of emotion or feeling: "General Buonaparte, citizen, do you consent to take as your lawful wife Madame Beauharnais, here present, to keep faith with her, and to observe conjugal fidelity?" When they both said "Citizen, I do," Napoleon drove her to their as yet unpaid-for home on rue Chantereine and gave her an angel hair gold necklace with an enamel plaque hanging from it inscribed with the words "*Au destin.*" Three days later he began the Italian campaign, leaving Josephine to her pleasure-seeking in Paris.

His orders from Paris clearly commanded Bonaparte to secure works of art for the enjoyment of the French people. He carried out this order with an ardor that was only surpassed during the Nazi rape of European treasures in World War II. In just under six weeks of campaigning, Napoleon had cowed all of central Italy and seized forty million francs in loot and indemnities ($85.9 million or £53.7 million) from the thrashed Italian princes. The founding principle of the revolutionary government in France had been that all works of art, jewels, and other treasures belonging to kings, nobles, and the church should be confiscated for the French people. In Bonaparte they had found their most competent and exacting administrator.

Though he hardly needed the encouragement, the Directory wrote to Napoleon while he was in Italy to keep up the good work and to "send back works of art to Paris to strengthen and embellish the reign of liberty." He did this with an eye to quality—and could tell schlock from the exceptional without any input from experts.

When Napoleon defeated the duke of Parma, in exchange for leaving the duke his title and lands unmolested, he exacted a huge indemnity. Among the myriad items listed in the treaty, he stipulated without advice that Correggio's *Dawn* should be among the prizes. Although this painting depicted the Madonna and child and could well be frowned upon by the irreligious Directory, Napoleon reasoned that "The million he [the duke] offers us will soon be spent . . . but the possession of such a masterpiece will adorn the capital for ages, and give birth to similar exertions of genius." Other priceless items included Galileo's manuscripts on fortifications and da Vinci's mirror-written scientific treatises.

Virtually every treaty that Napoleon signed had some wording relating to works of art, jewels, or other priceless treasures. The pope had to provide valuables from the Vatican. When Venice fell, Napoleon made sure that the four horses adorning St. Mark's Square, and which had been looted by the Venetians during the sacking of Constantinople in the Fourth Crusade, were sent to Paris. As was customary since the Dark Ages, soldiers were allowed to participate in the spoils of war, and were made rich beyond their own imagining by personally partaking in the booty along with the nation.

Having conquered much of Italy, and enriching himself and his country in the process, Napoleon returned to a Paris of which he disapproved. He discovered that Josephine had been having an affair with a young colonel, Hippolyte Charles, and only after she begged him for days not to divorce her, did he forgive his wife. But before he could consolidate his marriage, he was shipped out again to Egypt "in order to utterly destroy England." While the Egyptian campaign against the Turks and the British was a qualified scientific and educational success, militarily it was a fiasco, with many of the French soldiers dead of disease, and to a lesser extent, from fighting the Turks.

On this return to Paris, he again threatened to divorce Josephine, who he again suspected of unfaithfulness. Yet, in looking at his own entourage of friends, he realized that all France had become dissolute. For one, Paul Barras was described by his cousin the marquis de Sade as "selling any job to pay for his pleasures." The people, however, were poorer than ever, and the roads so unsafe that even Napoleon's baggage train had been attacked and looted on his return.

Napoleon resolved to rescue France from herself and addressed the Council of Five Hundred at the Palace of Saint-Cloud, with his army camped outside, to insist on a role as director and a new constitution to save the country. As he stood before them, Napoleon uttered fateful words:

> Representatives of the people, this is no normal situation. You are on the edge of a volcano. Allow me to speak with the frankness of a soldier. . . . I swear that the country has no more zealous defender than I. . . . I am entirely at your orders. . . . Let us save at all costs the two things for which I have sacrificed so much, liberty and equality. . . . In fact there are conspiracies being hatched in the name of the constitution. . . . I know about all the dangers that threaten you.

With an army at the ready outside the palace, it was not difficult for the Council of the Directory to see who was threatening their body and limbs. Napoleon was ordered from the chamber amid shouts of "Outlaw the dictator!" His brother Lucien Bonaparte, as its president, called the Council to order, having scribbled a note to be delivered to Napoleon telling him, "You have ten minutes to act." Within the ten minutes, the tables were turned, and Napoleon ousted the "assembly of outlaws," who were so terrified by the bayonet charge of Napoleon's soldiers that they jumped out of the windows of the chamber. This was the coup d'état of the 18th Brumaire. The French Revolution was over, and the Consulate, with Napoleon as first consul, had been launched.

The serious business of rebuilding France began at once. The treasury only had 167,000 francs in cash and debts amounting to 474 million francs. The civil service had not been paid in ten months, and the country was wallpapered with worthless paper money. Napoleon raised 3 million francs with French bankers, 2 million francs in Genoa, and 9 million francs from a lottery, thus staving off impending bankruptcy. Full-time income-tax collectors were employed for tax collection across the country, and he demanded receipt of 5 percent of all taxes collected at once. This gave him ten days' cash in advance, and within the year, this had increased to a month. From an organized income-tax collection system alone he was able to raise some 660 million francs—over 185 million more francs than Louis XVI had in 1788.

Napoleon was the first to introduce indirect taxes on wine and playing cards, two vice industries of the elite. By 1806 he had expanded these taxes to salt, and by 1811 to tobacco, which had become a state monopoly.

The loans he was forced to accept from the bankers in rebuilding the French nation were at a crippling interest rate of 16 percent per annum, despite the fact that he made his views known that any yearly rate over 6 percent was usurious. Dissatisfied with the terms the bankers had given him, Napoleon set up the Banque de France in February 1800 with an initial capital of 30 million francs and the ability to lend money up to that amount. For the convenience of the Parisian region, the bank also could issue banknotes to the extent of its gold reserves.

Whatever had remained of the crown jewels was still in pawn when Napoleon seized power, and he resolved to get them back with the improved financial outlook of the nation. Since the crown jewels had bought him the horses on which he rode to victory, Napoleon believed that these would continue to bring him good luck. Naturally, since the Regent was the largest and most prestigious of the stones in pawn, Napoleon set about recovering it first. The Amsterdam merchant Vanlenberghem took the gem from his wife's underclothes and returned it to Paris personally once his loans had been repaid in mid-February 1800.

France's single largest creditor was Baron Treskow, who had initially had the Regent in pawn. When he was reimbursed for his loans, and all the gems he still had in his possession were returned to the treasury, Napoleon set out in search of the Sancy. The amount to be reimbursed, ostensibly to the marquis d'Iranda, was a third of its value from the inventory of 1791: 300,000 francs in gold ($498,000 or £311,000 today). Whether Napoleon *knew* that the marquis d'Iranda had only been an intermediary acting for the account of Queen Maria Luisa of Spain was never recorded, but the fact remains that from the

Napoleon in his coronation regalia. Painting by Francois Gerard, 1805.

Queen Maria Luisa and the Spanish Royal Family. From left to right: Francisco de Paula, Duke of Cadiz; Maria Luisa, Queen Consort of Spain; Charles, Duke of Molina; Maria Isabella, Queen of the Two Sicilies; Charles IV, King of Spain; Maria Luisa, Queen of Etruria; Ferdinand VII, King of Spain. Stipple engraving by unknown artist, early 19th century.

time Iranda negotiated the deal with Napoleon for the Sancy to be used as security, the queen of Spain had had the Sancy diamond in her possession. Despite Napoleon's omniscience in almost every matter, it seems unlikely that he knew that Maria Luisa of Spain had tricked him out of the Sancy. By the time Napoleon was in a position to buy back the Sancy, the marquis had died, and his heirs claimed that the diamond had been sold. They did not divulge to whom, and since Napoleon was most anxious to normalize relations with France's numerous creditors, including Spain, he temporarily gave up his search for the Sancy. And so, reluctantly, on the 15th Thermidor of Year IX—

better known as August 2, 1800—Bonaparte, as France's new first consul, decreed:

> The Consuls of the Republic, on the report of the minister of finances, warrant that the minister of finance is authorized to receive into the treasury the sum of three hundred thousand francs in exchange for the value of a diamond weighing fifty-three carats and three quarters [old carats] and estimated for the same amount de minimus, following the invoice and testimony of the 30 Pluviose of Year IX [February 18, 1800] and that the heirs of the Marquis d'Iranda were unable to present the said diamond of which they were the depository at the time of surrender on the 6 Messidor last [June 25, 1800]. Bonaparte.

In other words, the heirs of the marquis officially received the Sancy in exchange for an earlier loan to France of 300,000 francs.

In less than a year in power, Napoleon had reversed the country's economic fortunes, restored order, and reclaimed 8.6 million francs' worth of crown jewels. His next tasks were to rebuild France and to make the rest of Europe a vassal state of France.

Napoleon had not given up hope of finding the Sancy again—after all, it had reappeared after its previous 120-year disappearance, and more recently been recovered from thieves. What he did not know was that Queen Maria Luisa de Parma, wife of the mad Bourbon king Charles IV, had succeeded through a ruse where Philip II two and a half centuries earlier had failed in armed combat, and the Sancy finally belonged to the Spanish crown.

25

Spain and His Most Catholic Majesty Joseph

1808–1828

THE BITTER RIVALRY that had long existed between France and England had been rekindled during the French Revolution. In January 1793, after France had invaded the Habsburg possession of Belgium and alarmed the politicians, merchants, and businessmen of both Austria and Britain, the British prime minister, William Pitt, who had received newly impoverished aristocratic French émigrés on Britain's shores, pronounced that the country was at war with France and that it would be "a war of extermination."

With Napoleon's rise to power in 1797, the war took on a highly personal nature. British political caricaturists portrayed the general in pamphlets and newspapers "seated on the back of the devil vomiting cannon and armies," according to the historian Christopher Hibbert. They continued to taunt Napoleon in 1799 when he was pictured running away from Egypt with all the gold. By the time Napoleon had proclaimed himself first consul, France had secured her natural frontiers by force of arms and had created satellite states of Switzerland and Holland, where his brother Louis had been made king.

The first consul decided it was time to make peace with France's most bitter enemy, Britain. He sent a Christmas message to George III asking, "Why should the two most enlightened nations of Europe . . .

go on sacrificing their trade, their prosperity, and their domestic happiness to false ideas of grandeur?" George III's first act of the New Year was to pen a reply to his new prime minister, Grenville, that it was "impossible to treat with a new, impious, self-created aristocracy." The response made to the "Corsican tyrant's" letter was a tactless lecture demanding restoration of the French Bourbons and a return to the frontiers of 1789. The war with France had already cost Britain £400 million ($20.4 billion or £12.8 billion today) and had sent the nation spiraling off the gold standard. And these sums did not take into account the loss of trade with Antwerp.

The political economist Edmund Burke wrote in support of the king's position to Grenville that "it is not the enmity but the friendship of France that is truly terrible. Her intercourse, her example, the spread of her doctrines are the most dreadful of her arms." Whether Napoleon's overture was genuine or a wily ploy like Hitler's over the Sudetenland is one of the great speculations of history. Nonetheless, one by one, other European nations sued for peace, until finally, with a change of government, Britain, too, was compelled to agree to a peace treaty, in 1802 at Amiens. The signatories were General Cornwallis and Napoleon's eldest brother, Joseph Bonaparte. Napoleon was so delighted that he kept a bust of Admiral Nelson and Charles James Fox, the leader of the Whig Peace Party, on his dressing table.

But the peace was not to last, primarily due to three seemingly unrelated matters. The first of these related to the Treaty of Amiens, also known as the Concordat, according to which the British were to evacuate Egypt, and the French, Malta. However, by 1803, neither had done so. The second issue that strained the peace was when Napoleon resumed his aggression on the Continent when he claimed he was "obliged" to replace King Charles Emmanuel on the throne of Piedmont. The third of his transgressions, and probably the most serious from Britain's viewpoint, came when Napoleon declared that Switzerland was a danger to the "new France." His invasion of Switzerland, and the subsequent formation of the Helvetic Republic, struck at the heart of the wealthy ruling class in Britain, which kept much of its money on deposit with Swiss banks. Napoleon rightly understood that England had long used Switzerland as "a second Jersey from which to encourage agitation." The English moneyed classes, shocked, demanded redress.

The political situation worsened again when British newspapers such as the *Times* and the *Morning Chronicle* (owned by the prince of Wales) personalized the rising political tensions—frequently portraying Napoleon as a pygmy or "an unclassifiable being, half-African, half-European, a Mediterranean mulatto." The first consul exploded with rage against the English, claiming that the king was "no gentleman" and that the English did not keep their treaties. It was, Napoleon claimed, that Britain broke the peace. All the other wars fought, he insisted, stemmed from the war with Britain.

In response, Napoleon instituted the Continental System, the first international sanctions, making it a crime to trade with Britain, and tried—unsuccessfully—to completely blockade the country and starve her people into peace for the next twelve years. The quest for Continental allies by the British would mean that all of Europe would reek from the caustic stench of gunpowder and the entire world would be plunged into war.

In 1804, after a serious assassination attempt by royalists, Napoleon seized the moment and declared himself emperor of the French with the approval of his Senate. He argued that this would consolidate the various revolutionary and royalist factions behind a new incorrupt and incorruptible sovereign. Only Josephine opposed him, on the grounds that it would look like the "sin of pride and ambition." In fact, she feared that since she was unable to have any more children, he would eventually divorce her now that he was the head of a new dynastic empire and would inevitably want a son and heir.

The coronation of Napoleon and Josephine on December 2, 1804, marked an official return to all the pomp and circumstance that the French Revolution had sought to wipe out. Napoleon would spend more on diamonds and jewels for this one event than Louis XIV had done in his entire reign. At Napoleon's disposal for his coronation were the crown jewels he had recovered, worth more than 8 million gold francs ($19.5 million or £12.2 million today). The Regent alone, which he had mounted in his coronation sword, was valued at 6 million gold francs. His solid gold laurel crown, comprising forty-four large leaves, twelve small ones, and forty-two buds, was invoiced at 8,000 francs; his gold and enamel scepter cost 2,800 francs, and the gold and enamel globe cost 1,350 francs.

When he made his entrance into the Cathedral of Notre-Dame in his purple velvet mantle lined with ermine and sewn with golden bees—the symbols of diligence used by Charlemagne—Napoleon was already wearing his golden laurel wreath. He sparkled so ostentatiously with all his jewels and finery that an observer called him a "walking looking glass." Another guest said that his costume might have looked fine as a drawing but that it was "terrible on the short, fat Napoleon, who resembled the king of diamonds."

Josephine, like her brothers-in-law Louis and Joseph, was dressed in white satin with a liberal smattering of diamonds. Once the pope, who officiated at the ceremony, had celebrated High Mass and placed the crown on Napoleon's head, the emperor himself placed the tiny crown over Josephine's diamond tiara after first placing it on his own head, "taking great pains to arrange this little crown" according to the French gem historian Bernard Morel.

But the seeds of family feuding had already been sown. Joseph Napoleon Bonaparte was Napoleon's eldest brother, with Louis, Lucien, and Jerome, his younger brothers, all vying for a share of the empire. Ruling Europe was nothing if not a family affair, and Napoleon's sisters Pauline, Caroline, and Eliza, like his brothers, all played important roles in his grand design for the future. Each sibling had one thing in common: a dislike of Josephine.

Never popular with the Bonaparte siblings, Josephine's coronation was particularly distasteful to the Bonaparte sisters, who had been obliged by Napoleon to hold the empress's train. One scowled while the second held smelling salts under her nose and the third let the empress's heavy, jeweled train drop. Louis and Joseph were barely on speaking terms with the emperor, since he had decided against naming either of them as his heir.

Yet this was only the beginning of the family feuds. With a great thud of gunfire, Napoleon set about conquering the rest of Europe. Louis was already on the throne of Holland. By 1806 the treaties of Tilsit and Pressburg had weakened Prussia and Austria, respectively—an important preamble for what was to follow. Marie Antoinette's sister Maria Carolina was the neurotic queen of Naples, and in Napoleon's own words "the criminal woman" had broken her pledge of neutrality and would pay by being "hurled from her throne." Joseph Bonaparte was placed on the throne of the Kingdom of Naples within months.

While Napoleon was rifling through official papers in Berlin, after his victories over the Prussians, he discovered secret documents from Queen Maria Luisa and Manuel de Godoy, her prime minister and lover, pledging to attack France in concert with Prussia. From that moment their cards were marked. Napoleon had been negotiating with Godoy, nicknamed the "prince of peace," for years to try to secure repayment of Spain's debts to France. The emperor knew that the Bourbon family's grip on Spain was tenuous at best—King Charles IV was demented, and Maria Luisa avaricious and bitter. When a popular uprising against the unpopular king and queen of Spain occurred in 1808, Napoleon offered them exile in France despite the fact that he loathed Godoy as much as the Spanish insurrectionists. But why?

The emperor described the "prince of peace" as a man "taking crumbs from his master's table and an insolent flatterer whose machinations of negotiating with lies" enraged him. By manipulating Godoy he hoped the royal family would see reason and leave Spain without further struggle. On June 22, 1808, the Spanish royal representative wrote from France to the head of the king's household that the "emperor was impatient for the inventory of diamonds," which he was demanding be handed over to France, and that this list must be provided to him at Bayonne *immédiatemente*.

The plan was simple: exile in exchange for all of the crown's wealth. Letters were drawn up, decrees made, and Napoleon even offered 16 million francs ($39 million or £24.4 million today) for the Spanish crown's diamonds. The majordomo of the king's household, Pedro de Cifuentes, replied that he understood the urgency but not the merit of creating an inventory for the emperor of France.

Cifuentes, like Godoy and the queen, knew that wherever Napoleon and his armies invaded, the treasures of that nation were pillaged. But having tricked the Directory out of the Sancy once by using the marquis d'Iranda as intermediary, Maria Luisa was not to be so easily defeated. While the dreaded inventory was being prepared, she handed her prize possession—the Sancy—to her lover Manuel de Godoy, so it would not be counted among her jewels.

History owes much of the mystery surrounding the Sancy during the next twenty years to, first, the Bonapartes, and then to the queen of Spain for trying to save her treasures. Despite the rumors, innuendos, and written words, Manuel de Godoy never owned the Sancy diamond. He merely acted as its guardian protector for the brief period of utter chaos in Spain's history when the Bonapartes took over the country. When Joseph Napoleon Bonaparte was proclaimed king of Spain at the head of a French army, the Spanish called his hated rule *el gobierno intruso*, or the invading government of Joseph Napoleon I.

While Godoy was certainly no angel, at least he was Spanish, his defeated countrymen reasoned. He rose from such extreme poverty that a chronicler of the court wrote that "he was often obliged to lie in bed while his only shirt was at the wash." Godoy had become the king's and queen's favorite and trusted adviser within two years of his arrival in the king's guard—who were popularly known at the time as *chocolateros*, or brownnosers. And as their favorite, Godoy made powerful enemies.

The most important of these was the king's and queen's son Ferdinand, prince of the Asturias, who had plotted in 1807 with Napoleon's stepson Eugène de Beauharnais to overthrow Godoy. The Spanish heir was a stammering, materialistic, nasty, and devious individual who conspired against his own parents for the throne. Ferdinand's plotting gave Napoleon the justification he needed to cross the Pyrenees and "liberate" the Spanish from his parents' and Godoy's misadministration. Yet the Spanish had already risen in revolt against injustices and restriction of freedoms of Godoy's making, and Charles IV abdicated in favor of his son, fleeing with his wife and Godoy to Bayonne in France. Napoleon's "saving" of Spain was nothing more than a sham. He ordered the insurrection to be put down, irrespective of the blood to be shed, and after putting two hundred thousand armed men into combat, Spain became his. Joseph was hastily removed from the throne of the Kingdom of Naples by his brother, and in July 1808 became His Most Catholic Majesty, king of Spain and India. On October 28, 1808, he left for Madrid "at the head of my army to crown the

King of Spain and plant my Eagles [the symbols of imperial France] personally on the fortresses of Portugal." Napoleon's power was at its pinnacle.

The deal he struck with the exiled Spanish royal family was enshrined in Napoleon's letter to his finance minister, Mollien, in Paris:

> I have concluded a secret treaty with King Charles, dated 5th May. I am now writing to instruct you as to its dispositions insofar as these concern you:
> 1. You must pay to this Prince, in equal monthly installments, from the 1st of May, an annual sum of 30 million reals, or 7.5 million francs, and put this Prince on my civil list.
> 2. You must also pay all his children 400,000 francs yearly. There are five I believe; which would make it 2 million annually. That makes a total of 9.5 million francs that must definitely be paid, but this sum must not appear on the budget. It must be itemized as a loan that will be reimbursed by Spain. It is probable that I will give 500,000 francs more to the Prince of the Asturias (Ferdinand), which will make it 10 million. All of these sums will be reimbursed by Spain.

Napoleon also had purchased the Spanish crown jewels for 8 million francs, not 16 million francs, as originally offered. The money, according to the Royal Archives in Madrid, was never paid. Even if it had been, both figures were derisory, since the value of the crown jewels was several times that sum.

The morning after this letter was written, the former king and queen of Spain left for the palace at Fontainebleau, which Napoleon had designated as their place of exile. Godoy would soon follow the royal family into French exile, but the crown jewels, like the crown of Spain, remained in Madrid. When or how Godoy passed the Sancy back to Joseph is as mysterious as any of the most inscrutable transactions involving the diamond, and we may never know the details for certain. Joseph never wrote about it to Napoleon, and it would have been uncharacteristic for him to have done so.

Joseph took the throne of Spain as a poisoned challis, having loved Naples. Despite this, Joseph found it difficult to deny his younger brother any request, and left Naples for Madrid without much of an argument. It was obvious that Napoleon did not trust his military prowess, having taken to the field personally to secure the country, and a prolonged bitterness settled between them for more than three years. In 1811 Joseph met his brother at Rambouillet, the *ferme ornée*, (lavish farm) of Marie Antoinette, to abdicate as Spain's monarch. Joseph insisted that he had had no authority or respect and that the underground Spanish Cortes (Assembly) remained loyal to Ferdinand despite his instituting all of Napoleon's usual increased freedoms of expression and religion to the country. The emperor's officers also ignored Joseph, and waged war against the British, who had jumped to Portugal's defense when Napoleon invaded Portugal. The British commander, Sir Arthur Wellesley (later the duke of Wellington), in intercepted dispatches further insulted Joseph's military prowess by not referring to him as king. Joseph had a royal title without power— and a crown without pomp or money. These soon became his reasons for abdicating.

Napoleon's system for collecting taxes was impoverishing Spain— not to mention its court—with all of the revenue either being sent back to France to pay off Spain's war debts or going to the generals in the field. Joseph became incensed and headed for France to tender his resignation to the emperor.

The two brothers talked for two days, rambling in the ornate corridors of Rambouillet, until Joseph realized that what his younger brother was telling him was true: he was no general, but he was flesh and blood—and therefore the only person Napoleon could trust. Joseph agreed to stay on as king on the proviso that his court would be provided with 500,000 francs each month—20,000 francs ($49,000 or £31,000 today) of which were spent on gold and diamonds.

Joseph left Rambouillet a happy man with hollow promises, and went to visit his wife, Julie, at their estate in Mortefontaine, where she preferred to live. She thought that Joseph had changed from the kind soul she had married to a man whose "frivolity was inconceivable and self-confidence was equally inexplicable. . . . He was surprised that we did not look at him with great admiration, so convinced was he that he had performed great deeds."

Joseph returned to his courtly life in Madrid, feeling invigorated and less aggrieved. He dedicated more lycées as centers of learning to overcome the superstitious influence of the church in matters of state and granted religious freedom to all, ending centuries of the Inquisition. He planted small parks to beautify Madrid, earning himself the title *rey de las plazuelas* (king of the garden squares). Spanish food—which he disliked—was always on the menu at court, and French philosophers took their place in the evenings alongside Cervantes and Calderón. Still, Joseph, as the head of an occupying force, remained loathed.

By August 1812 Wellington had made tremendous strides into the Iberian Peninsula, and the British redcoats were welcomed everywhere with near-hysterical cries of *Viva!* Even the great painter Francisco Goya entered into the mood of the moment by taking a partially finished portrait of Joseph on horseback and replacing his face with Wellington's.

Matters were at their most desperate. Joseph and General Soult had had serious disagreements about the military security of the country, and the king had written to Napoleon, who was preoccupied with his disastrous invasion of Russia, that Soult would simply need to be replaced. The French were persistently routed in battle after battle, and France's grip on Spain was slipping. Napoleon resisted, saying that Soult was the "only competent military brain in the Peninsula" and ordered Joseph to remove his court and government to Valladolid instead of Burgos, as Joseph had previously suggested. With the court went all the riches in the capital, including the Sancy and the other crown jewels.

But it was not until the Battle of Vittoria in July 1813 that Joseph Bonaparte, His Most Catholic Majesty, was finally "hurled from the throne," as was reported by the rabid British press. It was a battle that Joseph himself masterminded, and blame for the disastrous outcome lies entirely at his feet. The French were being forced eastward, carrying with them a huge baggage train filled with Spanish booty—including the crown jewels. The road to Bayonne, and escape, was threatened, and the only way out was through a series of small mountain roads to Pampeluna. Mark Urban retells an eyewitness account of the battle in his book *The Man Who Broke Napoleon's Codes:*

A political cartoon depicting Napoleon as a matador with King Joseph trampled by the bull. Cartoon by the artist James Gillray.

Entire brigades of infantry fled east, leaving behind their artillery. Vast holes appeared in the French line, and the British flowed through them like a torrent. There was total mayhem—shrieks, gunfire, the thundering of cavalry horses' hooves, shouting soldiers, crying women—with Joseph Bonaparte and his escort caught up in the middle. To make matters worse, the ground was boggy, and as discipline collapsed, wagons toppled into the roadside ditches, eventually blocking the way.

When the English realized that the coaches belonged to the French king of Spain and his ministers, the 18th Hussars indulged in an orgy of looting that was the most memorable of any of their careers, and one of them recorded that "all who had the opportunity were employed in reaping some personal advantage from our victory." In one portmanteau alone there were silver doubloons to the value of £1,000. The king's silver chamber pot was looted along with wagons crammed with silver plate, altarpieces, and religious artifacts as well as the treasure convoy carrying 5 million francs that Joseph had only just received from Paris. Only a small portion of the cash was ever recovered, the rest disappearing into the pockets of soldiers, the mouths of their children, or cash registers of bars and whores. Two thousand men were taken prisoner amid this scene of biblical pillage highly reminiscent of the looting of Charles the Bold's camp at Grandson. Yet mysteriously, there was no record of the crown jewels or the Sancy or other jewels having been looted.

Even more mysteriously, Napoleon's brother, once again simply "Joseph Bonaparte," disappeared for two weeks, then suddenly reappeared on his estate near Paris. Rumors kept surfacing that Joseph had fled Spain and buried the crown jewels, including the Sancy, somewhere in France so he could recover them later.

After his brother's abdication in 1814, Joseph left France for England and eventually settled in the United States, where he reputedly purchased a mansion at Breezy Point, New Jersey, with cash from the looted treasures of Spain. He returned periodically to Europe, eventually settling in Genoa, then Florence, Italy, where his near neighbors were Nikolai and Paul Demidoff, the future in-laws of his niece Princess Mathilda.

26

In the Hands of the Demidoffs

1828–1865

❧

WHILE AMERICA'S ROBBER BARONS were making the country great, Russia, too, had her own version of the Carnegies, Vanderbilts, and Mellons, who had come from quite humble origins and showed astounding entrepreneurship combined with ruthless business sense. The most unusual and perhaps the most exceptional of these families were the Sancy's next owners, the Demidoffs.

The vast Russian expanse of Siberia and the Urals is still rich with iron, minerals—and diamonds. Yet industrial production in the region remained of limited value to the country as a whole until the time of Peter the Great in the latter part of the eighteenth century. War rather than economic expansion was the catalyst for Russia to develop its own iron industry, since Peter had declared war against his primary source of iron for armaments, Sweden.

Nikita Demidoffich, later Demidoff, provided the czar with the answer to his prayers, and the czar gave Nikita untold wealth and power in return. The Demidoffs emerged from an obscure ironsmithing family during the economic revolution under Peter the Great. Nikita, who was said to be avaricious and brutal, and his son Akinfii Nikitich Demidoff set out to create a family industrial empire of simply awesome magnitude without concern for the rule of law. By the mid-eighteenth century the Demidoffs provided Russia with more than 40 percent of its iron requirements and had propelled Russia onto the world stage as an economic power. Russia, which had been regarded as an industrially wayward nation, became a dominant power in European iron production from the time the Demidoffs burst onto the world scene.

Bogged down in a system of arbitrary laws, service obligations to the czar, and a woefully inbred lack of understanding of commercial imperatives, Russia had a well-deserved reputation for stifling creative entrepreneurship. When Nikita, age thirty-five, first met Peter the Great in 1691, he had already won the czar's admiration as a talented maker of firearms. Law having little meaning to Nikita, he had run away from a miserably paying job at the Moscow Artillery Bureau to the land of the hostile Kalmyks to work the rich copper and iron ore deposits in exchange for his manufacturing military wares. Yet despite such treasonable behavior, Nikita's talent and self-publicized mystique not only won him a pardon from the czar himself but also a place at the head of Russia's fledgling arms manufacturing industry. Legend has it that the real reason why Demidoff won this highly prized honor was that Peter the Great visited Nikita's home, got hopelessly drunk in true imperial fashion, and honored Nikita by debauching his wife.

Whatever the truth of the matter, Nikita provided better armaments at a far lower price than any of the competition by obtaining his raw materials directly from his own smelting and processing factories in the Urals. Peter the Great appreciated his artistry so much that he agreed to pay him three times the going rate and showered him with priceless gifts, including diamonds.

Nikita's son Afkinfii built eleven iron and seven copper works and owned a further twenty-seven factories, while his younger brothers held another nine. The family's reputation had grown so much by 1713 that they were known as the "lords of the Urals." By 1718 they had diversified into leather. Incredibly, Afkinfii was granted statelike status when he claimed that their mines and factories were attacked by marauding bandits, and obtained a state license to take matters into his own hands. He executed this task with a brutality reserved in our minds for the Mafia. In the Urals there was one law, and it was called Demidoff.

Afkinfii was so sure of his position within Russia that he willingly risked the wrath of the imperial court and loss of essential court influence by taking untaxed, and therefore illegal, profits from the family silver operations. Yet despite all the allegations—most of which were true—of murder, land-grabbing, forced labor (slavery), theft on a gargantuan scale, and lawlessness, the Demidoffs remained respected citizens and were elevated to aristocratic status in 1721, making them the first industrialists—and peasants—to have this significant advantage.

This meant that they no longer had to apply for special permission to be given serfs, as this was now their right as aristocrats. They specialized in illegal inhibition of competition, seizing mines, abducting the foremen, stealing ore, and preventing other manufacturers from felling trees to use as fuel. Prospectors were beaten, state mines were shut down, and even the famous aristocratic family the Stroganoffs were attacked in their own bailiwick when the Demidoffs turned them out, claiming the lands to be uninhabited and therefore their own.

The *fiskaly* (revenue officials) finally stepped in, and after three years' investigation the Demidoffs were asked to desist from any further "oppression, red tape, and bribery." Yet the czar needed them so badly that a new edict was issued in 1720 stating, "neither the governor, nor the *voevoda* [military leaders] nor any other official is permitted to investigate Demidoff's factories or enterprises. No measure is allowed that would bring the factories to a halt. No insult against him is permitted under threat of His Imperial Majesty's wrath and fury." The Demidoffs thereafter enjoyed absolute power. And as is always the case, the absolute power corrupted absolutely.

The abuse of power continued under Empress Catherine the Great, who took the throne in 1725. Charges of embezzlement, tax delinquency, and general lawlessness prevailed, but other than having to pay taxes due, no other punishment was given. Yet, by the time the third generation rose to prominence, the sons of Afkinfii were well educated abroad, learned European languages, and went on the Grand Tour, behaving as other aristocrats of the time—visiting castles, palaces, and other monuments and entertained by the European aristocracy, merchant bankers, and ennobled industrialists. The second of Afkinfii's three sons, Pavel, or Paul, endowed Moscow University with a fabulous collection of minerals, books, medals, and antiques valued then at 300,000 rubles ($2 million or £1.3 million), with another 100,000 rubles in 1803 for the maintenance of students. He also gave a further 50,000 rubles toward the construction of Kiev and Tobol'sk Universities. The brutality of Nikita Demidoffich and Akinfii were now relegated to ancient history, replaced by the ethos of altruism and the conspicuous consumption of an aristocratic lifestyle. This altruism and aristocratic lifestyle gave the third generation their place in history. It also impoverished them.

The new head of the family at the end of the eighteenth century, Nikolai Demidoff, married Baroness Elizaveta Aleksandrovna Stroganova—of the famous Stroganoffs—in 1797 and had the wisdom to relinquish control of what remained of the Demidoff industrial empire to her family. Their first son Pavel, or Paul, was born in 1798, and was followed fifteen years later by a brother, Anatoli.

Nikolai was a gentleman of the household of Catherine the Great and a protégé of her favorite, Potemkin. Like many of the Russian aristocrats, he toured Europe, living for a year in Dresden, Paris, and London before buying a home in Paris. But when Napoleon declared war on Russia, Nikolai was forced to flee Paris and returned to Moscow to defend the nation against the French tyrant. As a colonel at the head of the Russian army whose tactics broke the Grand Army of France, Nikolai was hailed a national hero. With the restoration of the French monarchy in 1815, Nikolai returned to Paris, undoubtedly as the eyes and ears of the Russian court.

After the death of Elizaveta in 1818, the imperial court sent him to Florence as its special envoy. This position was much akin to the role that his wife's family played as envoys to Spain—spying on the elements in European society that could be of benefit, or harm, to Mother Russia.

The Russians had been brutally attacked by Napoleon, and the new czar, Alexander, defended his nation in many ways reminiscent of England's Elizabeth I, using a well-oiled spy network. For centuries, ambassadors and envoys were frequently used as conduits, not only for passing on important information but also for ferreting out secrets of any nature. Nikolai's two sons, Paul and Anatoli, also lived in Florence with their father during his long sojourn there.

The Napoleonic interlude affected all of Europe—including Russia—for much longer than the ten short years of the empire. The resources that were spent to halt him were huge. The wealth from the rich provinces that Napoleon had promised his army had been transported back to France (either in their pockets, or for the glory of France) from the vanquished regions. And nowhere was this shift of power and affluence more in evidence than in Florence and the Papal States when Nikolai had settled there. Florence, as the capital of Tuscany and former home of the de' Medici princes, had more than its fair share of riches that had caught Napoleon's eye.

Church valuables such as silver and gold altar vessels and priceless Renaissance paintings had been expropriated alongside private property, including the Medici Venus, and packed for dispatch to the Louvre. Despite their initial enthusiasm for the French, the Florentines were soon enraged by the outright looting of national treasures, and fought back as best they could by abusing their occupiers in the streets and tearing down the symbols of their authority. They were so fed up with the raft of decrees beginning with *nous voulons* (we want) that the Florentines gave the apt nickname to the French of *Nuvoloni* (Cloud of Locusts). Hundreds of precious treasures were taken from the Vatican and central Papal States by Napoleon and his army. The citizens of the Italian Peninsula—not as yet unified into one nation—felt that they had been raped of their heritage.

Demidoff's eldest son, Paul, was only sixteen when Napoleon was defeated in Russia. There is no doubt that Russia intended to translate her victory against Napoleon's Grand Army into political power in Europe. For this reason, trusted and loyal nobles like Nikolai Demidoff were sent to specific locales as privileged observers. Their primary job was to report back, but if they also could turn local nobles into Russian sleepers, then so much the better. The czar had advised Nikolai to transfer to Florence personally, and become his privileged observer of the activities of the House of Habsburg in Italy and in the whole of the Mediterranean. So when Nikolai arrived in Florence, it was reported in *Il Corregio* that he had retired there for his health, and he promptly got to work for Russia.

Nikolai's greatest success in this murky world may have been the enrollment in the Russian corps of a Florentine nobleman named

Serristori. When Serristori departed for Moscow, Nikolai leased his Palazzo di Serristori in Florence, and remained there until his death. Yet the undoubted ace in the hole was his friendship with the former king of Westphalia, Jerome Bonaparte—a near neighbor to the Palazzo di Serristori, and father of his future daughter-in-law, Mathilda. A frequent visitor to Jerome's household was his eldest brother, Joseph, who had settled some years earlier at Breezy Point, New Jersey, and who had spent much of his time in America justifying the "truth" of the Bonaparte legacy and his own role as the king of Naples and king of Spain.

Yet despite these friendships, and the entertainment that the Russians obviously created as well as the wealth they generated through their philanthropy and conspicuous consumption, they were not universally liked or even admired in Florence. A "confidential" police report from March 7, 1828—written at a time when the local powers that be were clinging to the vain hope that Florence would not be subsumed into a larger unified Italian state under the Risorgamento—describes a list of twenty-eight foreigners as being "licentious, debauched, gambling, womanizing, drunken" individuals who were corrupting the "flower of the pure youth of Italy." Numbers six and seven on the list were Paul and Anatoli Demidoff. Although Anatoli is remembered by history for his philanthropy, there are a number of reports of his dissolute life. As far as Paul is concerned, this is the only official blemish on his record. Any credence given to the highly xenophobic report must be made in light of the times in which it was written, an era when all aristocrats gambled and drank to excess.

There is little doubt that Nikolai knew of the police report, and as the unofficial head of the sizable Russian aristocratic contingent living in Florence at the time sought to mitigate any damage it might do to his family or to the broader Russian community. The Demidoffs, now immensely rich due to their exclusive license to mine gold in the Urals, lived in grand style—entertaining anyone who was anyone, and buying anything they fancied. Nikolai and his son Paul became great philanthropists and art collectors, but it is Anatoli who is best remembered for his love of art and the discovery of Russian art by the greater Italian public through his support of the artist Brjullov. Paul busied himself with his passion for archaeology and became a patron

Joseph Bonaparte as
king of Spain. Painting
by J. B. Joseph Wicar, 1808

of the Archaeological Society of Siena and an honorary member of
the Academy of Science and Arts of Arezzo and Siena, but remained
devoted to Russian art.

Other Russians and "foreigners" tried to fit in with the rather
exclusive and snobbish Florentine aristocracy of the time, often buying themselves Italian titles from impoverished nobles, as Anatoli did
many years later when he became known as the principe di San
Donato. While the Florentines lived in great luxury and wore elegant
and expensive clothing and jewels, the Russians stood out for their
astronomical wealth and penchant for eye-catching jewelry. Princess
Woronzoff, for example, had a collection of jewelry so astounding
that Florentines and visitors alike stopped in the streets to watch her
saunter by wearing her twelve ropes of flawlessly matching pearls that
reached down to her knees. Nikolai was undoubtedly envious of the
stir she created.

Being a great collector and friend of the Bonapartes, as well as a privileged observer for the czar, Nikolai would have known how to divine from the Bonaparte brothers the existence of booty from the Napoleonic era. He would have seen it as a unique opportunity to acquire their booty to return to Russia in compensation for its devastating losses. This attitude remained prevalent in Russian thinking during and after World War II and does receive some sympathy internationally. Precisely when he discovered the existence of the Sancy among the treasures looted from the Spanish crown jewels is not known, but the Sancy had been seen in Paris by King Charles X's jeweler earlier in 1828, when it was allegedly presented for sale by "an agent of Godoy." Charles X refused the stone, since he believed that it already belonged to the French crown and refused to "buy it twice."

There is no proof that the agent was Godoy's, but it had always been assumed, since Godoy had been the last person presumed to have had the Sancy. What we do know is that the agent was a lawyer acting on behalf of an "unnamed client." It is entirely likely that the lawyer worked for Joseph Bonaparte, who had dug it up from its secret hiding place, since he was again in great need of cash. Breezy Point had recently burned down in mysterious circumstances, and it would take the fortune that the Sancy could provide to rebuild another home.

In any event, Nikolai bought the Sancy in January 1828 and made it known in the Florentine circles of power that he was now the proud owner of this most historic and large diamond. Even Princess Woronzoff could not boast of owning such a fabulously important stone.

Three months after purchasing the Sancy, Nikolai was dead. The curse surrounding the diamond resurged, and there were great mutterings throughout the closely knit aristocratic community that the diamond was responsible, despite the fact that the curse should not have applied to a legal acquisition. It was even rumored that Paul would refuse to accept the stone. Some thought that Anatoli—the intended lover and future husband of Princess Mathilda—had naturally inherited the Sancy from her Uncle Joseph. Official shipping documents report, however, that the "entirety of the Nikolai Demidoff estate including paintings and furniture from the Palazzo di Serristori were shipped back to Moscow."

With Nikolai's death, Paul (who was thirty) and Anatoli (who was fifteen) inherited the Nizhnetagil branch of the Demidoff holdings, which included gold and platinum mines. It was during this return to Moscow that Paul met the stunningly beautiful Finnish-born Aurora Stjernwall-Walleen, a lady-in-waiting to the czarina. Aside from being a tremendous beauty, Aurora also was an intellectual, and a lifelong friend of Pushkin.

The fabulously wealthy Paul felt that he needed to have such a partner, and set out to win her heart. Paul, who had earned the nickname "Rothschild of Russia," was deemed to be one of the country's most eligible bachelors. Finally in 1836 they were married, and as is the custom in Nordic countries, Paul gave Aurora a morning gift when she awoke the day after the wedding ceremony. It was the Sancy diamond.

Aurora, despite being given the most historic diamond in Europe, apparently was not overly awed. She was, after all, an intellectual and understood the power of riches and their ability to corrupt.

There is a painting of Aurora hanging in the museum at Nizhnetagil, which Paul Demidoff founded. It was painted by his most important protégé, Brjullov. Since the only jewels in the painting are a bracelet and a wedding ring on her third finger, we have no visual record of how she had had the Sancy mounted. What the painting does bear out, however, is her haunting loveliness—she is dark-eyed and intelligent with peach-blossom skin, ample bosom, tiny waist, and exquisite dress.

Paul and Aurora spent their time in St. Petersburg and Moscow, and passing winters in Italy. In 1839 she gave birth to a son, also named Paul. Within the year, her husband was dead. Again, rumors bubbled to the surface that the diamond he had given her was unlucky, even cursed. She shrugged off the superstition and tried to live a life of Victorian circumspection—loathing the fashion to gamble and drink and shunning any form of loose morals. Anatoli took over the administration of her substantial holdings, which included the district of Tiraspol, the government of Cherson with 385 peasants, a

large stone house four leagues (about fourteen miles) from St. Petersburg, a house at Nizhni-Novgorod, and a half share in all the iron,
platinum, silver, and gold mines, while she devoted herself to the up-
bringing of her small son.

Then in 1846 she married Andreij Karmasin, a handsome captain
of the guards who was her intellectual equal. He devoted himself to
young Paul's education until 1854, when he went to serve in the Russian army during the Crimean War. Within the year, Aurora was wid-
owed, never to remarry again.

After Karmasin's death and the end of the Crimean War, Aurora
settled finally in Helsinki and lived quietly in relative obscurity. Anatoli still managed her holdings—more or less as he deemed fit—and
she maintained a lifelong friendship and closeness with her former
brother-in-law and frequently visited Florence.

Interestingly, it has been written that Paul Demidoff tried to sell
the Sancy to a Mr. Levrat, the head of the state mining services in
Grisons, Switzerland, who tried to cheat him out of the stone. It
seems that this tale may have been invented, since all sorts of law-
suits against the unscrupulous Levrat are on record, but none concerning a diamond.

When Aurora finally decided to sell the stone, she gave it to the
highly respected royal jeweler, Garrard & Co, as her agent. In 1865
Garrard sold the Sancy to Sir Jamsetjee Jejeebhoy of Bombay for the
princely sum of £20,000 ($1.5 million or £957,000 today).

And so the Sancy, after centuries of travel through the hands of
kings, princes, and scoundrels, returned to the country of its origin.
Whatever the nature of the Sancy's curse, Aurora lived to age ninety.

27

A Jewel of Historic Curiosity

1865–1906

THE SANCY'S NEXT OWNER, the second baronet Sir Jamsetjee Jejeeb-hoy, returned home to India with the diamond in 1865. Jejeebhoy's India had been dominated for more than two hundred years by the British Raj, or rule, and the country had become the backbone of the British Empire's vast wealth. The long-sought-after subcontinent had made European powers and entrepreneurs rich beyond any expectation for centuries, but the British, while merely the latest in a long line of invaders, believed that they would possess India forever and built an infrastructure that reflected this conviction.

The Raj had taken shape on the back of trade, and that trade had been dominated for more than two centuries by the English East India Company. When on New Year's Eve 1600 Elizabeth I had granted a royal charter to the East India Company, owned by a select group of merchants from the City of London, neither she nor those original investors could have foreseen how much it would dominate trade to all of Europe from the subcontinent and the Far East. By the mid-nineteenth century the East India Company's grasp stretched across most of India, Burma, Singapore, and Hong Kong, with a fiftieth of the world's population under its "governmental" authority. The company had, at various stages in its history, defeated China, occupied the Philippines, conquered Java, and even imprisoned Napoleon on its desolate island of St. Helena off the coast of Africa, all in the name of empire.

Yet there were always independent, entrepreneurial spirits who were not granted immediate access to the East India Company and all its riches, since the easy lifestyle with its clubs, churches, social functions, servants, and calling cards was the exclusive preserve of the "English gentleman." Jamsetjee Jejeebhoy was one of the East India Company's most successful challengers, and, like Nikita Demidoff, rose from extreme poverty to a coveted position of wealth and power. Unlike Demidoff, he used both for the public good.

Born in 1783 at Navsari and orphaned at age sixteen, Jamsetjee would become the stuff of legends by his midtwenties. On the death of his mother he went to Bombay to earn his livelihood with his cousin among the Parsee community, who thrived there.

The Parsees were remnants of the Zoroastrian Persian Empire who were defeated and fled before the sword of Islam. After years of hardship and wandering, the Parsees were finally given refuge in Gujarat, where the exiles from what is modern-day Iran earned their living mostly as farmers and weavers for more than a thousand years.

It was with the advent of the Raj that the rise of the Parsee community began; and with the achievements of Jamsetjee and others, the name Parsee became synonymous with a pioneering spirit, love of adventure, business integrity, public spirit, charity, and unswerving loyalty toward their rulers. The Parsees are still known as a great merchant community, and have contributed substantially to the rise of Bombay as India's commercial center.

When Jamsetjee arrived in Bombay, he had only 120 rupees in his pocket, or £12 ($672 or £420 today). His cousin Merwanjee Maneckjee Tuback took him under his wing and arranged for Jamsetjee to go on a voyage to China with him in 1799 in the capacity of clerk. On his return, aged only sixteen, Jamsetjee married the beautiful Avabye Framjee Bottlewalla and joined his father-in-law's trading business. Within a short time, Jamsetjee became his partner. Their primary commodities were cotton and opium. Jamsetjee thought that if they could establish trade links in these commodities with China—which the East India Company had been courting actively—their fortunes would be made. A daring second voyage to China was undertaken to trade all their worldly goods, thanks to an incredibly risky loan of 35,000 rupees at a time when the Napoleonic Wars were raging and state-sponsored piracy was the norm. Despite running into any number of French blockades, the voyage was a success, and on his return to Bombay, Jamsetjee repaid the loan with interest.

Illegality associated with the opium trade was nonexistent at that time, even though its narcotic qualities were well known. Opium was widely used both as a recreational drug and as an analgesic by people of all classes and walks of life, from Queen Victoria in the form of laudanum to the Chinese peasant farmer in his cheroot. The opium trade represented approximately 5 percent of India's international trade, with the majority of the exports from India sold into China via the East India Company, whose perennial need for bullion to buy tea for Britain became the driving force for both the company and others, such as Jamsetjee, exporting Indian-grown opium to China.

Yet the Chinese emperor objected to the opium imports, since the nation had been overwhelmed into a narcotic stupor and was dependent on the imports to feed its habit. The company, not wishing to cross the emperor, claimed openly that nothing should be done to put its vital tea trade with China in jeopardy and that "useful as the opium revenue was to India, it was less to be desired than the China trade monopoly."

Yet the Chinese continued to consume Indian opium in huge quantities, most of which was imported openly by Jejeebhoy or secretly by the East India Company. By the 1830s the company had become hooked on the opium trade to China, despite earlier efforts to exercise commercial responsibility and good governance. It had come under pressure from Indian merchant adventurers in the trade with China, such as Jejeebhoy, and used this as a flimsy excuse to step up its own operations.

To keep a larger share of the profits from the sales to China and to knock out the middlemen, in 1814, while the Napoleonic Wars were drawing to a close in Europe, Jejeebhoy and his father-in-law bought a fleet of ships, the first of which was named the *Good Success*. Jejeebhoy believed that there would be a sharp rise in the price of cotton throughout Continental Europe as a result of the wars, and arranged to ship thousands of bales there. According to Jejeebhoy's biographer, writing in 1859:

> The [Napoleonic] wars had spread blood and desolation from Cadiz to Moscow, and from Naples to Copenhagen; they had wasted the means of human enjoyment, and destroyed the instruments of social improvement. Nor was the contest confined to Europe only, but it had made its appearance even in India, where like hungry lions they were lying in ambush to pounce upon their first victim.

The profits from the expedition of the new fleet were colossal, and set up Jejeebhoy and his family in truly princely style for the rest of their lives. On his father-in-law's death, he broke through the religion barrier and took in two other partners to Jamsetjee Jejeebhoy & Co.—a Hindu and a Muslim. In 1821 the firm cornered the entire import trade of China, with the firm of Jardine Mathieson & Co. as their principal agent in China for the opium trade. The company continued to flourish, and in 1836 Jamsetjee's eldest son, Setts Cursetjee, joined the firm as a partner, and the word "Sons" was introduced to the company name.

In 1840 the firm suffered heavy losses during the China War, known to us today by the catchy title coined in the *Times* of London, the Opium Wars. In part, these wars were, of course, about opium, but more about the opening up of China to trade generally. The utter defeat of the weakened Chinese Empire by the East India Company in the name of the British crown in 1842 led to the humiliating Treaty of Nanking and the opening of treaty ports, including Shanghai, to foreign trade. Hong Kong was ceded to the British, and Jejeebhoy's hold on the China trade was lost.

Jejeebhoy responded by extending his business to Bengal, Madras, the western coast of Sumatra, Singapore, Siam (today's Thailand), the Malay Archipelago (today's Indonesia), Alexandria in Egypt, and England. By the time he was twenty-four, according to the *Memorandum of the Life and Public Works of Sir Jamsetjee Jejeebhoy*, he was so wealthy that he was able to "spread his money amongst the people of Bombay in unostentatious charity and ameliorating the condition of his poor countrymen."

Jejeebhoy not only knew how to live in style but also how to give back to the community. He built his family a palatial home, was reputed to eat from real gold spoons, and when one surprised visitor to the house remarked about it, he gave all of his guests their gold spoons as a souvenir. At the same time, he built a new dispensary in Bombay; the first civil hospital (1843); the first maternity home (Sir Jamsetjee Jejeebhoy Obstetric Institution); gave a sizable grant for books, prizes, and general funds to the Grant Medical College; built the first causeway from Mahim to Bandra for the people going to and from Salsette; improved a vast number of roads and schools; and pioneered female education (19 girls' schools) and the first waterworks for the citizens of Poona.

He led a blameless life and donated thousands of gifts to worthy causes. He became a fellow of Bombay University and was granted the freedom of the City of London in 1855. His philanthropy was unmatched anywhere in the world, since it touched everyone with whom he came into contact.

His integrity in resisting the widespread system of private influence in the morally corrupt practice termed *khuput*, by which wealthy natives remitted large sums of money to their agents at Bombay, was an example to all. According to Bartle Frere, the representative of the British government in Scinde, the high-mindedness of Sir Jamsetjee was described as:

When the petitioner is of rank, a favourite device is to take him to call on some gentleman, with whom his conductor converses in English, and easily persuades his up-country friend that his affairs have been the subject of conversation. . . . Some gentlemen, I am sure, without any idea of the deception to which they lend themselves, or the mischief they do, are a kind of permanent unconscious accomplices of fraud of this kind . . . one very striking exception in Sir Jamsetjee Jejeebhoy, who with every inducement from his great influence, and the exceeding benevolence of his character, never, as far as my experience goes, lends himself to the dangerous practice of patronizing parties engaged in obtaining redress of their grievances, real or supposed, by indirect influence.

On his death in 1859, Sir Jamsetjee left the following balance sheet of his public works:

For British and General Objects:
The JJ Hospital, Mahim Bridge and Approaches,
Mahim Road, Bridge at Earla Parla, Deepening a Tank at
Bandora, Dhurmsalla, or House of Charity in Bellasis Road
Including an Endowment of £5000, Waterworks at Poona,
Dhurmsalla at Khundalla, Contributions to Suffers by Fire
At Surat and Syed Poora, Payments to the settlement of
Sundry private and family disputes referred to him for
Arbitration, Bridge at Bartha, Subscriptions and Donations
[Elphinstone Professorship], Byculla Schools, District Benevolent
Society, Proposed Sailors' Home, School of Industry,
Free School Calcutta, Relief of the Scotch and Irish,
Naval School at Devonport, Wells on the Esplanade
In Bombay, wells with an aqueduct in Musjid Bunder,
Same at Calaba, Reservoir at Poona, Relief to a distressed
Friend and family [not Parsee], sums paid to release poor
Debtors in 1822, 1826 and 1842, book and prize fund Grant
Medical College, contribution to a road at Bandora,
Public tank at the hospital, the obstetric institution, contribution
To the Fund in Bombay for the Benefit of European
Pensioners and their Widows, Wellington Testimonials,
Endowment of a school of Design in Bombay   £110,432

For Parsee Objects:
Donation to the Parsee Benevolent Institution,
Parsee Place of Worship at Poona, Endowment
For the Performance in Bombay and Guzerat of
Various Parsee rites and ceremonies, a new
Building and ground for celebration of certain public
Festivals among the Parsees, sums remitted to the
Relief of the poor Parsees at Surat from 1840–47,
Redemption of the Body tax levied by Gackwar on
The Parsees of Nowsaree, Parsee Cemetaries in
Various places, sums given in aid of distressed
Members of respectable Parsee families, building and
Repairs of various Parsee places of worship, Trustee
Fund for the benefit of the poor Blind at Nowsaree,
Subscriptions to the Parsee Punchayet, for charitable
Works, Fund for general expenses of poor Parsees
At Gundavee, near Nowsaree, Dhurmsalla at Nowsaree,
Endowment for poor Parsees at Surat and Nowsaree,

Zend Avesta School for Parsees, buildings at Nowsaree
And cemetery for the religious observances for Parsees   £113,380

For Hindu Objects:
Subscriptions to the Pinjra-pol in Bombay, out of respect
To the deceased Motichund Amichund, to the Pinjra-pol at Patton
For the same motive, endowment for the relief of poor Hindoos
In Guzerat in memory of Motichund Amichund   £10,460

In today's values that equals $17.9 million or £11.2 million.

Exceptionally, Jamsetjee was knighted by Queen Victoria for his phenomenal good works and contributions to India. He was the first colonial Briton to be given such an honor. Sir George Arthur presented to Jamsetjee, at a special durbar, or reception, a diamond-studded gold medal. On its obverse it bore the queen's face encircled with diamonds, and on its reverse was inscribed "Sir Jamsetjee Jejeebhoy, Knight, from the British Government in Honour of his munificence and patriotism."

Sir Jamsetjee gladly accepted the honor and adopted a coat of arms that said "Industry and Liberality," with a peacock holding a flower on a knight's helmet. Inside the coat of arms there is a hand surrounded by two bees and the sun rising over mountains, with an oasis and water below.

But the *Bombay Times* of June 13, 1856, was outraged that he had been given a "mere Knighthood" when it wrote, "We trust Her Majesty's Government will no longer permit the opportunity to pass unimproved, of indicating some more worthy mark than a mere Knighthood, their estimation of a munificence which finds no parallel in history."

His eldest child, Setts Cursetjee, later the second Baronet Jamsetjee, was born on October 9, 1811, and it was superstitiously remarked at the time that since his birth Sir Jamsetjee had been very successful and prosperous in all his ventures. Yet for all his generosity and success, Jamsetjee did not die a popular man. During the Dog Riot and the Parsi-Muslim Riot of 1851, he took an outspoken position that was decidedly pro-British. His biographer, writing eight years later, wrote:

Summer heat and water shortage led to many cases of hydrophobia [rabies]. The Government ordered a general massacre of dogs. This hurt the feelings of some Parses and Hindus. It led to the Dog Riot.

The rioters of both the communities badly manhandled two police officers on duty. Jamsetjee rightly argued that stray dogs were dangerous and the Government was doing its duty. Besides, it was an unlawful act to manhandle the police. He firmly stated that citizens had no right to take the law into their own hands. If all were to do this there would be anarchy in the country. As he refused to take sides with the Parsee rioters, he became unpopular.

For days the frenzied Muslim mobs terrorized the people of Bombay. Parsee houses were pillaged, shops looted, and settling of old scores by murder was commonplace. The police claimed to be helpless, but the Parsees blamed them for the chaos through a noninterventionist policy. Jamsetjee, by now nearly seventy, could no longer influence the community of which he had become the leader.

When he died on April 15, 1859, the *Bombay Times* voiced the feelings of the masses:

> Did he not feed the hungry? Did he not clothe the naked? Did he not help the distressed and succour the afflicted? To the fatherless, was he not a father? To the widows and orphans, had he not been a breadwinner? Did he not build hospitals for the sick? For the ignorant, did he not endow schools? For the thirsty, did he not sink wells and tanks and build waterworks? For the homeless, did he not build *dharamsalas* [almshouses]?

The second Baronet Jamsetjee Jejeebhoy was said to be a perfect English gentleman—in society an agreeable companion, and he was always among the first to further a good cause. Like all English gentlemen, he was especially fond of the social functions and his club, and the English viceroy deemed it an honor to play cards with him at his palatial home. He was reputed to be an excellent public speaker, and as chairman at various public meetings, he displayed knowledge and acumen that were impressive.

While still a philanthropist, the second baronet enjoyed his amusements and was always the first to promote any scheme for the amusement of the Bombay public, being one of the earliest patrons of the Royal Italian Opera and of the theatrical corps of the Parsees, which played in English by the name P. Elphinstone Club.

He adored England and all things English, and during his trip to England in 1865 he acquired "the polish of European refinement in his habits and manners" as well as the Sancy diamond. The Sancy would become his symbol of wealth, frequently worn at the front of his turban for state occasions and as a visible link to royal European history. Since the Sancy was also essentially Indian, it had the importance that any treasured object has to a collector and connoisseur with a keen sense of profound history.

This was clearly demonstrated when two years after he acquired the Sancy diamond, he allowed it to travel back to France for the International Exhibition at Paris in 1867. There it was reunited with the Regent and was valued at 1 million francs for the voyage. The tremendously wealthy maharajah of Patiala created quite a stir at the time by insinuating that Jejeebhoy did not own the "real" Sancy, but rather that he was the true owner of the "sixty-carat" stone. The maharajah was obviously confused—or confounded by whoever sold him his diamond—and had taken the weight of the Sancy as the one put forward by Harlay de Sancy in the 1600s when he tried to sell it, including its mounting. This naturally added to the myths and mysteries surrounding this most historic stone, and upset the second baronet to no end. The maharajah was, after all, Indian royalty, and Jejeebhoy was nouveau riche.

Fortunately for the baronet, at the International Exhibition at Paris the great Parisian jeweler Lucien Falize met Jejeebhoy and created his magnificent watercolors of the stone set in its flawless necklace. Falize's interest in Jejeebhoy's diamond was as good as the *Good Housekeeping* seal of approval and put the spurious rumors in their place. Interestingly, Falize was rumored as early as the 1890s to have acquired the Sancy from Jejeebhoy, but according to Falize's biographer Katerine Purcell, he would never have had the funds available to purchase the Sancy.

Twenty years after the exhibition, Germain Bapst, head of a family of French crown jewelers and a lapidary historian, took advantage of the Sancy's European expedition to Paris to compile the definitive history of the stone, claiming once and for all that it did *not* belong to Charles the Bold based on evidence put forward by both Nicolas Harlay de Sancy and Robert de Berquen. Bapst cannot be faulted for his reasoning, since the information available to him at the time was not of the same caliber as the vast quantities seen in the twenty-first century.

A year after Bapst wrote his definitive history of the Sancy and other crown jewels of the French crown, he was called on to head a committee to select which of the French crown jewels should be retained and which should be sold, in the greatest catastrophe and dispersal to befall the collection ever. In the lead up to the dispersal—and for years afterward—the international diamond market was severely depressed, and anyone wishing to dispose of a large stone was simply unable to do so.

If Sir Jamsetjee Jejeebhoy wanted to sell the Sancy from 1886 to 1896, he would have been foolish to do so. Yet in 1906, he did sell the stone for reasons unknown to William Waldorf Astor, great-grandson of John Jacob Astor, America's first millionaire.

28

The Last Private Owners: The New "Royals"

1906–1976

❧

WILLIAM WALDORF ASTOR LEFT NEW YORK for good in 1889 after serving as a congressman and American ambassador to Rome because he firmly believed that America was "no place for a gentleman to live." He claimed that his move had nothing to do with the fact that his family had come under threat of kidnapping, and everything to do with his desire to build his own landscape in England distinct from the Astor landscape that made New York City great. Ten years later, when his son Waldorf was twenty, William Waldorf and his clan became British citizens. The popular U.S. press inveighed against him as "the richest man that America ever owned and that disowned America."

The Astor name had long been synonymous with the state of New York and New York City real estate, and in 1890 William Waldorf was purported to have inherited $175 million (£36 million), worth $3.5 billion or £2.2 billion today. His annual income from New York rentals was a staggering $6 million a year. The tycoon also gave birth to the modern meaning of the "five-star hotel" on the site of the Empire State Building; the hotel was later moved to the Waldorf-Astoria's current location on Park Avenue. He carried his talent, flair, and creativity for art and architecture back to Europe—first to England with his faultless restoration of Cliveden, home to the second duke of Buckingham; to Hever Castle, Anne Boleyn's castle given to her by Henry VIII; then on to Italy, where he painstakingly reinvented Villa Labonia and Villa Sirena.

Each of William Waldorf's homes was a living museum of extraordinary value, yet sadly today only at Hever Castle can we sense the sheer quantity and quality of his collections. Hever's library boasts twenty-five hundred leather-bound volumes of rare or unique books. Portraits by Scrots, Clouet, Holbein, and other sixteenth- or seventeenth-century old masters pepper the walls. Large Flemish and French tapestries that hang in the public areas are among the finest examples in existence today. And above all, to give Hever Castle its historic context, Astor scoured Europe for any objects connected with the court of Henry VIII, such as Anne Boleyn's prayer book, which she is alleged to have taken with her to the executioner's block; her embroidery; and even her autograph. Hever also boasts ecclesiastical vestments, furniture, Persian carpets, and eighteenth-century porcelain, and it is difficult to imagine, as impressive as Hever is, that it represented only a quarter of his total acquisitions.

At Astor's home in London, Temple Place, there were more than four hundred autographs, including letters from the duke of Marlborough; London's chronicler Samuel Pepys; George Washington; Shelley; Dickens; and Mary, queen of Scots. The library housed Chaucer, five Shakespeare folios, and thirteen illuminated books of hours from the fifteenth century. There were books bearing the coats of arms or monograms from Cardinal Richelieu, Henry III, Talleyrand, Catherine de Medici, Madame du Barry, Marie Antoinette, and James II, among others. There was even a Latin treatise with margin notes by Queen Elizabeth I. The library also held a treasure trove of oddities such as ancient lutes, a spinning wheel, and Napoleon's hat.

The collections Astor amassed in his homes allowed him to wander—usually alone—and revel in the past world of illusion he had created for himself. It was a world of taste and splendor, a world of romance, removed from the sordid daily grind of moneymaking. It was a world of permanence and illustrious ancestry.

It was in this world that William Waldorf brought up his family, living mostly at Cliveden in Berkshire. Years later, a family friend, Lady Ottoline Morrell, wrote of her experiences at the Astor household:

> Think, too, what it must mean to a small child to be brought up in the midst of historical associations and treasures from every land, and to wander from early years in beautiful rooms filled with such things as other children only see in museums. How I loved to finger and caress the pearl drop from King Charles' ear, and to lock up and hide my first precious letters in a casket given by King William III, with keys that are a pattern of beauty and delicacy, and to play and act with King Henry VIII's ruby-studded dagger.

William Waldorf was a collector extraordinaire of diverse things, acquiring newspapers as he did artworks and homes. In 1892, a year after his wife's death, he bought the *Pall Mall Gazette* followed by the *Observer* in 1911. It is no wonder that this man simply had to own the most historic diamond—no longer the largest diamond by a long shot—yet the most enduring of diamonds, the Sancy. There is no doubt that Astor would have known *everything* that there was to know about the Sancy, and would have appreciated the controversy over its past, and the hands that held the diamond as well as those who lusted after it. To a keen scholar on the subject of Napoleon, the mystery, alleged curse, and uncertain history all added to its allure.

Some sources claim that William Waldorf purchased the Sancy in 1894 for his wife, and others in 1906. The former date can hardly be true, because his wife had died in 1891. Since William Waldorf burned most of his private papers just prior to his death and no invoice for purchase has been made public, it is impossible to say for certain when the stone was acquired from Sir Jamsetjee Jejeebhoy or his agent, and for that matter why the second baronet sold the stone. Whatever the truth of the matter, William Waldorf certainly gave the Sancy to his new daughter-in-law, Nancy Langhorne Shaw, as a wedding gift, and it was placed at the center of her magnificent diamond tiara. The tiara was valued in 1906 for $75,000. The "other" wedding gift to the young couple was the magnificently restored Cliveden.

Although his generosity might indicate otherwise, Nancy Lang-horne Shaw was not William Waldorf's ideal choice of daughter-in-law for his son and heir, Waldorf. Though deemed a great beauty—Nancy's younger sister was the original "Gibson Girl"—she was auto-cratic, phenomenally single-minded, outspoken, outrageously funny, and one of those people who instantly became the center of attention when she entered a room. As if that were not enough to condemn her in William Waldorf's mind, she was a teetotaling, staunch Epis-copalian (at the time) and a southern belle divorcée with a small son, Bobbie. The fact that he had long hoped that Waldorf would marry the daughter of some English noble house also weighed heavily with the tycoon.

In fact, to the staid upper-crust layers of English society of the early twentieth century Nancy Shaw was simply shocking. One of the first anecdotes about her arrival in England comes from a conversa-tion with Lady Edith Cunard, wife of the owner of Cunard Lines, who looked down her nose at Nancy and asked, "I suppose you have come over here to get one of our husbands?" Without batting an eyelash, Nancy responded, "If you knew how much trouble I had getting rid of my husband, you'd know I don't want yours."

It was aboard ship that Nancy Shaw met the ascetic, quiet—almost to the point of being painfully shy—Waldorf Astor, who claimed that it was love at first sight. While they seemed to be like oil and water—she was a wild, highly emotional, talkative extrovert and he a self-controlled, reflective man who enjoyed listening to other points of view—both were very serious young people. Waldorf felt it was his paternalistic duty to do something "useful" with his life and give back to the people of Britain something of importance, something that would truly help improve their lives. Nancy was driven by a moral fervor steeped in religious conviction drawn from the hard times she had had as a child. Their son Michael described his parents best when he said, "His approach to life was that of reason and he allowed his intuition very little play; consequently his methods, though admirably tenacious, were stern and not relieved by those flights of fancy and spontaneous outbursts which so enlivened my mother's life."

Another diamond wedding present received by Nancy on April 2, 1906, was a diamond bow modeled on a piece from the crown jewels

of Louis XV. This was a gift from her unsuccessful suitor Lord Revel-
stoke. When the couple were married on May 3, 1906, William Waldorf pleaded illness and did not attend the wedding, ambling instead
through his private world at Hever Castle, where public eyes would not
pry into his innermost thoughts. On the surface he seemed more than
generous to his new daughter-in-law and son by giving them Cliveden as the family home, and to Nancy the astounding wedding present
of the famous Astor diamond tiara with the Sancy diamond crowning
it at the center, which she gratefully accepted.

Still, it was an uneasy relationship. William Waldorf had toyed
with writing short stories over the years, and now the proud owner of
the *Times* of London, he found no difficulty in being published. His
cruel streak, which few dared to remark upon, extended to Nancy.
Shortly after the marriage, he promised to send her an advance copy
of his latest story "The Vengeance of Poseidon," which contained the
following description:

> The father had begun life as a country lad, had found employment
> on the nearest railway, and in twenty years had made his way into
> the phalanx of millionaires. He was forever telling stories—much
> embellished—of his own past exploits . . . speaking in the Western
> nasal vernacular and smiled so sourly at his own jokes, that in mirth-
> ful sallies his lips reminded me of a nutcracker. As for the daughter,
> I remember pausing to observe the soulless mechanism she had
> caught from her father and reflected in herself. . . . Her voice was
> shrill and she spoke in a leisurely drawl.

Nancy could not fail to notice that she and her father, Chillie
Langhorne, had been lampooned by her father-in-law, and similarly
had been told that he found her newfound Christian Science "offensive and blasphemous." But Nancy Astor never flinched in the face
of criticism and gave as good as she got, albeit in a ladylike fashion.
She and Waldorf were determined to lead a different kind of life from
William Waldorf, and if he wanted to be part of that life he would
have to accept them as they were. It was no surprise to her father-in-
law that she plowed through the interior decor at Cliveden claiming
that "the Astors have no taste" and dispersed the priceless collection.
This comment came from the same woman who wrote to her sister

shortly after she had met Waldorf in 1905, "What I like most about rich people is their money."

The elder Astor's reply on seeing the classical statuary, mosaic floors, painted ceilings, and leather upholstery replaced by parquet floors, drapes, and chintz was simply, "The house has been somewhat altered in decoration and furniture, and without objecting to these changes, it is no pleasure to me to see them."

In view of this grumbling background history, it is interesting to ponder why William Waldorf, in addition to the splendid wedding gift of Cliveden that would have one day come to his son as part of his inheritance, gave the Sancy diamond in its tiara to Nancy. Was it a peace offering? An early inheritance, as Cliveden was for Waldorf? Or was it another cruel message? The Sancy had been rumored by the twentieth century to be truly cursed, since most of its owners had met terrible ends. Since William Waldorf was a keen lover of history and historical quirks, we cannot completely eliminate this possibility.

Whatever the elder Astor's motivations were, the Sancy certainly did not appear to bring the young couple bad luck or misfortune—at least not immediately. Waldorf and Nancy passed their time as part of the rich and famous set at the pinnacle of society, surrounding themselves with interesting people such as Hilaire Belloc, George Bernard Shaw, H. G. Wells, Oxford dons, journalists, editors, national statesmen, and international diplomats. Waldorf was determined to become a politician, and unlike his fellow elected Members of Parliament (MPs), he bought a home in his constituency of Plymouth and sought to serve the people rather than his own political ambition. It was Waldorf Astor who laid the foundations for the National Health Service in Britain by creating the Ministry of Health.

But his career in the House of Commons was cut short abruptly by a simple act of generosity: in 1916 William Waldorf Astor was created Lord Astor and received a barony in the New Year's Honours List. Not only was this a shock, but also the honor symbolized the life of selfish privilege that Waldorf and Nancy abhorred. The peerage ended up completely destroying any vestige of a relationship between the two men, since it meant that on William Waldorf's death, Waldorf would have to quit the House of Commons and go to the House of Lords.

Waldorf pleaded with his father to refuse the honor, but the old man was adamant: King Edward VII had kept him from having a peerage because of political differences, and as he wrote to Nancy, "the love of success is in my blood and personally speaking, I am delighted to have rounded these last years of my life with distinction." In a last-ditch effort to save himself, Waldorf put a bill before the House of Commons that would allow heirs to titles to refuse them, but the bill was resoundingly defeated. He was trapped and never completely forgave his father, since he viewed the peerage as his father's last victory, defeating the man he wanted to become to the core. While Nancy tried to heal the rift as best she could, the damage was irretrievable.

Yet being the serious young man that he was, Waldorf Astor soon turned his attention back to the work at hand, and what he could do to serve in the immediate future. The Astor newspaper empire in Britain, the Astor money, William Waldorf's influence, and Waldorf's political prowess made the family powerful allies to cultivate for any government. In the hotbed of World War I, Waldorf worked tirelessly as a member of the war cabinet of Prime Minister Lloyd George, analyzing the Bolshevic Russian developments, monitoring the "Irish question," and advising with an honest passion. His passion never clouded his thinking, as it sometimes did with Nancy. Waldorf was the first government minister to identify Ulster extremism as the main obstacle to finding an equitable solution to the Irish question. His crusade to establish a Ministry of Health was a resounding success, but his passion to introduce Prohibition was an utter failure.

Then 1919 came. In setting out the terms of his will, William Waldorf struck one last blow. He wanted his eldest son and heir to have tangible proof of his disappointment in him and so distributed his wealth equally between Waldorf and his brother John. Two trusts were created where neither could touch most of the capital, one for his grandsons (more than $20 million in 1916, worth $335.7 million or £209.8 million today), the other for $50 million in 1919 (worth $840.3 million or £525.2 million today), to be divided between Waldorf and John. Within a month of the second trust having been created, William Waldorf Astor, elevated to viscount by this time, was dead.

Waldorf immediately inherited the dreaded title of "Lord" Astor and had to remove himself to the House of Lords, and his parliamentary seat of Plymouth would need to be contested. As *Huckleberry Finn* had breathed new life into the American novel thirty-five years earlier, Nancy Astor was about to take the British establishment by storm. As the wife of the former MP, and an attractive and outspoken proponent for the common man, Nancy was a shoo-in. Although she was not the first woman in Britain to be elected to Parliament, she was the first woman to actually take her seat there.

It would be unfair to say that she became the mouthpiece for Waldorf, though he certainly wrote her early major speeches. Her concerns were the poor and downtrodden, women's and children's rights, and delivering society from "demon drink." Parliament would become the stage for her theatrical personality. She wanted women on the police force, strong guardianship of infants, widows' pensions, juvenile courts, good education for all, and proper housing, and she tried to end sweatshops and child abuse. Her incredible outspoken manner and quick wit gave spiritual flight to her supporters and enraged her foes. Within no time she set the dubious Commons record for interrupting her colleagues' speeches and using "unparliamentary" language about her opponents. She was noted for dreaming up insults such as "the village donkey" or "loud speakers and big-mouthed fellows with flapdoodle hearts and no heads" to describe her fellow parliamentarians. Extraordinarily, she would remain in Parliament espousing her causes until 1954. Throughout this time Lady Nancy Astor would accompany Waldorf, now Viscount Astor, to state occasions and don her tiara with the Sancy at its summit, playing the part of the perfect viscount's wife, or hostess.

Even Winston Churchill trained his powerful verbal guns at Nancy Astor, when on August 17, 1931, he wrote in the *Sunday Pictorial*:

She successfully exploits the best of both worlds. She reigns in the Old World and the New, and on both sides of the Atlantic, at once as a leader of smart fashionable society and of advanced feminist democracy. She combines a kind heart with a sharp and wagging tongue. She embodies the historical portent of the first woman member of the House of Commons. She applauds the policies of the Government from the benches of the Opposition. She denounces

Lady Nancy Astor, defender of the rights of the common man, wearing the Sancy in her crown. Portrait by Dorothy Wilding, 1937.

The Sancy diamond is mounted at the center of Lady Astor's crown.

the vice of gambling and keeps an almost unrivalled racing stable. She accepts Communist hospitality and flattery and remains the Conservative member for Plymouth. She does all those opposite things so well and so naturally that the public, tired of criticizing, can only gape.

It was precisely her outspokenness and the Astors' love of intelligent conversation and frank exchange of ideas that got them into trouble in 1938 when the "Cliveden Set"—as those who went to Cliveden as part of the intelligent circle of Astor friends were labeled—became synonymous with Nazi-sympathizers. While now it is a widely held belief that the Astors themselves were certainly *not* Nazi-sympathizers, wild comments by Nancy in the Commons such as "Only a Jew like you would *dare* to be rude to me" did nothing to further their cause when rival newspapers printed these slurs.

The Astors were public property, with all the glamour of Hollywood stars, and it would be years before honesty crept back into the reporting about those who were invited down to Cliveden. Although Joachim von Ribbentrop was a guest there, so were Charlie Chaplin (later alleged to be a Communist during the McCarthy era), Sean O'Casey, T. E. Lawrence, Prime Minister Neville Chamberlain, and Mahatma Ghandi. In the 1930s George Bernard Shaw promoted the Astors' fact-finding trip to Russia—a trip that later created a stir when the U.S. Senate Foreign Relations Committee requested the Astors appear before them to give their views on the new Russia.

The Astors were adopted American royalty, and when they came on their many trips to America all of America's "royal-watchers" buzzed around Washington, D.C., in the hope of seeing something of a "royal walkabout." They were not disappointed. R. J. Cruikshank, a reporter for the *News Chronicle* (London), wrote to his passionate public:

> Across the grounds of Capitol Hill this morning I saw that bustling, trim, masterful figure which is commanding all eyes in Washington these days—Lady Astor, England's best known American and America's best known Englishwoman.
> Southern Senators, wearing Robert E. Lee hats and Bohemian ties, made sweeping bows of old-fashioned chivalry as she sped by.

Children waved to her, Congressmen beamed, hostesses dashed after her with invitations to lunch.

Lady Astor has returned and seen and conquered.

As the clouds of war gathered over Europe with each new day, Nancy and Waldorf Astor believed, and had believed for some considerable time, that the United States had to help Europe conquer the Nazi threat. As early as June 4, 1922, Nancy prophetically stated in an interview for the *Observer* of London that:

> I have urged that America is great enough and strong enough to rise above the fear of "entanglement." American mothers have no wish to send their sons to fight foreign wars in remote countries, on behalf of strange peoples, for possibly unworthy causes. But that is not Europe's claim on America. I have tried to show that Europe needs the moral support of America even more than her money or her men.

As the years in Parliament stretched behind her, Nancy's relationship with Waldorf grew more and more frayed. She had become obsessed with her "causes" and unable or unwilling to see that everything else around her— including her family—was having to pay as a result. The number one advocate of temperance had become hooked on power, and like most drug-dependent individuals, held the firm belief that she could quit when *she* wanted to, but not before *she* wanted to quit. In the final seven years of Waldorf's life, he and Nancy saw each other only a dozen or so times, for family gatherings; when she was at Cliveden, he would be in London or Brighton or vice versa. When the end came, she was completely repentant and had the ailing Waldorf brought back "home" to Cliveden, arriving too late herself from an engagement to say her good-byes personally.

With such a larger-than-life and globetrotting mother it must have been difficult to grow up in the Astor sanctuary at Cliveden, since despite giving of herself so completely to her public, Nancy also was an intensely possessive mother. She was jealous of women who came into her sons' lives, and remained the only woman in her first son's life, ever. Cliveden was the castle, and there was only one queen: Nancy. She doted on and indulged Bobbie, her eldest and only child with Bobbie Shaw of Boston. The family discovered that Bobbie was gay in a very public way: he was tried and convicted of "importuning young men," a criminal offense at the time in Britain, and was whisked off to prison for a five-month sentence. He served four months of it, and Nancy bore the matter well. Perhaps this was made much easier for her since no newspaper carried the story.

The eldest son of Nancy and Waldorf, William fared better, but only up to a point. Unlike Bobbie, Bill conformed, striving to please his parents, and frequently becoming the "piggy in the middle" between Nancy and Waldorf. According to Bill's third wife and widow, Bronwen Astor, whenever Nancy entered the room, his face would "turn the color of the ceiling." She remained convinced that the aortic aneurysm that killed Bill prematurely was the result of the anxiety and tension that had pervaded his youth. Yet Bill's early death was perhaps unkindly attributed to the most infamous incident to have occurred at Cliveden, the Profumo Affair.

Bill Astor is probably the most misunderstood and mistakenly maligned of all the British branch of the Astor family. By now Lord Astor, Bill had done some incredibly important work for refugees from World War II through the International Disaster Relief Committee and Chatham House's Royal Institute for International Affairs (cofounded by his father), and continued his work for refugees as an active member of the House of Lords. He was involved in private charity work supporting vocational training centers in Israel, aiding Russian refugees in Germany, and acting as chairman for the Great Ormond Street Hospital Institute of Child Health. As early as 1961 he was a founder member of the parliamentary campaign for Britain to join the Common Market, now the European Union.

Yet, unlike his illustrious parents, he did not always allow parliamentary business to come first. In May 1963 he complained to Lord Shackleton: "Really, to have your Division on Divorce on the Friday of Ascot week is very difficult, because clearly most of the Peers who have sympathy for the Division are likely to be at the races. However, I will do my best. . . . The best moment would be 7 P.M., which would allow one to get up from the races and go out after."

These facts make the tragic circumstances that led to the sensational Profumo Affair all the more tragic. Bill's wife and former model, Bronwen, had been living at Cliveden with him since the autumn of

1960, and shared in his pride of the estate's history as well as being its perfect hostess. The only dark cloud on the horizon was an osteopath named Stephen Ward, whom Bill had allowed to live at Spring Cottage on the estate. Bronwen had heard about him, and when she met him concluded that he was the devil incarnate; somehow this message got back to Ward. Ward had now been ensconced at Spring Cottage for four years, and had been introduced to the rich and glamorous who passed through Cliveden—thereby building up his practice. Bill swore by Ward's healing hands, and soon his friends used Ward, too. Ward, who was a middle-aged roué, would have felt threatened by Bronwen's influence over Bill, and under pressure to do something drastic to save his position.

This was a difficult time politically for Britain. A year earlier, the Soviets had captured U-2 pilot Francis Gary Powers, and the Cold War was in full flow. The English turncoat spies Guy Burgess and Donald Maclean had been unmasked, and their partners were still being sought by British intelligence. Britain was perceived as an "untrustworthy ally" by America as a result, and the government was working hard to dispel American fears as unfounded.

Bill Astor's trouble began in early 1961, when Ward met the Soviet naval attaché, Captain Eugene Ivanov—a Russian military intelligence officer who had befriended him in the hope of being invited to Cliveden frequently. Cliveden was a playground for the powerful and wealthy, and could provide Ivanov with a happy hunting ground. His hopes were soon realized.

Minister for War John Profumo was invited to Cliveden with his wife for the weekend of July 7–9, 1961, by the Astors. Also arriving as houseguests were Lord Mountbatten; General Ayub Khan, president of Pakistan; and Bill's aunt, Pauline Spender-Clay. The Profumos had been patients of Ward for some years, so Ward knew that they were going to be at Cliveden, and he knew Profumo's weakness for "sweet young things." The rest, as they say, is history. Christine Keeler, Mandy Rice-Davies, and Captain Ivanov were invited to Spring Cottage as Ward's guests on the same weekend.

Despite the court case that followed, there is substantial evidence today to show that Stephen Ward's plight was worsened by British intelligence, MI5, which had planned to entrap Ivanov and turn him into a double agent. Notwithstanding this, Ward would become the scapegoat for the entire escapade, and Bill Astor's reputation would be in tatters.

On the Saturday evening several members of the Astor party came out to the swimming pool to see a new bronze statue that Bill had recently purchased. Bill and Jack Profumo walked through the door to the pool area first, when they saw Stephen Ward and his guests. Christine Keeler had been running around the edge of the pool stark naked, and at the sight of Bill and Profumo quickly scampered into her swimsuit. According to Bill, no one saw anything untoward, but Christine Keeler's account was spicier—and the one that was widely held by the press to be the truth.

According to her, Bill and Jack Profumo playfully chased her around the pool; then, when the others arrived, she hastily put on her swimsuit. Later, according to Keeler, Profumo pursued her through the rooms of the house and dressed her up in a suit of armor, in which she paraded around to everyone's general amusement. With the benefit of time and hindsight, Christine Keeler's account sold newspapers—Bill Astor's did not—and so her story was the one generally believed.

What was true, however, was that Jack Profumo began an affair with Christine Keeler—as had Captain Ivanov. Washington got wind of the matter, and the wheels of power churned remorselessly against Profumo, since Ivanov was the Soviet Union's military expert in Western Europe and could have been told state secrets. Within two months of the incident, the Berlin Wall was erected, Profumo's career was in tatters, and Bill's reputation was ruined. The family did all they could to keep the incredible stream of newspaper harangues from the ailing Nancy, who by then had become detached from active life, with a considerable degree of success.

Three years later, in 1964, Nancy died after a long illness. In her last weeks she murmured "Waldorf . . . Waldorf" repeatedly, still regretting the final dozen years when power had outshone love. Then in 1967, Bill Astor died suddenly of an aortic aneurysm, and the Sancy passed to his fifteen-year-old son William, who became the fourth viscount.

29

Epilogue or Epitaph?

1976–Present

❦

FORTUNATELY, WILLIAM ASTOR CONTINUED in the family tradition of honor and duty, as well as politics, and treated the Sancy with great respect, lending it for the Louvre's special exhibition in 1967 of "The Diamonds of the French Crown," where it was reunited with the Regent and the Hortensia for the first time in nearly two centuries.

It was this special exhibition that eventually led to the Louvre's success in acquiring the diamond from the fourth viscount for an undisclosed sum, which some French lapidaries have set at £1 million ($7.6 million or £4.8 million today). Whether this was indeed the actual sum for which the Sancy was acquired is a matter of speculation, since the documents from the Banque de France, which purchased the stone on behalf of the Louvre, are not made available to the public.

The Sancy rests in a display case resembling an open coffin, six feet long by four feet wide. In the top of the case is a silk, rose-colored slope to which the Sancy is pinned, and to the left are the Regent and the Hortensia. A replica of the crown of Louis XV, with paste copies of the Sancy and the Regent, stands to the far left of the display. The Sancy is slightly tilted upward to better disguise the surface scratches from all the historic events that it has endured. It is surrounded by a simple circle of white gold that seems to squeeze the diamond into a somewhat smaller pear shape. Next to the Sancy, the

311

The Sancy diamond in its "Astor" setting, 1976.

Regent sparkles magnificently—more than three times larger than the Sancy. On the far left, the peach-blossom Hortensia, with its pentagonal eighteenth-century cut, and while smaller than the Sancy, also looks more important.

At the other corners of the display case are other remnants of the French crown jewels. When compared to the British crown jewel collection it is, frankly, a sorry affair. In April 2002, the plaque in front of the Sancy simply stated, "Part of the Crown Jewels of France, in the crown of Louis XIV and Louis XV, given to the Louvre by Viscount Astor."

Shock more than disappointment ran through me when I first saw the Sancy. Surely the Louvre would display the diamond better than that? So I listened to the audiotape in both French and English for an account of the litany of the Sancy's famous owners and those who had lusted after it, and was again shocked to learn that there was none. The Regent had an explanation on the tape, as did the crown of Louis XV, whereas the Sancy rated only a mention as having been set "at the crown's summit."

On my second visit to see the diamond, in July 2002, an updated display sign included the wording "allegedly belonging to Charles the Bold" at the beginning of the plaque, and the diamond had been repositioned and apparently repolished—thus hiding its historic scratches. Whether this had anything to do with my advising the museum that I was writing this book, I could not say.

What is interesting to me is why the Louvre would have gone to the lengths it did to acquire the Sancy if it had no intention of either acknowledging the "fantasy" (their word, not mine) surrounding the diamond, or finding out its true history. All that has been written about the Sancy, prior to my book, relies on just a few French writers, secondary sources, or the lies of Harlay de Sancy or Robert de Berquen. I have cleared the fog surrounding the Sancy's history to some extent by going back to original sources in France, Belgium, Holland, England, Portugal, Germany, Spain, Switzerland, and Italy, revealing many—but not all—of the Sancy's secrets. The Louvre, too, holds its own secret as to why it has not chosen to enlighten its patrons about this amazing diamond's past.

When I said my last good-bye to the Sancy, I felt that the description of the gem's phenomenal history was woefully lacking. Now that I have spent the past year researching, debunking previously written "histories," speaking to other European curators and diamond experts, and sometimes falling in and out of love with the Sancy, I am more convinced than ever that this jewel has been metaphorically hidden away in its display case, and instead of its sojourn in the Louvre being its safe haven, or its epilogue, the blandness of the presentation has become the Sancy's epitaph.

Selected Bibliography

Archival Sources

Account of the history of the royal finances, marquess of Winchester, April 1571. Arundel 151, fol. 195. British Library, London.

Account of jewels presented to the queen, 1572–1587. Add. 40796. British Library, London.

AD Nord B 2069/65017, AD Nord B 3500, B 3501/123745, AD Nord B 3378, 3495–3496, 3501–3502, 3507–3512, 3514, 20144, 20159, 20160. Dated 1386–1477. Series B. Archives départementales du Nord, Lille.

Add. 15858, fol. 201, letters re arrears on Henrietta Maria's dowry. Add. 32092, fol. 316, letter from Richelieu regarding the marriage of Henrietta Maria to Charles. Add. 28857, letters of Charles I to Henrietta Maria. Add. 46930, fol. 151–152b—original letters of Charles to Henrietta Maria, 1646. British Library, London.

Add. 61698, DXCVIII ff. 35 (*Inventaire des Portraits, et Tableaux du feu Roy Charles 1er; qui furent estimés, et vendus par les Rebelles, en 1641*), Charles I inventory of portraits and paintings, which were valued and sold by the rebels in 1641. Blenheim Papers. British Library, London.

Affaitadi, Grand Livre A (inventory), fol. 142, 1540–1555. Staatsarchief, Antwerp.

Aranda Huerte, Amelia. *La Vuelta à los Modelos clàsicos en la joyerìa española de los siglos XVIII y XIX*, CHEA. Departamento de Historia del Arte, U.N.E.D., Madrid, 1994.

Basler Kleinodienhandel, STA, Staedlische Urkunde 2604. Verkaufsurkunde zwischen Basel und den Fuggern vom September 16, 1504.

Birch, Thomas. *An Historical View of the Negotiations between the Courts of England, France and Brussels from the Year 1592 to 1617*. London, 1769. Rare Books, British Library, London.

Bonaparte, Joseph. *Biographical Sketch of Joseph Napoleon Bonaparte, Count de Survilliers* (handwritten manuscript). London: James Ridgway, 1833. Rare Books, British Library, London.

Boone, M. Apologie d'un banquier medieval. Tommaso Portinari et l'État bourguignon—le moyen age (n.d.). Series CV. Archives civiles, Dijon.

Bouchon, manuscript of Swiss chronicler Jean de Troyes. Berner Historisches Museum, Bern.

Boullemier, Abbé. Oeuvres historiques et archeologiques (n.d.). MS 938. Fonds Bourguignon, Dijon.

Bourbon. *Bulletin Historique et philologique du Comité des Travaux Historiques et Scientifiques.* Paris, 1901. Periodicals, Bibliothèque Nationale de France, Paris.

Burgunderbeute. Manuscript, Swiss. Fonds Bourguignon. National Archives, Basel.

Cabala, Ed. *Mysteries of the State,* 1654, letter from Viscount Kensington to Buckingham. British Library, London.

Calendar of Close Rolls. Edward IV, 1469. Bodleian Library, Oxford.

Calendar of State Papers. Domestic, 1603–1610. HMSO, 1897. British Library, London.

————. Edward VI, 1547–1553. Bodleian Library, Oxford.

————. Foreign, 1578–1579. Public Records Office, 1909. British Library, London.

————. Henry VIII, vol. 21, part II, 1546–1547. Bodleian Library, Oxford.

————. Venetian, 1579–1580. Public Records Office, 1904. British Library, London.

————. Venetian, vol. 7, 1558–1580. London: Brown & Bentinck, 1890. British Library, London.

————. Venetian, vol. 8. Public Records Office, 1904. British Library, London.

————. Venetian, etc., vol. 9, 1592–1603. HMSO, 1897. British Library, London.

————. Venetian, vol. 18, no. 438, November 16, 1624; vol. 19, no. 59, May 25, 1625. Appendix I, no. 605. Public Records Office, 1910. British Library, London.

————. Venetian, vol. 24, no. 414, vol. 25, vol. 26. HMSO, 1924. British Library, London.

Cartas latinas de Damiao de Gois. Published for Joaquim de Vasconcelas, 1901. Arquivo Historico Portugues VI e VII, Lisbon.

Caukercken in Paperochius. Annales Antverpienses ab urbe condita, tome II. Torré do Tombo, Lisbon.

Charles the Bold. *l'Ordonnance de Charles le Téméraire.* Hatton 13. Bodleian Library. Oxford.

Chastellain, Georges. *Chronique des Ducs de Bourgogne*. Tome III, 1827. Paris: Hippolyte, Tillard.

————. Oeuvres historiques inedites, 1832. Paris: Pantheon Litteraire.

Cletscher, Thomas. Sketchbook (n.d.). Bouymans Museum, Rotterdam.

Commines, Philip de. *Mémoires*. Eulogy to Charles the Bold (n.d.). Manuscripts, British Library, London.

Corro Cronologica. Parte I, tomo I, maco 20, fol. 329, no. 49. Torré do Tombo, Lisbon.

————. Parte I, tomo I, maco 5, fol. 30–68. Torré do Tombo, Lisbon.

————. Parte II, maco 26, fol. 225. Torré do Tombo, Lisbon.

Cosnac. *Les Richesses du Palais Mazarin*. Coll. Richelieu. La Bibliothèque Nationale de France, Paris.

Cotton MS, fols. 211, 295 (now 246), transcription of letter of Elizabeth. Nero B1. British Library, London.

Daily Telegraph. June 21, 1859. Collindale Library. British Library, London.

Da Prato, Cesare. *Firenze ai Demidoff, Pratolino es Donato, Relazione storica e descrittiva, Preceduta da cenni Biografici sui Demidoff*. Firenze, 1887. Rare Books, British Library, London.

D'Auvergne, Edmund. *Godoy: The Queen's Favourite*. London: Stanley Paul & Co., 1912. Rare Books, British Library, London.

De Berquen, Robert. *The Marvels of Occidental and Oriental India, or New Treatise of Precious Stones and Pearls Containing their True Nature, Hardness, Colors and Virtues*. Rare Books, British Library, London.

De Tillières. *Mémoires* (privately published, n.d.). Rare Books, British Library, London.

Diamond Sutra, A.D. 868. Virtual Reading Room. British Library, London.

Dossiers Bleus 349, pieces 70–81, fol. 73. Coll. Richelieu. Bibliothèque Nationale de France, Paris.

Egerton 2542, fol. 335–341, loans from Lord Jermyn and Cardinal Mazarin; Egerton 2554, fol. 27, marriage contract between Charles I and Henrietta Maria; Egerton 2618, fol. 13; Egerton 2619, original letters of Henrietta Maria to Charles, 1642–1645. British Library, London.

Enault, Louis. *Les Diamants de la couronne*. E. Bernard et Cie, Paris, 1884. Coll. Richelieu. Bibliothèque Nationale de France, Paris.

French State Papers E 2503–2515, 2517–2520, 2523, 2524 (*1774–1776 arrêts du conseil du roi règne de Louis XVI. Inventaire analytique T. 1 [10 mai 1774 au 12 mai 1776 par ministère Turgot]*), E 2521–2550, 2475, 2784, 2660, 2661, 1776–1778. Coll. Richelieu. Archives Nationales, Paris.

Fugger *Ehrenspiegel* (inventories), 1508 and 1525, extracts. Manuscripts, British Library, London.

Godefroy, Frederic. Dictionnaire ancienne langue francaise, t. 2–5, 11th–15th centuries. 1883. Bibliothèque Nationale de France, Paris.

Goris, J. A. Étude sur les colonies marchandes meridionales (Portugais, Espagnols, Italiens) à Anvers de 1488–1567. Rare Books, Bibliothèque Nationale de France, Paris.

Green, M. E. A., ed. *Letters of Henrietta-Maria to Charles.* London, 1857. Rare Books, British Library, London.

Greiff, B., ed. *Tagbuch des Lucas Rem aus den Jahren 1494–1541.* Rare Books, Torré do Tombo, Lisbon.

Hardwicke State Papers, vol. I, pp. 535–536. Lord Carlisle [Viscount Kensington] to Prince Charles, October 7, 1624. British Library, London.

Harlay de Sancy, Nicolas. *Discours de la négociation de MM. De Bouillon et de Sancy en Angleterre (en 1596).* Paris, 1641. Rare Books, British Library, London.

————. *Discours sur l'occurrence de ses affaires.* Paris, 1610. Rare Books, Bibliothèque Nationale de France, Paris.

————. *L'extrait d'un discours d'estat de M. de Sancy, Général de l'armée estrangère qu'il amena au Roy Henry III, en l'année 1589.* In *Mémoires* of the duke of Nevers, 1665, t. II. Rare Books, Bibliothèque Nationale de France, Paris.

Harleian 6986, art. 39 (in the king's own hand). Nero. British Library, London.

Illustrated London News. March 11, 1865. Sale of the Sancy diamond by Messrs. Garrard & Co, London. Collindale Library. British Library, London.

Inventaire de Philippe le Hardi de 1420. Fonds Bourguignon. Bibliothèque Municipale de Dijon, Dijon.

Inventaire des diamants de la couronne, perles, pierreries, tableaux, Pierres gravées et autres Monumens des Arts et des Sciences existans au Garbe Meuble, Imprimé par ordre de l'Assemblée Nationale, Par ses Commissaires MM Bion, Christin et Delattre, Deputés a l'Assemblée nationale, Partie Première. Paris, 1791. Bibliothèque Nationale de France, Paris.

Inventaires des arrêts du Conseil du Roi, Règne de Louis XV (arrêts et commandements) inventaire analytique par M. Antoine, T. I, 1715–1720. E 1957, 1977, 1980, 1983–2051, 2061– . *T.2, 1721–1723.* Archives Nationales, Paris.

Inventory of Queen Elizabeth I's jewels. Sloan, 814. British Library, London.

Jefferson, Thomas. *Memoirs, Correspondence, and Private Papers.* Vol. II. London: Henry Colburn and Richard Bentley, Publishers, 1829. Rare Books, British Library, London.

Laborde. Les comptes des Ducs de Bourgogne, 1872. Series B. Collections des Inventaires Sommaires Nord. Archives civiles, Lille.

Lachenal, Jean. *Inventaire des joyaux d'or et d'argent reliques ornaments de chapelle, livres tapisserie apparentenant au duc de Bourgogne (par la suite de la mort de Jean sans Peur, son père) et baillés par l'inventaire en garde à Jean de Lachenal dit Boulogne, garde des joyaux du duc, commence à Dijon le 12 VII 1420.* Series 500 de Colbert, 127. Bibliothèque Nationale, Paris.

————. *Inventaire des joyaux et vaisselles d'or et d'argent venus au duc de Bourgogne par le décès de sa mère, Marguerite de Bavière, et bailés par inventaire à Jean de Lachenal dit Boulogne, garde des joyaux du duc, fait à Dijon le 1. VIII 1424.* Collection Moreau, vol. 802, fol. 42–46. Bibliothèque Nationale, Paris.

Lachenal, Jean. Manuscript B 296, jewel purchases of Philip the Bold. Collection d'Arbaumont. Archives civiles, Dijon.

————. Manuscript B 1476, jewel purchases of Charles the Bold. Collection d'Arbaumont. Archives civiles, Dijon.

Lee, Sidney, ed. *Autobiography of Lord Herbert of Cherbury.* 1886. Rare Books, British Library, London.

Les comptes des Ducs de Bourgogne. 1372–1477. Inventaire des Archives Departementales Nord. Series B, Nos. B 3229–3389. Archives civiles, Lille.

————. 1423–1424. Inventaire des Archives Departementales Nord. Series B, No. 3495. Archives civiles, Lille.

Letters to Henry III, Catherine de' Medici and Charles IX, 1572–1574. Add. 20779 ff. 2–8. British Library, London.

Loans to the crown, 1591–1594. Add. 33924 ff. 13–15. British Library, London.

Marche, Olivier de la. *Mémoires* (n.d.) Bibliothèque de Bourgogne. Bibliothèque Royale, Brussels.

Mazarin, Jules. Last Will and Testament, 1661. Coll. Richelieu. Bibliothèque Nationale de France, Paris.

Mémoires pour servir à l'histoire de France et de Bourgogne contenant un journal de Paris sous les règnes de Charles VI et Charles VII, 1729. Paris: Julien-Michel Gandouin.

Memorandum of the Life and Public Works of Sir Jamsetjee Jejeebhoy. Printed for private circulation, May 24, 1905, India Office Library. India and Oriental Coll. British Library, London.

Mody, Jehangir, R. P. *Jamsetjee Jejeebhoy: The First Indian Knight and Baronet.* Bombay: Jehangir R. P. MODY, 1959. India and Oriental Coll. British Library, London.

Molinet. *Mémoires* (n.d.) Manuscripts, British Library, London.

MS 1753. Collection d'Arbaumont. Archives civiles, Dijon.

MS Fr 16942, fols. 7, 274. Manuscripts, Bibliothèque Nationale de France, Paris.

MS Fr 262, fol. 268. Coll. Godefroy. Bibliothèque Nationale de France, Paris.

MS Fr 7131, fol. 438. Coll. Richelieu. Bibliothèque Nationale de France, Paris.

Musée du Louvre, Département des objets d'art. Sancy Dossier OA 10630. Paris.

————. Valuation of the Sancy for Charles X (unmarked MS). Paris.

Nazir, Cooverjee Sorabjee. *The First Parsee Prophet.* Bombay: Union Press, 1866. Rare Books, British Library, London.

Nero B 1, fol. 295 (now 246). Portugal, 1582. Nero Collection. British Library, London.

Olschki, Leo S. *I Demidoff a Firenze e in Toscana, a cura di Lucia Tonini, Florence.* Cultura e Memoria Provincia di Firenze, 1996.

Paradin. *Annales* (n.d.). Fonds Bourguignon. Swiss National Archives, Basel.

Patrimonio Nacional. Casa Real de Tesoria General, caja 308, exp. 11, *inventario* 48, fol. 15. Archivo Réal. Palacio Nacional, Madrid.

————. Manuscrito Archivo General de Palacio, *Renados José I*, no. 59, fols. 5, 6. Archivo Réal. Palacio Nacional, Madrid.

Paviot, J. *Portugal et Bourgogne au Xvème Siecle*. Commission nationale pour les commemorations des découvertes portugaises. Bibliothèque Nationale de France, Paris.

Pazzi, Piero di. *I Diamanti nel Commercio, nell'arte e nelle Vicende Storiche di Venezia*, 1986. Stampato nel mese di Dicembre. Monastero di San Lazzaro degli Armeni, Venice.

Plancher, Dom. *Histoire générale et particulière de Bourgogne avec les preuves justificatives*, tome IV, 1781. Louis-Nicolas Frantin, Imprimeur du Roi, Dijon.

Polo, Marco. *The Most Noble and Famous Travels of Marcus Paulus, one of the nobility of the State of Venice into the East parts of the world, as Armenia, Persia, Arabia, Turkey with many other kingdoms and Provinces*. Trans. Ralph Newbury. London, 1579.

Prevost-Paradol, M. *Elisabeth et Henri IV 1595–1509*. Paris: Michel Levy Frères, 1863. Coll. Richelieu. La Bibliothèque Nationale de France, Paris.

Prost, B. and H. *Inventaires Mobiliers et extraits des comptes des Ducs de Bourgogne, 136301477*. Tome II, 1378, 1399, inventaires, item 1409. Fonds Bourguignon. Bibliothèque Municipale de Dijon, Dijon.

Registre journal du règne de Henri III. Tome IV (jewels). Fonds Royales. Bibliothèque Nationale de France, Paris.

Renan, Ernest. *Valentine de Milan et Christine de Suece, Deux Enigmes Historiques* (privately published, n.d.), no. 129 of 200. Manuscript Collection, British Library, London.

Resolution of the English commanders to pursue the Spanish Armada. Add. 33740, fol. 6. British Library, London.

Rohan, L. R. E., Cardinal de. *Pièces justificatives pour M. le Cardinal de Rohan accuse. Déclarations authentiques selon la forme anglaise*, 1786. Coll. Richelieu. Bibliothèque Nationale de France, Paris.

Royal letters, commissions, warrants, etc., 1595–1598. Sloane 33. British Library, London.

Schick, L. Jacob Fugger, S.E.V.P.E.N. Bibliothèque Nationale de France, Paris.

Schrenk, Gilbert. "Nicholas Harlay de Sancy." Doctoral thesis, University of Geneva, 2000.

Société pour l'histoire du droit et des institutions des anciens pays bourguignons, comtois, et romands, 1939–1942. Collections Sommaires Nord. Archives civiles, Lille.

State Papers. Dom 1629–1631. Foedera VIII, pt. iii. The British Library, London.

State Papers. Exchequer E 404/151 and E 404/157; Treasury Books T56/1 Lists "Expected Improvements" for example from new impositions. Public Records Office, London.

————. 10/15, fol. 41. Public Records Office, London.

————. 78/37. Letter from Sancy to Burghley dated April 14–24, 1596, plus fol. 139, 140, 141, 143, 145, 150, 157, 160, 164, 170, 172, 176, 184, 189, 221, 227, 234. Harlay de Sancy correspondence. Public Records Office, London.

————. 78/51, fol. 149. Harlay de Sancy correspondence. Public Records Office, London.

————. Relating to Elizabeth I's foreign policy, 1559–1588. Sloane 2442, ff. 20–156b. British Library, London.

Stowe 322, fol. 54. Revenue and disbursements of Queen Henrietta Maria, 1633. Stowe 561, fols. 2–21. Ordinances of the King's and Queen's households. Manuscripts, British Library, London.

Streeter, Edwin. *Precious Stones and Gems.* London: Chapman & Hall, 1877. De Beers Library, London.

Tavernier, Jean Baptiste. *The Six Voyages of Jean Baptiste Tavernier, A Noble Man of France now living, through Turkey into Persia and the East-Indies finished in the year 1670 giving an account of the State of Those Countries.* London, 1678.

Treaties and negotiations with Portugal. Cott. Nero., B. i. 85, Cott. Galba. D, V. 99, 331, and Cott. Galba. E, vi. 5, 7, 13. British Library, London.

Treaty with Portugal 1576. Add. 40795, fol. 1. British Library, London.

Wootton, Sir Henry. *Life & Death of George Villiers, Duke of Buckingham,* 1642. Rare Books, British Library, London.

Interviews and Correspondence

All interviews were conducted by the author.

Ajuda Palace, Lisbon. Personal correspondence.

Bank of England Information Centre, London. Personal correspondence.

Dennisen, Sabine. Curator, Diamond Museum, Antwerp. Interview, July 9, 2002.

Huerte, Amelia Aranda. Curator of jewels, Patrimonio Nacional, Madrid. Interview, June 15, 2003.

Louvre Département des objets d'art, Paris. Interviews with various staff members, April and July 2002.

Margadant, Silvio. Curator, State Archives, Grisons, Switzerland. Telephone interview, June 20, 2003.

Pike, Corinna. Curator, Garrard & Co., London. Telephone interview, September 12, 2002.

Tolkowsky, Gabi. Master diamond cutter, Antwerp. Interview, July 8, 2002.

Wins, Hans. Diamond historian, Antwerp. Interview, July 10, 2002.

Other Sources

Aristide, Isabelle. *La Fortune de Sully*. Paris: Comité pour l'histoire économique et financière de la France, 1990.

Balfour, Sir Ian. *Famous Diamonds*. 4th ed. London: Christie's, 2000.

Boyajian, James C. *Portuguese Trade in Asia under the Habsburgs, 1580–1640*. Baltimore: Johns Hopkins University Press, 1993.

Calmette, Joseph. *The Golden Age of Burgundy*. Trans. Doreen Weightman. London: Phoenix Press, 1962.

Clay, C. *Economic Expansion and Social Change*. Vol. 2, *Industry, Trade & Government*. Cambridge: Cambridge University Press, 1984.

Cockshaw, P., C. Lemaire, and A. Rouzet, eds. *Charles le Téméraire, 1433–1477*. Brussels: Bibliothèque Royale Albert Ier, 1977.

Collas, Émile. *Valentine de Milan Duchesse d'Orléans*. Paris: Librairie Plon, 1911.

Collins, A. J. *Jewels and Plate of Queen Elizabeth I*. London: Trustees of the British Museum (edited from Harley MS 1650, Stowe MS 555), 1955.

Cowles, Virginia. *The Astors: The Story of a Transatlantic Family*. London: Weidenfeld & Nicolson, 1979.

Cronin, Vincent. *Napoleon*. London: HarperCollins, 1994.

da Silva, J. Gentil. *Strategie des Affaires à Lisbonne entre 1595 et 1607, Lettres marchandes des Rodrigues d'Evora et Veig*. Paris: Librairie Armand Colin, 1956.

Denucé, J. *L'Inventaire des Affaitadi, Banquiers Italiens a Anvers de l'Année 1568*. Antwerp: Éditions de Sikkel, 1934.

Dulong, Claude. *La Fortune de Mazarin*. Paris: Perrin, 1990.

Dyer, Christopher. *Making a Living in the Middle Ages*. New Haven, Conn.: Yale University Press, 2002.

Ehrenberg, Richard. *Le Siècle des Fugger*. Abridged and trans. from German. Paris: Larousse, 1955.

Fraser, Antonia. *Marie Antoinette*. London: Weidenfeld & Nicolson, 2001.

Graves, F. M. *Louis I, Duc d'Orléans et Valentine Visconti, Sa Femme*, Paris: Libraire spéciale pour l'histoire de France, 1913.

Harte-Davis, Adam. *What the Tudors and Stuarts Did for Us*. London: BBC Books, 2002.

Hering, Ernst. *Die Fugger*. Leipzig: Wilhelm Goldmann, Verlag, 1939.

Hibbert, Christopher. *Florence: Biography of a City*. London: Penguin, 1994.

———. *The French Revolution*. London: Penguin, 1980.

———. *Napoleon: His Wives and Women*. London: HarperCollins, 2003.

———. *The Rise and Fall of the House of Medici*. London: Folio Society, 1998.

Hudson, Hugh D. Jr. *The Rise of the Demidov Family and the Russian Iron Industry in the Eighteenth Century*. Newtonville, Mass.: Russian Biography Series, no. 11, Oriental Research Partners (Georgia State University), 1986.

Jacobs, Henri. *Le Diamant*. Paris: Librairie de l'Académie de Médcine, 1884.

Journal of Economic and Business History. Vol. II, 1929–1930. *Lettres marchandes d'Anvers.* Staatsarchief Antwerp, Antwerp.

Khalidi, Omar, *The Romance of Diamonds.* Ahmedabad, India: Mappin, 1999.

Massie, Robert K. *Peter the Great: His Life and World.* London: Phoenix Press, 1980.

Mattingly, Garrett. *The Spanish Armada.* London: Folio Society, 2002.

McCusker, John J. *Money and Exchange in Europe and America, 1600–1775: A Handbook.* New York: Macmillan, 1978.

Mears, Kenneth. *The Crown Jewels,* Historical Royal Palaces, HMSO. London, 2001.

Michel, Patrick. *Mazarin, Prince des Collectionneurs.* Paris: Éditions de la Réunion des Musées de France, 1999.

Mitchell, B. R. *British Historical Statistics.* Cambridge: Cambridge University Press, 1988.

Mitford, Nancy. *Madame de Pompadour.* London: Penguin, 1958.

————. *The Sun King.* London: Hamish Hamilton, 1966.

Morel, Bernard. *Les joyaux de la couronne de France.* Antwerp: Fonds Mercator; Paris: Albin Michel, 1988.

Mouawad, Robert. *Diamonds.* Paris: Vilo Adam Biro, 2001.

Ortiz, Lambert Elizabeth, ed. *The Encyclopedia of Herbs, Spices, and Flavourings.* London: BCA, 1998.

Paviot, Jacques. *Jacques de Bregilles, garde des joyaux des ducs de Bourgogne, Philippe le Bon, et Charles le Temeraire.* Lille: *Revue du nord* 77, 1995.

Petrie, Sir Charles, ed. *Harleian Miscellany.* Vol. 8, *Letters of Charles I.* London: Cassell, 1935.

Pipes, Richard. *Russia under the Old Regime.* Ithaca, N.Y.: Cornell University Press, 1974.

Plowden, Alison. *Henrietta Maria, Charles I's Indomitable Queen.* London: Sutton Publishing, 1992.

Porter, Roy. *England in the Eighteenth Century.* London: Folio Society, 1998.

Purcell, Katherine. *Falize: A Dynasty of Jewelers.* London: Thames & Hudson, 1999.

Rietbergen, Prof. Dr. P. J. A. N. *A Short History of the Netherlands.* Amersfoort, Netherlands: Bekking Publishers, 2002.

Rose, Norman. *The Cliveden Set: Portrait of an Exclusive Fraternity.* London: Jonathan Cape, 1933.

Scarisbrick, Diana. *Jewellery in Britain 1066–1837: A Documentary, Social, Literary, and Artistic Survey.* Wilby, Norwich, Eng.: Michael Russell Publishing, 1994.

————. *Tudor and Jacobean Jewellery.* London: Tate Publishing, 1995.

Sharpe, K. *The Personal Rule of Charles I.* New Haven, Conn.: Yale University Press, 1992.

Sinclair, David. *Dynasty: The Astors and Their Times*. London: J. M. Dent & Sons, 1983.

Spufford, Peter. *Handbook of Medieval Exchange*: London, Royal Historical Society, 1986.

Starkey, David. *Elizabeth*. London: Vintage, 2000.

Strong, Roy. *The Story of Britain: A People's History*. London: Pimlico, 1998.

Sykes, Nancy. *The Life of Lady Astor*. London: Panther, 1979.

Tolkowsky, Marcel. *Diamond Design*. London: E. & F. N. Spon, 1919.

Treveleyn, G. M. *A History of England: England under the Stuarts*. London: Folio Society, 1996.

Urban, Mark. *The Man Who Broke Napoleon's Codes*. London: Farber & Farber, 2001.

von Klarwill, Victor. *The Fugger News-Letters*. Trans. Pauline de Chary and John Lane. London: Bodley Head, 1924.

Walton, Guy. *Louis XIV's Versailles*. London: Viking Press, 1986.

Weir, Alison. *Lancaster and York: The Wars of the Roses*. London: Pimlico, 1995.

Wild, Antony. *Remains of the Raj: The British Legacy in India*. London: Harper-Collins, 2001.

Wilson, Derek. *The Astors: Landscape with Millionaires*. London: Weidenfeld & Nicolson, 1986.

Index